Practical Reporting with Ruby and Rails

David Berube

Apress®

Practical Reporting with Ruby and Rails

Copyright © 2008 by David Berube

ISBN-13 (pbk): 978-1-59059-933-4

ISBN-10 (pbk): 1-59059-933-0

ISBN-13 (electronic): 978-1-4302-0532-6

ISBN-10 (electronic): 1-4302-0532-6

Printed and bound in the United States of America 9 8 7 6 5 4 3 2 1

Lead Editors: Steve Anglin, Jason Gilmore
Technical Reviewer: Nick Plante
Editorial Board: Clay Andres, Steve Anglin, Ewan Buckingham, Tony Campbell, Gary Cornell,
    Jonathan Gennick, Kevin Goff, Matthew Moodie, Joseph Ottinger, Jeffrey Pepper, Frank Pohlmann,
    Ben Renow-Clarke, Dominic Shakeshaft, Matt Wade, Tom Welsh
Project Manager: Beth Christmas
Copy Editor: Marilyn Smith
Associate Production Director: Kari Brooks-Copony
Production Editor: Liz Berry
Compositor: Dina Quan
Proofreader: April Eddy
Indexer: Broccoli Information Management
Artist: April Milne
Cover Designer: Kurt Krames
Manufacturing Director: Tom Debolski

Distributed to the book trade worldwide by Springer-Verlag New York, Inc., 233 Spring Street, 6th Floor, New York, NY 10013. Phone 1-800-SPRINGER, fax 201-348-4505, e-mail orders-ny@springer-sbm.com, or visit http://www.springeronline.com.

For information on translations, please contact Apress directly at 2855 Telegraph Avenue, Suite 600, Berkeley, CA 94705. Phone 510-549-5930, fax 510-549-5939, e-mail info@apress.com, or visit http://www.apress.com.

Apress and friends of ED books may be purchased in bulk for academic, corporate, or promotional use. eBook versions and licenses are also available for most titles. For more information, reference our Special Bulk Sales–eBook Licensing web page at http://www.apress.com/info/bulksales.

The source code for this book is available to readers at http://www.apress.com.

This book is dedicated to my parents.

Contents at a Glance

About the Author xi
About the Technical Reviewer xiii
Acknowledgments xv
Introduction xvii

PART 1 ■ ■ ■ Introducing Reporting with Ruby

■CHAPTER 1   Data Access Fundamentals 3
■CHAPTER 2   Calculating Statistics with Active Record 19
■CHAPTER 3   Creating Graphs with Ruby 33
■CHAPTER 4   Creating Reports on the Desktop 51
■CHAPTER 5   Connecting Your Reports to the World 75

PART 2 ■ ■ ■ Examples of Reporting with Ruby

■CHAPTER 6   Tracking Auctions with eBay 111
■CHAPTER 7   Tracking Expenditures with PayPal 133
■CHAPTER 8   Creating Sales Performance Reports with SugarCRM 155
■CHAPTER 9   Investment Tracking with Fidelity 171
■CHAPTER 10   Calculating Costs by Analyzing Apache Web Logs 189
■CHAPTER 11   Tracking the News with Google News 215
■CHAPTER 12   Creating Reports with Ruby and Microsoft Office 233
■CHAPTER 13   Tracking Your Ads with Google AdWords 261

■INDEX   285

Contents

About the Author xi

About the Technical Reviewer xiii

Acknowledgments xv

Introduction xvii

PART 1 ■ ■ ■ Introducing Reporting with Ruby

■CHAPTER 1   Data Access Fundamentals 3

Choosing a Database 3

Using Active Record As a Database Access Library 5

Calculating Player Salaries 6

Calculating Player Wins 11

Summary 17

■CHAPTER 2   Calculating Statistics with Active Record 19

Grouping and Aggregation 19

Analyzing Data with Grouping and Aggregates 22

Calculating Salary Distribution 25

Calculating Drink/Win Distribution 26

Summary 31

■CHAPTER 3   Creating Graphs with Ruby 33

Choosing a Graphing Utility 33

Graphing Data 37

Creating a Line Chart 37

Creating a Line Chart 45

Summary 49

▪CHAPTER 4   **Creating Reports on the Desktop** 51

Choosing a Desktop Format 51
Exporting Data to Spreadsheets 52
      Generating an Excel Spreadsheet 52
      Creating a Spreadsheet Report 53
Creating GUIs with Ruby 60
      Using FXRuby 61
      Graphing Team Performance on the Desktop 63
Summary 73

▪CHAPTER 5   **Connecting Your Reports to the World** 75

Choosing a Web Framework 75
Live Intranet Web Reporting with Rails 76
      Setting Up the Database 78
      Creating the Models for the Web Report 82
      Creating the Controller for the Web Report 85
      Creating the View for the Web Report 85
      Examining the Web Report Application 87
Graphical Reporting with Rails 91
      Creating the Controller for the Graphical Report 92
      Creating the Models for the Graphical Report 95
      Creating the View for the Graphical Report 96
      Examining the Graphical Reporting Application 99
Summary 107

PART 2 ▪▪▪ Examples of Reporting with Ruby

▪CHAPTER 6   **Tracking Auctions with eBay** 111

Using eBay APIs 111
Obtaining Competitive Intelligence via eBay Web Services 113
      Installing Hpricot and LaTeX 114
      Coding the eBay Report 115
Summary 131

■**CHAPTER 7**   **Tracking Expenditures with PayPal**........................133

Gathering Data from PayPal......................................133
Reporting PayPal Expenses.....................................136
    Using FasterCSV...137
    Converting PayPal CSV Data 138
    Analyzing the Data..144
Summary..153

■**CHAPTER 8**   **Creating Sales Performance Reports with SugarCRM**....155

Installing SugarCRM 155
Sales Force Reporting..156
    Updating the Database 156
    Creating PDFs from HTML Documents....................157
Summary..169

■**CHAPTER 9**   **Investment Tracking with Fidelity**........................171

Writing a Small Server to Get Report Data 171
Tracking a Stock Portfolio 173
    Creating an XML Server with Mongrel......................173
    Creating the Graphical XML Ticker 180
Summary..187

■**CHAPTER 10**   **Calculating Costs by Analyzing Apache Web Logs** 189

Speeding Up Insertions with ActiveRecord::Extensions 190
Creating PDFs with PDF::Writer 191
Cost-Per-Sale Reporting...192
    Creating the Controllers 193
    Creating the Layout and Views 198
    Downloading a Parser Library 201
    Creating the Routing File 201
    Setting Up the Database and Schema 201
    Defining the Models 203
    Examining the Log Analyzer and Cost-Per-Sale Report 203
Summary 212

█**CHAPTER 11**   **Tracking the News with Google News**................215

Using FeedTools to Parse RSS 216
Company News Coverage Reporting 217
    Loading the Data 217
    Creating the News Tracker Report Application.................226
Summary...232

█**CHAPTER 12**   **Creating Reports with Ruby and Microsoft Office** 233

Interacting with Microsoft Office 233
    Working with Microsoft Excel 234
    Working with Microsoft Word 234
    Working with Microsoft Access.............................236
Importing Web-Form Data into an Access Database.................236
    Creating the Web Interface.................................237
    Importing the XML Data into Microsoft Access 251
Summary...260

█**CHAPTER 13**   **Tracking Your Ads with Google AdWords** 261

Obtaining Google AdWords Reports.............................262
Planning an AdWords Campaign.................................267
    Loading the XML into a Database...........................267
    Creating the AdWords Campaign Reporter Application.........272
Summary...284

█**INDEX** 285

About the Author

DAVID BERUBE is a Ruby developer, trainer, author, and speaker. He has used both Ruby and Ruby on Rails for several years, starting in 2003 (he became a Ruby advocate after writing about the language for *Dr. Dobb's Journal*). Prior to this, David worked professionally with PHP, Perl, C++, and Visual Basic. He is the author of the Apress book *Practical Ruby Gems*.

David's professional accomplishments include creating the Ruby on Rails engine for CoolRuby.com (http://coolruby.com), a site that tracks the latest Ruby developments, and working with thoughtbot (http://www.thoughtbot.com) on the Rails engine that powers Sermo's Top Doctor contest. Additionally, he has worked on several other Ruby projects, including the engine powering CyberKnowHow's Birdflubreakingnews.com search engine. He currently works with the Los Angeles digital-casting services firm The Casting Frontier.

David's journalism has been in print in more than 65 countries, in magazines such as *Linux Magazine*, *Dr. Dobb's Journal*, *Red Hat Magazine*, and *International PHP Magazine*. He has also taught college courses, guest lectured—notably at Harvard University—and spoken publicly on topics such as "MySQL and You" and "Making Money with Open Source Software."

About the Technical Reviewer

 **NICK PLANTE** is a programmer, author, entrepreneur, and (most of all) a nice guy. As a freelance programmer and a partner in Ubikorp Internet Services, Nick specializes in helping web startups accelerate their development with Ruby and Rails. He is a co-organizer of the New Hampshire Ruby Users Group and the Rails Rumble coding competition, and contributes to numerous open source projects.

When he is not dreaming up new applications or gushing about how great Ruby is, Nick enjoys independent music and film, as well as hiking, biking, and snowshoeing. He currently lives with his wife Amanda in the New Hampshire seacoast area, an hour north of Boston.

You can contact Nick at nap@zerosum.org or visit his programming blog on the Web at http://blog.zerosum.org. If you find something useful there, feel free to buy him comic books or an alpaca ranch.

Acknowledgments

I'd like to thank my parents and my sisters; I can't imagine writing this book without them. I'd also like to thank the many friends who have supported me; in particular, I'd like to thank Wayne Hammar, Matthew Gifford, and Michael Southwick.

I'd also like to thank the vast array of professional associates I've worked with and learned from, and in particular, I'd like to thank Joey Rubenstein. I'd also like to thank Jason Gilmore for teaching me quite a bit about the publishing business and about writing, and for that matter, for putting up with my incessant questions.

Finally, I'd like to thank my editors, originally Jason Gilmore and later Steve Anglin, as well as my technical reviewer and co-conspirator Nick Plante, my project manager Beth Christmas, and my copy editor Marilyn Smith.

Introduction

This book is about general and scalable ways to create reports with Ruby. It covers using a huge array of tools—Rails, Gruff, Ghostscript, and many more—but a common thread links them all: they are powerful tools that will serve you even if you have a huge amount of data. Using the reporting tools and techniques described in this book, you will be able to solve almost any reporting problem, from small to very, very large.

This book assumes you have some knowledge of Ruby and Rails, as well as access to a machine with Ruby, RubyGems, Rails, and MySQL installed. If you need to learn more about Ruby, I recommend reading *Beginning Ruby: From Novice to Professional* by Peter Cooper (Apress, 2007).

Practical Reporting with Ruby and Rails is divided into two parts. Part 1 covers the fundamentals of reporting with Ruby. You'll find information about data access, data analysis, and graphing, as well as presenting your graphs on the desktop and on the Web. Part 2 gives specific, real-life examples of useful reports, ranging from monitoring eBay auctions, to tracking sales performance with SugarCRM, to conducting Google AdWords campaigns.

If you would like to contact me, you can do so through my web site at `http://berubeconsulting.com` or via e-mail, at `djberube@berubeconsulting.com`. I would love to hear from you.

PART 1

■ ■ ■

Introducing Reporting with Ruby

CHAPTER 1

■■■

Data Access Fundamentals

Businesses all over the globe produce data, and they are producing it at a faster pace than ever before. Most of this data is stored in databases, but often it's publicly available only in inconvenient forms, such as Word documents, Excel spreadsheets, web pages, and comma-separated values (CSV) files.

As an unfortunate result, the data you need often isn't in a useful format. And even when the data is in an accessible format, you may need to process it heavily to achieve a useful result. For example, you might need to find the average sales of a certain region, rather than just a list of individual sales.

Of course, once you've analyzed the data and extracted some useful information, you'll need to present it intelligently; raw numbers are rarely useful outside academia. Today's business world requires powerful, attractively designed reporting, with features like charts, graphs, and images.

Essentially, this book will cover these three points: importing foreign data into a database, analyzing that data to get a useful result, and then formatting that data in a way that can be easily examined. To begin, you'll need a database in which to store your data and a library to access it. This chapter introduces two useful open source databases and Active Record, a powerful database access library.

Choosing a Database

A wide variety of connection adapters are available for various databases, including Oracle, Microsoft SQL Server, DB2, SQLite, MySQL, and PostgreSQL.

The examples in this book use MySQL, a fast, lightweight, open source database. You can download and use it for free, although a paid version with technical support is available from `http://www.mysql.com/`. MySQL is a good choice for applications that are not large enough to warrant purchasing an expensive database license. MySQL is also commonly used in web applications, because MySQL support is provided by a high percentage of Internet web hosts.

A number of high-profile organizations and web sites—Apple, Craigslist, Google AdWords, Flickr, Slashdot, and many others—use MySQL. Slashdot, shown in Figure 1-1, handles more than 150 million page views per day.

Figure 1-1. *Slashdot.org is a high-traffic site that uses MySQL.*

The techniques covered in this book will also generally work without modification on PostgreSQL, a fast and full-featured open source database. You can download and use PostgreSQL for free from `http://www.postgresql.org/`. PostgreSQL includes a number of features that are comparable to those available with large, commercial databases, and it performs just as well (and in some cases, better) as those databases. Therefore, you can use PostgreSQL in many situations where you need a powerful, scalable database.

PostgreSQL also has a fair number of large users, like Skype, TiVo, the Internet Movie Database, the US Department of Labor, Apple Remote Desktop (see Figure 1-2), and Radio Paradise. Radio Paradise is an Internet radio station with roughly 30 thousand users and more than 2 million file requests per day.

■**Tip** Often, convincing bosses, investors, or coworkers to use open source technology can be a hassle. Pointing to high-profile, high-load sites and companies using the technology can help in this endeavor. You can find a detailed list of significant MySQL users at `http://en.wikipedia.org/wiki/Mysql#Prominent_users`. Similarly, you can find a list of PostgreSQL users at `http://en.wikipedia.org/wiki/Postgresql#Prominent_users`.

Figure 1-2. *Apple's Remote Desktop is a high-traffic site that uses PostgreSQL.*

Using Active Record As a Database Access Library

Most of the examples in this book use Active Record as a database access library. Active Record is a simple way to access databases and database tables in Ruby. It is a powerful object-relational mapping (ORM) library that lets you easily model databases using an object-oriented interface. Besides being a stand-alone ORM package for Ruby, Active Record will also be familiar to web application developers as the model part of the web-application framework Ruby on Rails (see `http://ar.rubyonrails.org/`).

Active Record has a number of advantages over traditional ORM packages. Like the rest of the Rails stack, it emphasizes configuration by convention. This means that Active Record assumes that your tables and fields follow certain conventions unless you explicitly tell it otherwise. For example, it assumes that all tables have an artificial primary key named `id` (if you have a different primary key, you can override it, of course). It also assumes that the name of each table is a pluralized version of the model (that is, class) name; so if you have a model named `Item`, it assumes that your database table will be named `items`.

Active Record lets you define one or more models, each of which represents a single database table. Class instances are represented by rows in the appropriate database table. The fields of the tables, which will become your object's attributes, are automatically read from the database, so unlike other ORM libraries, you won't need to repeat your schema in two places or tinker with XML files to dictate the mapping. However, the relationships between models in Active Record aren't automatically read from the database, so you'll need to place code that represents those relationships in your models.

Creating a model in Active Record gives you quite a few features for free. You can automatically add, delete, find, and update records using methods, and those methods can make simple data tasks very trivial.

Let's look at two examples to demonstrate data manipulation with Active Record.

Calculating Player Salaries

Suppose you work for a game development company, Transmegtech Studios. The company's initial game releases were well received, but subsequent releases have been lambasted due to poor artificial intelligence and game balance. Management has concluded that programmers and graphic designers, who were responsible for testing the previous releases of the game, do not have the game-playing experience necessary to determine problems that occur only at superior skill levels. To remedy the problem, the company has hired a number of professional game players to test the next game before it's released. The testers will be paid according to their gaming performance, calculated based on their number of total wins per day.

The testers play a set number of games per day, and they record their wins. The company wants you to use Active Record to manage the list of players and to find their average salary/win ratio—that is, how much money each player costs per win. Transmegtech feels that this calculation will aid in determining how useful the player is to the company, on the assumption that the more skilled players are more valuable, since they presumably have a better knowledge of the game at hand. (Of course, this may or may not be true, but the goal of a report is to provide the data that the end user requests.)

Fortunately, Active Record makes this fairly easy. With Active Record and MySQL installed, you can create a simple schema, populate it with your data, and then find the average salary.

Listing 1-1 shows the code to create a player table schema.

Listing 1-1. *Simple Player Table Schema (player_schema.sql)*

```
CREATE DATABASE players;
USE players;

CREATE TABLE players (
  id int(11) NOT NULL AUTO_INCREMENT,
```

```
    name TEXT,
    wins int(11) NOT NULL,
    salary DECIMAL(9,2),
    PRIMARY KEY (id)
)
```

Save this file as `player_schema.sql`. Then run the following MySQL command:

```
mysql -u your_mysql_username -p < player_schema.sql
```

Next, you can write the code to declare a model to wrap the newly created database table, establish a connection to the database, add a few records, and then calculate the average win/salary ratio. Listing 1-2 shows this code.

Listing 1-2. *Calculating Player Salaries (player_salary_ratio.rb)*

```
require 'active_record'

ActiveRecord::Base.establish_connection(
    :adapter  => 'mysql',
    :host     => 'localhost',
    :username => 'your_mysql_username_goes_here',
    :password => 'your_mysql_password_goes_here'   :database => 'players')


class Player <  ActiveRecord::Base
end

Player.delete_all

Player.new do |p|
  p.name = "Matthew 'm_giff' Gifford"
  p.salary = 89000.00
  p.wins = 11
  p.save
end

Player.new do |p|
  p.name = "Matthew 'Iron Helix' Bouley"
  p.salary = 75000.00
  p.wins  = 4
  p.save
end
```

```
Player.new do |p|
  p.name = "Luke 'Cable Boy' Bouley"
  p.salary = 75000.50
  p.wins = 7
  p.save
end

salary_total = 0
win_total=0

players = Player.find(:all)
players.each do |player|
  puts "#{player.name}: $#{'%0.2f' % (player.salary/player.wins)} per win"
  salary_total = salary_total + player.salary
  win_total = win_total + player.wins
end

puts "\nAverage Cost Per Win : $#{'%0.2f' % (salary_total / win_total )}"
```

■Note If you connect to MySQL via Unix sockets, and it's in a nonstandard location, you can add a `:socket=>'path/to/your/socket'` option to the `ActiveRecord::Base.establish_connection` call.

Save this script as `player_salary_ratio.rb`. You can run this script using the following command:

```
ruby player_salary_ratio.rb
```

```
Matthew 'm_giff' Gifford: $8090.91 per win
Matthew 'Iron Helix' Bouley: $18750.00 per win
Luke 'Cable Boy' Bouley: $10714.36 per win

Average Cost Per Win: $10863.66
```

Let's take a closer look at the techniques used to manipulate the database in this example.

Dissecting the Code

In Listing 1-2, first the `ActiveRecord::Base.establish_connection` method is used to establish a connection to the database, as follows:

```
ActiveRecord::Base.establish_connection(
  :adapter  => 'mysql',
  :host     => 'localhost',
  :username => 'root',  # This is the default username and password
  :password => '',      # for MySQL, but note that if you have a
                        # different username and password,
                        # you should change it.
  :database => 'players')
```

The `adapter` parameter is of particular interest. As you can infer from this line, you can use other adapters to connect to other database types. The remainder of the parameters specify details of the connection: the server location, the name of the database, access credentials, and so forth.

All of the models will use this connection by default, since you called `establish_connection` on `ActiveRecord::Base`. However, you can also call `establish_connection` on individual models that inherit from the Active Record base class, which lets you have some models refer to one database and other models refer to a different database.

Next, you create a model:

```
class Player <  ActiveRecord::Base
end
```

As you can see, it's not at all complicated to create a simple model in Active Record. All of your record names are automatically read from your database, and you can access them with simple getter and setter methods. The two lines used to create the `Player` class are very powerful. They declare the new class as a subclass of `ActiveRecord::Base`. This gives you access to a number of built-in methods and, through introspection and pluralization rules, obtains the name of the underlying database table. The fact that Active Record is now aware of the table's name means that it can create methods to match the field names and automatically generate SQL statements to interact with the database.

One of the methods you inherit from `ActiveRecord::Base` allows you to delete all of the records from previous runs (of course, there won't be any the first time through):

```
Player.delete_all
```

Next, you use the new method to add a record:

```
Player.new do |p|
  p.name = "Matthew 'm_giff' Gifford"
  p.salary = 89000.00
  p.wins = 7
  p.save
end
```

The new method has a few different forms. In this case, you're passing it a block, and it passes a new Player object to your block. You could also use this form:

```
p = Player.new
p.name = "Matthew 'm_giff' Gifford"
p.salary = 89000.00
p.wins = 7
p.save
```

Alternatively, you could use this form:

```
p = Player.new(:name=> "Matthew 'm_giff' Gifford", :salary => 89000.00, :wins => 7)
p.save
```

All three of these forms are just variations that perform the same action.

The methods you use to set your fields—name and salary—are provided by Active Record, and they are named after their associated fields. Remember that both getter and setter methods are automatically created for each field name declared in your schema (Listing 1-1).

After you create the first player, you create two more in similar fashion. Then you need to perform the analysis:

```
salary_total = 0
win_total = 0

players = Player.find(:all)
players.each do |player|
  puts "#{player.name}: $#{'%0.2f' % (player.salary/player.wins)} per win"
  salary_total = salary_total + player.salary
  win_total = win_total + player.wins
end

puts "\nAverage Cost Per Win : $#{'%0.2f' % (salary_total / win_total )}"
```

This code finds all of the players using the `Player.find` class method (inherited from `ActiveRecord::Base`) and saves them into an array. It then loops through the array while totaling the salaries and wins. For each player, it prints out the player's salary/wins ratio— that is, how much the player costs the company for each win. Note that although you calculated the average manually for demonstration purposes, you would normally use MySQL's statistical functions to get this kind of information, as discussed in Chapter 2.

■**Note** The `find` method has quite a few options, as you'll see in upcoming chapters. For example, the `:conditions` parameter specifies conditions for the record retrieval, just like a SQL `WHERE` clause. The `:limit` parameter specifies a maximum number of records to return, just like the SQL `LIMIT` clause. In fact, the `:conditions` parameter and the `:limit` parameter are directly translated into `WHERE` and `LIMIT` clauses, respectively.

Finally, the code prints out the average salary, which is calculated by dividing the total salary by the number of players:

```
puts "\nAverage Cost Per Win : $#{'%0.2f' % (salary_total / win_total )}"
```

Notice the use of the % operator. This lets you format the output using two decimal points. It is very similar to the C/C++ `sprintf` function; in fact, it calls the `kernel::spintf` function. You can find out more about the various formatting options at http://www.ruby-doc.org/core/classes/Kernel.html#M005962.

This example was fairly simple, but you can see how trivial it is to do data manipulations with Active Record.

Calculating Player Wins

Now suppose that the new game release was a success, and Transmegtech has hired professional game players to beta test all of the company's games. Your boss now wants you to calculate which player has the highest wins for each individual title, as well as which player has the most wins overall.

For this report, you'll need more than one table. Fortunately, Active Record has a rich set of associations that describe the relationships between tables: the `has_many` relationship describes a one-to-many relationship, the `has_one` association describes a one-to-one relationship, and so forth. Those relationships are created inside your model definitions. Once you've created them, you get a number of helper methods for free. A method named after the association is added to the class, which can be enumerated, inserted into, and so forth. For example, if you have a model named `Customer` and a model named `Order`, and the `Customer` model has a `has_many` relationship with the `Order` model, you can access the `Orders` associated with each `Customer` object via the `orders` method.

Let's begin by creating two more tables. You can do so using the SQL shown in Listing 1-3.

Listing 1-3. *Player Schema Modifications (player_schema_2.sql)*

```
DROP DATABASE IF EXISTS players_2;
CREATE DATABASE players_2;
USE players_2;

CREATE TABLE players (
  id int(11) NOT NULL AUTO_INCREMENT,
  name TEXT,
  salary DECIMAL(9,2),
  PRIMARY KEY (id)
);

INSERT INTO players (id, name, salary)
            VALUES (1, "Matthew 'm_giff' Gifford", 89000.00);
INSERT INTO players (id, name, salary)
            VALUES (2, "Matthew 'Iron Helix' Bouley", 75000.00);
INSERT INTO players (id, name, salary)
            VALUES (3, "Luke 'Cable Boy' Bouley", 75000.50);

CREATE TABLE games (
  id int(11) NOT NULL AUTO_INCREMENT,
  name TEXT,
  PRIMARY KEY (id)
);

INSERT INTO games (id, name) VALUES (1, 'Eagle Beagle Ballad');
INSERT INTO games (id, name) VALUES (2, 'Camel Tender Redux');
INSERT INTO games (id, name) VALUES (3, 'Super Dunkball II: The Return');
INSERT INTO games (id, name) VALUES (4, 'Turn the Corner SE: Carrera vs CRX');

CREATE TABLE wins (
  id int(11) NOT NULL AUTO_INCREMENT,
  player_id int(11) NOT NULL,
  game_id int(11) NOT NULL,
  quantity int(11) NOT NULL,
  PRIMARY KEY (id)
);
```

```
INSERT INTO wins (player_id, game_id, quantity) VALUES (1, 1, 3);
INSERT INTO wins (player_id, game_id, quantity) VALUES (1, 3, 5);
INSERT INTO wins (player_id, game_id, quantity) VALUES (1, 2, 9);
INSERT INTO wins (player_id, game_id, quantity) VALUES (1, 4, 9);

INSERT INTO wins (player_id, game_id, quantity) VALUES (2, 1, 8);
INSERT INTO wins (player_id, game_id, quantity) VALUES (2, 3, 5);
INSERT INTO wins (player_id, game_id, quantity) VALUES (2, 2, 13);
INSERT INTO wins (player_id, game_id, quantity) VALUES (2, 4, 5);

INSERT INTO wins (player_id, game_id, quantity) VALUES (3, 1, 2);
INSERT INTO wins (player_id, game_id, quantity) VALUES (3, 3, 15);
INSERT INTO wins (player_id, game_id, quantity) VALUES (3, 2, 4);
INSERT INTO wins (player_id, game_id, quantity) VALUES (3, 4, 6);
```

Save this file as `player_schema_2.sql`. Then run the following MySQL command:

```
mysql -u your_mysql_username -p < player_schema_2.sql
```

Note that the SQL has the data already loaded into it (as specified with `SQL INSERT` statements), so the script does not need to handle the data insertion directly.

Next, you need some code to analyze our data. The code shown in Listing 1-4 does just that.

Listing 1-4. *Analyzing Player Wins (player_wins.rb)*

```ruby
require 'active_record'

ActiveRecord::Base.establish_connection(
  :adapter  => 'mysql',
  :host     => 'localhost',
  :username => 'root',  # This is the default username and password
  :password => '',      # for MySQL, but note that if you have a
                        # different username and password,
                        # you should change it.
  :database => 'players_2')


class Player <  ActiveRecord::Base
  has_many :wins
  def total_wins
    total_wins = 0
    self.wins.each do |win|
```

```ruby
      total_wins = total_wins + win.quantity
    end
    total_wins
  end
end
class Game <  ActiveRecord::Base
  has_many :wins
end
class Win <  ActiveRecord::Base
  belongs_to :game
  belongs_to :player
end


games = Game.find(:all)

games.each do |game|
  highest_win=nil
  game.wins.each do |win|
  highest_win = win if highest_win.nil? or
                                  win.quantity > highest_win.quantity
  end

  puts "#{game.name}: #{highest_win.player.name} with #{highest_win.quantity} wins"
end


players = Player.find(:all)

highest_winning_player = nil

players.each do |player|
  highest_winning_player = player if
                  highest_winning_player.nil? or
                  player.total_wins > highest_winning_player.total_wins
end

puts "Highest Winning Player: #{highest_winning_player.name} " <<
     "with #{highest_winning_player.total_wins} wins"
```

Save this script as `player_wins.rb`. You can run this script using the following command:

```ruby
ruby player_wins.rb
```

```
Eagle Beagle Ballad: Matthew 'Iron Helix' Bouley with 8 wins
Camel Tender Redux: Matthew 'Iron Helix' Bouley with 13 wins
Super Dunkball II: The Return: Luke 'Cable Boy' Bouley with 15 wins
Turn the Corner SE: Carrera vs CRX: Matthew 'm_giff' Gifford with 9 wins
Highest Winning Player: Matthew 'Iron Helix' Bouley with 31 wins
```

Let's take a look at each of the techniques used in this script.

Dissecting the Code

First, the script in Listing 1-4 connects to the database, as in the previous example. However, the models are more complicated than the model in that example, because they have relationships defined between them and a custom method on the Player model. You can see those in the following code:

```
class Player <  ActiveRecord::Base
  has_many :wins
  def total_wins
    total_wins = 0
    self.wins.each do |win|
    total_wins = total_wins + win.quantity
    end
    total_wins
  end
end
class Game <  ActiveRecord::Base
  has_many :wins
end
class Win <  ActiveRecord::Base
  belongs_to :game
  belongs_to :player
end
```

The Player model defines a has_many relationship with the Win model, as does the Game model. This adds a wins method to instances of the Player and Game classes, which can be used to iterate through the associated wins from either a Player or a Game object. (A savvy reader will notice from the schema in Listing 1-3 that the Win model is a join table with an extra attribute, quantity; the quantity attribute is why it is a model in its own right.) The Win model defines a belongs_to relationship with both the Player and Game models, thus adding player and game methods to each instance of the Win model. Calling one of these methods lets you access the particular Player and Game objects with which the Win object is associated. The Player model also has an extra method: an instance method called total_wins, which is used to loop through all of a player's wins, returning the total quantity. This method uses the wins method added by the has_many relationship with the Win model.

Note Every time the total_wins method is called, a query is made on the wins table, which could conceivably take a while. In a production environment, it might be worthwhile to cache the result in the parent table.

The script loops through each game and finds the player who has the most wins for that game:

```
games = Game.find(:all)

games.each do |game|
  highest_win=nil
  game.wins.each do |win|
    highest_win = win if highest_win.nil? or
                             win.quantity > highest_win.quantity
  end

  puts "#{game.name}: #{highest_win.player.name} with #{highest_win.quantity} wins"
end
```

As you can see, it uses the aforementioned wins property of each Game object. The method returns an array of wins for the current game, so we loop through each and find the win with the highest quantity. At that point, the name of the game is printed out, as well as the name of the winning player and the quantity.

Next, a very similar loop goes through all of the players and finds the player with the highest total wins:

```
players = Player.find(:all)

highest_winning_player = nil

players.each do |player|
  highest_winning_player = player if
                  highest_winning_player.nil? or
                  player.total_wins > highest_winning_player.total_wins
end
```

```
puts "Highest Winning Player: #{highest_winning_player.name} " <<
    "with #{highest_winning_player.total_wins} wins"
```

You loop through each player and use the `total_wins` method to sum the player's quantity of wins. The player with the highest result from `total_wins` is selected, and that player's name and total wins are printed out. As you can see, it's easy to use Active Record to process data.

Summary

In this chapter, you got started using MySQL and Active Record with Ruby to produce some simple reports. Active Record is a powerful, easy-to-use library. Although Active Record is best known for web applications, it can be used quickly and easily for virtually all types of Ruby database connectivity, including reporting.

In both the examples in this chapter, you did all of the statistical calculations manually in Ruby code. Instead, you can use MySQL's and Active Record's statistical functions to get statistics, group data, and more. The next chapter covers calculatiing statistics with Active Record.

CHAPTER 2

■■■

Calculating Statistics with Active Record

The previous chapter discussed the fundamentals of accessing and manipulating data with Active Record. The statistical analyses—the highest salary, average salary, and so forth—were done manually using Ruby code. While that's a plausible approach, it's easier and often quicker to let the database do the work for you.

Databases typically have numerous built-in features for speeding up data access. Indexes, for example, are subsets of your table data, which are automatically maintained by your database and can make searching much faster. You can think of indexes like the table of contents in a book. It's much faster to find something by using the table of contents than it is to read every page of the book looking for the desired information. Additionally, the database's query planner uses speed-enhancing techniques automatically. This query planner has access to statistical information on the various tables and columns that your query uses, and it will formulate a query plan based on that information. In other words, it estimates how long each method of retrieving the data you requested will take, and it uses the quickest method. Because of the capabilities of the database, it's typically best to use the techniques described in this chapter, as they are considerably faster than doing your statistics in your Ruby code.

In this chapter, you'll learn how to use the database to perform two common tasks: *grouping* and *aggregation*. Let's look at how these tasks are useful, and then work through an example that uses them for reporting.

Grouping and Aggregation

Grouping refers to a way to reduce a table into a subset, where each row in the subset represents the set of records having a particular grouped value or values. For example, if you were tracking automobile accidents, and you had a table of persons, with their age and number of accidents, you could group by age and retrieve every distinct age in the database. In other words, you would get a list of the age of every person, with the duplicates removed.

If you were using an Active Record model named Person with an age column, you could find all of the distinct ages of the people involved, as follows:

```
ages = Person.find(:all, :group=>'age')
```

However, to perform useful work on grouped queries, you'll typically use aggregate functions. For example, you'll need to use aggregate functions to retrieve the average accidents per age group or the count of the people in each age group.

You've probably encountered a number of aggregate functions already. Some common ones are MAX and MIN, which give you the maximum and minimum value; AVG, which gives you the average value; SUM, which returns the sum of the values; and COUNT, which returns the total number of values. Each database engine may define different statistical functions, but nearly all provide those just mentioned.

Continuing with the Active Record model named Person with an age column, you could find the highest age from your table as follows:

```
oldest_age = Person.calculate(:max, :age)
```

Note that calculate takes the max function's name, as a symbol, as its first argument, but Active Record also has a number of convenience functions named after their respective purposes: count, sum, minimum, maximum, and average. For example, the following two lines are identical:

```
average_accident_count = Person.calculate(:avg, :accident_count)
average_accident_count = Person.average(:accident_count)
```

Both print out the average number of accidents for all rows.

■Note The calculate form takes the abbreviated version of the function name, such as avg for average. However, the shortcut form takes a longer version. For example, you could use either Person.calculate(:avg, :age) or Person.average(:age). This is confusing, but the idea is that the calculate form passes your function directly to your database, so you can use any statistical function defined in your database, whereas the convenience functions are fixed, so they can have easier to understand names.

You can also combine grouping and aggregate functions. For example, if you wanted to print the average accident count for each age, you could do so as follows:

```
Person.calculate(:avg, :accident_count, :group=>'age').each do |player|
  age, accident_count_average = *player
  puts "Average Accident Count #{'%0.3f' % accident_count_average} for age #{age}"
end
```

Note that the object passed to the block is an array. In the array, the grouped field comes first, followed by the calculated field. (If you wanted to group by more than one field, it would be in the order specified by the group parameter.)

Depending on your data, your results would look something like this:

```
Average Accident Count 3.000 for age 18
Average Accident Count 2.020 for age 19
Average Accident Count 1.010 for age 20
. . .
```

However, for more complex queries, you may need to craft a SQL statement manually. Specifically, you can use find_by_sql to search for any arbitrary SQL query, and this allows you to ask for virtually any type of information. For example, if a vehicle_model column existed in your Accident model, you could group by vehicle_model and run two aggregate functions: average age and average accident_count. This would give you an average owner age and an average number of accidents per vehicle, so you could get some idea whether, say, a Ford Explorer was a safer ride than a Honda CRX. (Of course, driver control would play a significant part, and hence the average age is a helpful statistic.) You can't use multiple aggregate functions with calculate, but you can with find_by_sql, like this:

```
sql = "SELECT vehicle_model,
            AVG(age) as average_age,
            AVG(accident_count) AS average_accident_count
        FROM persons
        GROUP
          BY vehicle_model
     "
Person.find_by_sql(sql).each do |row|
  puts "#{row.vehicle_model}, " <<
      "avg. age: #{row.average_age}, " <<
      "avg. accidents: #{row.average_accident_count}"
end
```

The output would look something like this:

```
Ford Explorer, avg. age: 43.010, avg. accidents: 0.400
Honda CRX, avg. age: 18.720, avg. accidents: 1.250
. . .
```

Let's put this knowledge to use with a more complicated example.

Analyzing Data with Grouping and Aggregates

The examples in Chapter 1 involved Transmegtech Studios, a hypothetical game development company. Now let's suppose Transmegtech Studios has merged with another small studio, J. Lee Games, and they want to analyze their combined base of game testers. Specifically, they want to answer two questions:

How many players are at each salary rate? Answering this question should give the merged companies a way to get a handle on their total beta-testing expenditures. This question can be answered with simple grouping in Active Record, so that will be tackled first.

Which drink leads to the highest performance? The Transmegtech people are having a dispute with the new personnel from J. Lee Games. The new testers and programmers drink Fresca, whereas the Transmegtech team prefers the Moxie energy drink. Both sides claim their drink is superior, and leads to higher productivity and mental agility. The management would like to know which drink leads to the highest performance, with the data broken down by wins per game. In the interests of fairness, they've agreed to analyze data only from new titles developed by the joint company, so old data won't cloud the analysis. This question can be answered with a combination of grouping and aggregate functions, and that will be tackled second.

For the examples in this chapter, you'll use the schema shown in Listing 2-1.

■**Note** This and upcoming chapters use subqueries. Subqueries were not introduced into MySQL until version 4.2. If you have an older version of MySQL, you'll need to upgrade to follow these examples.

Listing 2-1. *Player Schema Mark III (player_schema_3.sql)*

```
CREATE DATABASE players_3;
USE players_3;

CREATE TABLE players (
  id int(11) NOT NULL AUTO_INCREMENT,
  name TEXT,
  drink TEXT,
  salary DECIMAL(9,2),
```

```
  PRIMARY KEY (id)
);

INSERT INTO players (id, name, drink, salary) VALUES
                (1, "Matthew 'm_giff' Gifford", "Moxie", 89000.00);
INSERT INTO players (id, name, drink, salary) VALUES
                (2, "Matthew 'Iron Helix' Bouley", "Moxie", 75000.00);
INSERT INTO players (id, name, drink, salary) VALUES
                (3, "Luke 'Cable Boy' Bouley", "Moxie", 75000.50);
INSERT INTO players (id, name, drink, salary) VALUES
                (4, "Andrew 'steven-tyler-xavier' Thomas", 'Fresca', 75000.50);
INSERT INTO players (id, name, drink, salary) VALUES
                (5, "John 'dwy_dwy' Dwyer", 'Fresca', 76000.75);
INSERT INTO players (id, name, drink, salary) VALUES
                (6, "Ryan 'the_dominator' Peacan", 'Fresca', 75000.50);
INSERT INTO players (id, name, drink, salary) VALUES
                (7, "Michael 'Shaun Wiki' Southwick", 'Fresca', 75000.50);

CREATE TABLE games (
  id int(11) NOT NULL AUTO_INCREMENT,
  name TEXT,
  PRIMARY KEY (id)
);

INSERT INTO games (id, name) VALUES (1, 'Bubble Recycler');
INSERT INTO games (id, name) VALUES (2, 'Computer Repair King');
INSERT INTO games (id, name) VALUES (3, 'Super Dunkball II: The Return');
INSERT INTO games (id, name) VALUES (4, 'Sudden Deceleration: No Time to Think');

CREATE TABLE wins (
  id int(11) NOT NULL AUTO_INCREMENT,
  player_id int(11) NOT NULL,
  game_id int(11) NOT NULL,
  quantity int(11) NOT NULL,
  PRIMARY KEY (id)
);

INSERT INTO wins (player_id, game_id, quantity) VALUES (1, 1, 3);
INSERT INTO wins (player_id, game_id, quantity) VALUES (1, 3, 8);
INSERT INTO wins (player_id, game_id, quantity) VALUES (1, 2, 3);
INSERT INTO wins (player_id, game_id, quantity) VALUES (1, 4, 9);
```

```
INSERT INTO wins (player_id, game_id, quantity) VALUES (2, 1, 8);
INSERT INTO wins (player_id, game_id, quantity) VALUES (2, 3, 10);
INSERT INTO wins (player_id, game_id, quantity) VALUES (2, 2, 7);
INSERT INTO wins (player_id, game_id, quantity) VALUES (2, 4, 5);

INSERT INTO wins (player_id, game_id, quantity) VALUES (3, 1, 8);
INSERT INTO wins (player_id, game_id, quantity) VALUES (3, 3, 4);
INSERT INTO wins (player_id, game_id, quantity) VALUES (3, 2, 20);
INSERT INTO wins (player_id, game_id, quantity) VALUES (3, 4, 8);

INSERT INTO wins (player_id, game_id, quantity) VALUES (4, 1, 8);
INSERT INTO wins (player_id, game_id, quantity) VALUES (4, 3, 9);
INSERT INTO wins (player_id, game_id, quantity) VALUES (4, 2, 8);
INSERT INTO wins (player_id, game_id, quantity) VALUES (4, 4, 3);

INSERT INTO wins (player_id, game_id, quantity) VALUES (5, 1, 7);
INSERT INTO wins (player_id, game_id, quantity) VALUES (5, 3, 1);
INSERT INTO wins (player_id, game_id, quantity) VALUES (5, 2, 9);
INSERT INTO wins (player_id, game_id, quantity) VALUES (5, 4, 4);

INSERT INTO wins (player_id, game_id, quantity) VALUES (6, 1, 2);
INSERT INTO wins (player_id, game_id, quantity) VALUES (6, 3, 12);
INSERT INTO wins (player_id, game_id, quantity) VALUES (6, 2, 8);
INSERT INTO wins (player_id, game_id, quantity) VALUES (6, 4, 9);

INSERT INTO wins (player_id, game_id, quantity) VALUES (7, 1, 2);
INSERT INTO wins (player_id, game_id, quantity) VALUES (7, 3, 1);
INSERT INTO wins (player_id, game_id, quantity) VALUES (7, 2, 4);
INSERT INTO wins (player_id, game_id, quantity) VALUES (7, 4, 9);
```

Save this file as player_schema_3.sql. (Note that this listing increments the database version number, so you can still go back and run the previous examples, which have different database structures.) Next, run the following command:

```
mysql -u your_mysql_username < player_schema_3.sql
```

Now that you have the data loaded into your database, let's tackle the first question.

Calculating Salary Distribution

You want to find how many players are at each salary rate. It's reasonably simple to use Active Record's count function and grouping ability to calculate the distribution of the salary, and Listing 2-2 does just that.

Listing 2-2. *Calculating Salary Distribution (salary_distribution.rb)*

```ruby
require 'active_record'

# Establish a connection to the database. . .
ActiveRecord::Base.establish_connection(
  :adapter  => 'mysql',
  :host     => 'localhost',
  :username => 'root',  # This is the default username and password
  :password => '',      # for MySQL, but note that if you have a
                        # different username and password,
                        # you should change it.
  :database => 'players_3')

# . . . set up our models . . .
class Player <  ActiveRecord::Base
  has_many :wins
end
class Game <  ActiveRecord::Base
  has_many :wins
end
class Win <  ActiveRecord::Base
  belongs_to :game
  belongs_to :player
end

# . . . and perform our calculation:

puts "Salary\t\tCount"

Player.calculate(:count, :id, :group=>'salary').each do |player|
  salary, count = *player
  puts "$#{'%0.2f' % salary}\t#{count} "
```

```
# Note that the '%0.25f' % call formats the value as a float
# with two decimal points. The String's % operator works
# similarly to the C sprintf function.
```

end

Save this script as salary_distribution.rb. You can run it as follows:

ruby salary_distribution.rb

Salary	Count
$75000.00	1
$75000.50	4
$76000.75	1
$89000.00	1

As you can see, it's reasonably trivial to use the calculate function to do simple grouping and report the results.

Dissecting the Code

Most of Listing 2-2 is code to connect to the database and initialize the models, as you've seen in other examples. The work actually performed by this script is done by the following code:

```
Player.calculate(:count, :id, :group=>'salary').each do |player|
  salary, count = *player
  puts "$#{'%0.2f' % salary}\t#{count} "
end
```

Essentially, this code groups by the salary field and counts the ids in each group. Since each player has a unique id, this is equivalent to counting the rows themselves. For each row, the array is split into its component parts: salary and count. As before, the order of the array passed to your block is the grouped fields followed by the calculated field.

Calculating Drink/Win Distribution

Next, let's try answering the second question: which drink leads to the highest performance? Listing 2-3 uses find_by_sql to do that.

Listing 2-3. *Calculating Drink/Win Distribution (drink_win_distribution.rb)*

```ruby
require 'active_record'

# Establish a connection to the database. . .

ActiveRecord::Base.establish_connection(
  :adapter  => 'mysql',
  :host     => 'localhost',
  :username => 'root',  # This is the default username and password
  :password => '',       # for MySQL, but note that if you have a
                         # different username and password,
                         # you should change it.
  :database => 'players_3')

#  . . . set up our models . . .
class Player <  ActiveRecord::Base
  has_many :wins
end
class Game <  ActiveRecord::Base
  has_many :wins
end
class Win <  ActiveRecord::Base
  belongs_to :game
  belongs_to :player
end

def puts_underlined(text, underline_char="=")

  # This function will be used to print headers which are underlined
  # by an ASCII character such as the equal sign. This makes it
  # clear that it's a header and not part of the output data.

  puts text
  puts underline_char * text.length
end

#  . .. and create our report.

# First, we print overall results for each drink:

sql = "SELECT drink,
```

```
              COUNT(*) as total_players,

              (SELECT SUM(quantity) FROM wins
                WHERE wins.player_id=players.id) as total_wins

          FROM players

        GROUP
           BY players.drink

           ;"

puts_underlined "Overall"

puts "Drink\t\tWins\tPlayers\tWins/Players"

Player.find_by_sql(sql).each do |player|

  puts "#{player.drink.ljust(12)}\t" <<  # ljust is a function of String
                                        # that ensures the output is always
                                        # twelve characters long, so it lines up
                                        # nicely.
       "#{player.total_wins}\t" <<
       "#{player.total_players}\t" <<
       "#{'%0.3f' % (player.total_wins.to_f / player.total_players.to_f) }"
end

# Print results per drink and per game:

sql = "SELECT drink,
            games.name as game,

            COUNT(*) as total_players,

            (SELECT SUM(quantity) FROM wins
              WHERE wins.player_id=players.id
                    AND wins.game_id=games.id) as total_wins

        FROM players,
           games
```

```
        GROUP
          BY games.name,
             players.drink


             ; "


current_game=nil
Player.find_by_sql(sql).each do |player|
  if current_game != player.game
    puts "\n"
    puts_underlined player.game
    puts "Drink\t\tWins\tPlayers\tWins/Players"
    current_game = player.game
  end
  puts "#{player.drink.ljust(12)}\t" <<
       "#{player.total_wins}\t" <<
       "#{player.total_players}\t" <<
       "#{'%0.3f' % (player.total_wins.to_f /
                    player.total_players.to_f ) }"
end
```

Save this script as `drink_win_distribution.rb`. You can run the script as follows:

```
ruby drink_win_distribution.rb
```

You should get the following results:

```
Overall
=======
Drink         Wins    Players Wins/Players
Fresca        28      4       7.000
Moxie         23      3       7.667


Bubble Recycler
===============
Drink         Wins    Players Wins/Players
Fresca        8       4       2.000
Moxie         3       3       1.000
```

```
Computer Repair King
====================
Drink          Wins     Players Wins/Players
Fresca         8        4       2.000
Moxie          3        3       1.000


Sudden Deceleration: No Time to Think
=====================================
Drink          Wins     Players Wins/Players
Fresca         3        4       0.750
Moxie          9        3       3.000


Super Dunkball II: The Return
=============================
Drink          Wins     Players Wins/Players
Fresca         9        4       2.250
Moxie          8        3       2.667
```

As you can see, it appears that the results for Moxie and Fresca are very close. Fresca has exactly 7.0 wins per player, and Moxie has approximately 7.6 wins per player. Although the Moxie drinkers have a higher overall win ratio, the Fresca drinkers have a higher ratio for Bubble Recycler and Computer Repair King. Of course, a total of seven players is not enough to really draw a conclusion—it could be coincidence. However, the approach could easily be scaled up to thousands or even hundreds of thousands of records.

Dissecting the Code

First, the script in Listing 2-3 connects to the database and sets up the models, as you've seen in previous examples. Essentially, the remainder of the script runs two SQL statements and prints out the results in a nice format.

The first SQL statement returns the overall results for all games combined. To retrieve that result, the query groups by the drink field, and then uses a correlated subquery to retrieve the total number of wins:

```
sql = "SELECT drink,

          COUNT(*) as total_players,

          (SELECT SUM(quantity) FROM wins
            WHERE wins.player_id=players.id) as total_wins
```

```
        FROM players

     GROUP
        BY players.drink

        ;"
```

The grouping ensures that the main statement produces one row per drink. The correlated subquery produces a sum for each of those rows by looping through the wins table and totaling all of a player's wins. The code then proceeds to loop through the results and print them out.

Next, the second query produces a result specific to each game:

```
sql = "SELECT drink,
            games.name as game,

            COUNT(*) as total_players,

            (SELECT SUM(quantity) FROM wins
               WHERE wins.player_id=players.id
                     AND wins.game_id=games.id) as total_wins

        FROM players,
             games

     GROUP
        BY games.name,
           players.drink

        ; "
```

This uses a cross join and grouping. In other words, it produces one row for every combination of game and drink. For each of those rows, the subquery totals all wins that refer to the current game and to players who drink the current drink.

Once you have this query, it's reasonably trivial to print out the results.

Summary

Reporting often involves arduous statistical calculations. When you write code to perform these calculations by hand, you're reinventing the wheel—writing code that has been written countless times before. It's also easy to write slow code when you create it by hand. Fortunately, database systems contain fast, easy-to-use methods to create blazingly quick queries, and Active Record can make creating those queries even easier.

In the examples so far, you've seen how to print the results in a readable format. As you'll learn in the next chapter, you can use other formats. Chapter 3 discusses ways that you can take data and turn it into an attractive graph or chart.

Creating Graphs with Ruby

For reporting, you'll often need to format data as charts, which can come in a variety of formats—line, bar, area, and more. Such graphs won't be judged on functionality alone. Their appearance is a very important factor, so you must strive to make your graphs as attractive and understandable as possible.

Fortunately, graphing is a very common task, and several graphing utilities are available. This chapter introduces a few of these utilities, and then demonstrates how to build charts with Gruff, a powerful Ruby-based graphing library.

Choosing a Graphing Utility

You have many choices for creating charts with Ruby. For example, you can do simple charting in straight Hypertext Markup Language (HTML) and Cascading Style Sheets (CSS). Chapter 7 shows you how to use Markaby, a templating language for Ruby, to create your own HTML bar charts. Chapter 11 demonstrates how to use CSS helpers to create charts in Rails. Here, we'll look at the Gruff and Scruffy graphing libraries, and then use Gruff in a couple of examples.

Gruff (http://gruff.rubyforge.org/) provides a simple, Ruby-based interface to enter data and display details. After writing the code, you call a simple command to render the graph to a file. For example, if you had a collection of vintage guitars and wanted to display a simple bar chart with their values, you could do so as shown in Listing 3-1.

■**Note** You'll need Gruff, ImageMagick, and RMagick installed to run this example. ImageMagick, an image-manipulation toolkit used by Gruff, is available from http://imagemagick.org. RMagick is the Ruby interface to ImageMagick that Gruff uses. Install them by running the commands gem install -y gruff and gem install rmagick.

Listing 3-1. *Creating a Simple Chart with Gruff (guitar_chart.rb)*

```
require 'gruff'

line_chart = Gruff::Bar.new()
line_chart.labels = {0=>'Value (USD)'}
line_chart.title = "My Guitar Collection"

{"'70 Strat"=>2500,
 "'69 Tele"=>2000,
 "'02 Modded Mexi Strat Squier"=>400}.each do |guitar, value|
  line_chart.data(guitar, value )
 end

line_chart.write("guitar_chart.png")
```

You can run the example as follows:

```
ruby guitar_chart.rb
```

The resulting chart is shown in Figure 3-1.

As you can see, it's not particularly complicated to make a simple chart. The `labels` attribute takes a hash of labels for each column, so you can have multiple columns if you so desire. The `data` method takes a label for the row of data, as well as an array of values for that row. (If you have only one value, as in Listing 3-1, you don't need to pass it as an array.)

You can get Gruff documentation, sample graphs, and sample code from http://nubyonrails.com/pages/gruff.

Scruffy (http://scruffy.rubyforge.org/) is another popular graphing library. Scruffy offers a number of features that are not available with Gruff, but it's slightly more difficult to use than Gruff. Currently, Gruff has much more documentation available online and is more mature than Scruffy.

With Scruffy, you can mix graph types in the same graph, so you could, for example, have a chart with both line and bar elements. Suppose you were charting the output of a factory that builds widgets and sprockets. You could use the code in Listing 3-2 to create a bar and line chart with the data.

■**Note** To run this example, you'll need to install Scruffy with the command `gem install scruffy`. You'll also need RMagick installed, so install that with `gem install rmagick`, if you haven't already done so.

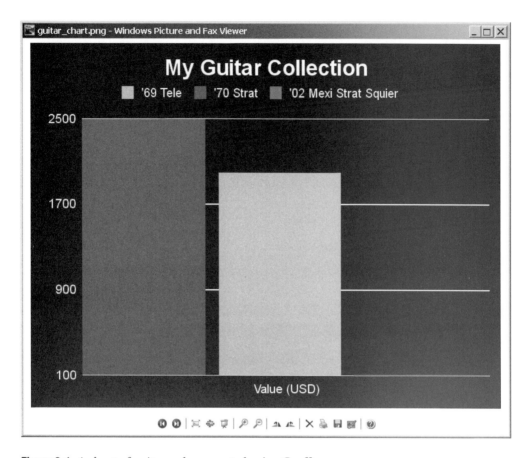

Figure 3-1. *A chart of guitar values created using Gruff*

Listing 3-2. *Creating a Simple Chart with Scruffy (widget_chart_scruffy.rb)*

```ruby
require 'scruffy'

sprocket_output = [["Jan",500],
                   ["Feb",750],
                   ["Apr",380]]

widget_output =   [["Jan",350],
                   ["Feb",650],
                   ["Apr",560]]

graph = Scruffy::Graph.new(
                   :title => "Widget and Sprocket Output",
                   :theme => Scruffy::Themes::Keynote.new)
```

```
graph.add(:bar, 'Sprockets', sprocket_output.map { |s| s[1] })
graph.add(:line, 'Widgets', widget_output.map { |w| w[1] })

graph.point_markers = widget_output.map { |w| w[0] }

graph.render(    :width => 800,
                 :as=>'PNG',
                 :to => 'widgets_and_sprockets.png')
```

Save this as `widget_chart_scruffy.rb`. You can run the script in Listing 3-2 as follows:

```
ruby widget_chart_scruffy.rb
```

If you open the file `widgets_and_sprockets.png`, you should see something similar to Figure 3-2.

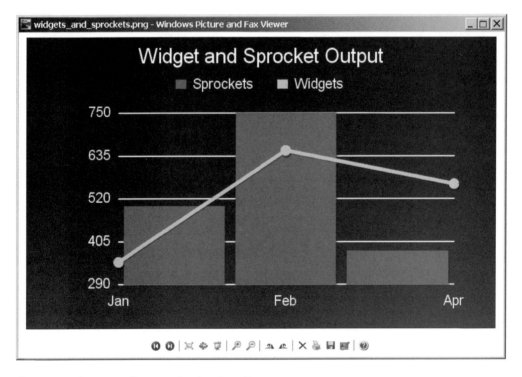

Figure 3-2. *Player graph created using Scruffy*

As you may have surmised from Listing 3-2, you can add data to a Scruffy graph using a command like this:

```
graph.add(:some_chart_type, 'Some_text_for_the_legend', some_array_of_values)
```

The add command is quite similar to Gruff's data method. This example is a bit more complex, as it parses some hashes and uses the keys of the first hash as labels for the x axis. (This assumes that they both have the same keys, which may or may not be true.)

You can find out more about Scruffy's various chart types at the Scruffy home page (`http://scruffy.rubyforge.org/`).

■**Tip** A graphing plug-in for Rails called ZiYa offers very attractive graphs and is easy to use. Unfortunately, it's based on a commercial SWF component, called XML/SWF Charts, so not only will your users need Flash, but you'll also need to purchase the component. (Actually, you can use ZiYa without paying, but if your users click the graph, they'll be taken to the XML/SWF Charts home page, which is unacceptable for many purposes.) If you're looking for a commercially supported graphing library, ZiYa may be a good choice. Another option is an open source Flash charting plug-in, one of which is covered in Chapter 5.

Now let's use Gruff to generate some interesting graphs.

Graphing Data

With Gruff, you can create bar charts, area charts, line charts, and more. To see how it works, you'll create a couple of charts for Transmegtech Studios, the fictional game development company used in the examples in Chapters 1 and 2.

Creating a Line Chart

Suppose that Transmegtech Studios is close to releasing its new strategy game, but the artificial intelligence is still not very good. Without a competitive artificial intelligence for single-player mode, players will quickly become bored with the game, which means that they will stop playing.

Your boss would like to dramatically improve the artificial intelligence. He wants to analyze the strategy of each player by producing a "scorecard" that shows the player's average time to accomplish each major goal in the game. The theory is that the order in which goals are achieved will reveal a significant amount about the player's strategy, and if the programmers can mimic that order, they can build a better computer player. (This is a strategy that has worked well for other real-time strategy games.) The Transmegtech game has a variety of goals, from building a company's data center (DC) component all the way to the player's company going public, which is the game-winning event.

Before you can use Gruff to graph the data, you must first load the data into a database. Listing 3-3 shows some of the SQL you'll need, but much of the data has been omitted for space considerations. You can download the full listing from `http://`

rubyreporting.com/examples/player_4.sql, or from the Source Code/Downloads area of
the Apress web site (http://.www.apress.com).

Listing 3-3. *Team Performance SQL (player_4.sql)*

```
DROP DATABASE IF EXISTS players_4 ;
CREATE DATABASE players_4;
USE players_4;

CREATE TABLE players (
  id INT(11) NOT NULL AUTO_INCREMENT,
  name TEXT,
  nickname TEXT,
  drink TEXT,
  salary DECIMAL(9,2),
  PRIMARY KEY (id)
);

INSERT INTO players (id, name, nickname, drink, salary) VALUES
                (1, "Matthew Gifford", 'm_giff', "Moxie", 89000.00);
INSERT INTO players (id, name, nickname, drink, salary) VALUES
                (2, "Matthew Bouley", 'Iron Helix', "Moxie", 75000.00);
INSERT INTO players (id, name, nickname, drink, salary) VALUES
                (3, "Luke Bouley", 'Cable Boy', "Moxie", 75000.50);
INSERT INTO players (id, name, nickname, drink, salary) VALUES
                (4, "Andrew Thomas", 'ste-ty-xav', 'Fresca', 75000.50);
INSERT INTO players (id, name, nickname, drink, salary) VALUES
                (5, "John Dwyer", 'dwy_dwy', 'Fresca', 89000.00);
INSERT INTO players (id, name, nickname, drink, salary) VALUES
                (6, "Ryan Peacan", 'the_dominator', 'Fresca', 75000.50);
INSERT INTO players (id, name, nickname, drink, salary) VALUES
                (7, "Michael Southwick", 'Shaun Wiki',  'Fresca', 75000.50);

CREATE TABLE games (
  id INT(11) NOT NULL AUTO_INCREMENT,
  name TEXT,
  PRIMARY KEY (id)
);

INSERT INTO games (id, name) VALUES (1, 'Bubble Recycler');
INSERT INTO games (id, name) VALUES (2, 'Computer Repair King');
INSERT INTO games (id, name) VALUES (3, 'Super Dunkball II: The Return');
```

```
INSERT INTO games (id, name) VALUES (4, 'Sudden Deceleration: No Time to Think');
INSERT INTO games (id, name) VALUES (5, 'Tech Website Baron');

CREATE TABLE plays (
  id INT(11) NOT NULL,
  player_id INT(11) NOT NULL,
  game_id INT(11) NOT NULL,
  won TINYINT NOT NULL,
  PRIMARY KEY (id)
);

CREATE TABLE events(
  play_id INT(11) NOT NULL,
    event VARCHAR(25) NOT NULL,
    time INT(11) NOT NULL
);

INSERT INTO plays (id, player_id, game_id, won) VALUES (0, 5, 5, 1);
INSERT INTO plays (id, player_id, game_id, won) VALUES (1, 5, 5, 1);
INSERT INTO plays (id, player_id, game_id, won) VALUES (2, 5, 5, 0);
INSERT INTO plays (id, player_id, game_id, won) VALUES (3, 5, 5, 1);
. . .
INSERT INTO events (play_id, event, time) VALUES(0, 'Built DC', 2146.8);
INSERT INTO events (play_id, event, time) VALUES(0, 'Built MC', 27867);
INSERT INTO events (play_id, event, time) VALUES(0, 'Built PR', 65349);
INSERT INTO events (play_id, event, time) VALUES(0, 'Went Public', 86104);
INSERT INTO events (play_id, event, time) VALUES(1, 'Built DC', 8466.0);
INSERT INTO events (play_id, event, time) VALUES(1, 'Built MC', 29454);
INSERT INTO events (play_id, event, time) VALUES(1, 'Built PR', 57896);
INSERT INTO events (play_id, event, time) VALUES(1, 'Went Public', 79587);
INSERT INTO events (play_id, event, time) VALUES(2, 'Built DC', 31455.6);
. . .
```

You can create the database using the following command:

```
mysql -u your_username -p your_mysql_password
```

As you can see from Listing 3-3, the schema in this example is quite similar to the previous schemas, except that it gives a bit more information. Each time a game is played, there is an entry in the plays table. Every time a major game event happens, there is a row in the events table. This allows you to analyze the average time it takes the player to achieve each goal. Note that the games table is included only for compatibility with the previous database, since you have data for only one game. (This allows you to easily expand if you're asked to create a similar report for a different game.)

Now that you have the data loaded into your MySQL database, you can create a simple bar chart for each player, as shown in Listing 3-4.

Listing 3-4. *Creating Player Bar Charts (player_bar_charts.rb)*

```ruby
require 'gruff'
require 'active_record'

game_id_to_analyze = 5

ActiveRecord::Base.establish_connection(
  :adapter  => 'mysql',
  :host     => 'localhost',
  :username => 'root',  # This is the default username and password
  :password => '',      # for MySQL, but note that if you have a
                        # different username and password,
                        # you should change it.
  :database => 'players_4')


class Player <  ActiveRecord::Base
  has_many :plays
end

class Game <  ActiveRecord::Base
  has_many :plays
end

class Play <  ActiveRecord::Base
  belongs_to :game
  belongs_to :player
end

class Event < ActiveRecord::Base
  belongs_to :plays
end

columns = Event.find(:all, :group=>'event DESC')
pic_dir='./player_graph_pics' #Used to store the graph pictures.
Dir.mkdir(pic_dir) unless File.exists?(pic_dir)
```

```ruby
Player.find(:all).each do |player|
  bar_chart = Gruff::Bar.new(1024)
  bar_chart.legend_font_size = 12
  total_games = Play.count(:conditions=>['game_id = ? ' <<
                                         'AND player_id = ?',

                                          game_id_to_analyze,
                                          player.id]).to_f


  total_wins = Play.count(:conditions=>['game_id = ? ' <<
                                        'AND player_id = ? ' <<
                                        'AND won=1',

                                         game_id_to_analyze,
                                         player.id]).to_f


  win_ratio = (total_wins / total_games * 100).to_i unless total_games == 0
  win_ratio ||= 0
  bar_chart.title = "#{player.name} " <<
                    "(#{win_ratio}% won)"
  bar_chart.minimum_value = 0
  bar_chart.maximum_value = 110

  sql = "SELECT event, AVG(time) as average_time

         FROM events AS e
               INNER JOIN
              plays AS p
                ON e.play_id=p.id
        WHERE p.game_id='#{game_id_to_analyze}'
               AND
              p.player_id='#{player.id}'
        GROUP
            BY e.event DESC;"
  data = []
  Event.find_by_sql(sql).each do |row|
    bar_chart.data row.event, (row.average_time.to_i/1000)
  end
  bar_chart.labels = {0=>'Time'}
  bar_chart.write("#{pic_dir}/player_#{player.id}.png")
end
```

Save this script as `player_bar_charts.rb`. You can run the script using the following command:

```
ruby player_bar_charts.rb
```

When you run that command, the script creates a directory called `player_graph_pics` and creates one graph for each player. The graphs are saved in PNG format as `player_1`, `player_2`, and so forth. You can see two of the graphs in Figures 3-3 and 3-4.

■**Note** Chapter 10 includes an example that uses Gruff to graph cost-per-sale figures from Apache web logs. Chapter 10 also covers using `.rpdf` views to embed those graphs in a PDF file, which is probably a more convenient way to e-mail graphs than as PNG files.

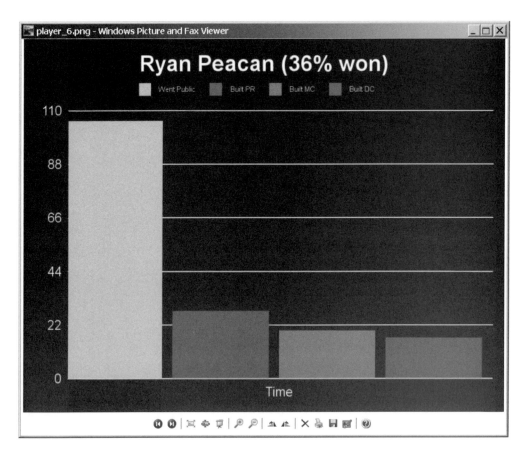

Figure 3-3. *Graph for one player*

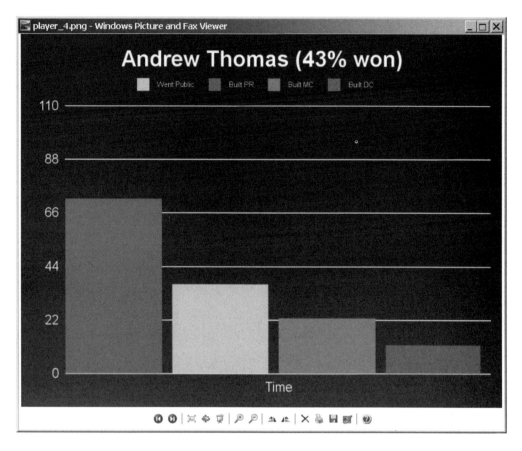

Figure 3-4. *Graph for another player, with a different build order*

Dissecting the Code

The bulk of the program in Listing 3-4 consists of a loop that iterates through each player in the database, creating a report and writing it to a file:

```
Player.find(:all).each do |player|
  bar_chart = Gruff::Bar.new(1024)
  bar_chart.legend_font_size = 12
```

The script creates a new Gruff::Bar object. The legend_font_size attribute is the font size of the chart's legend in points, The default is 20 points, but this graph has too much information for the larger text size, so you reduce it to 12 points.

Next, the script sets the title of the chart:

```
total_games = Play.count(:conditions=>['game_id = ? ' <<
                                        'AND player_id = ?',

                                        game_id_to_analyze,
                                        player.id]).to_f

total_wins = Play.count(:conditions=>['game_id = ? ' <<
                                       'AND player_id = ? ' <<
                                       'AND won=1',

                                       game_id_to_analyze,
                                       player.id]).to_f

win_ratio = (total_wins / total_games * 100).to_i unless total_games == 0
win_ratio ||= 0
bar_chart.title = "#{player.name} " <<
                  "(#{win_ratio}% won)"
```

The title of the chart is set to the player's name, followed by a win/loss ratio. The calculation uses the count aggregate function (discussed in Chapter 2).

Next, you set the scale of the chart:

```
bar_chart.minimum_value = 0
bar_chart.maximum_value = 110
```

The minimum_value and maximum_value attributes specify the scale. Without these attributes, the chart will automatically scale according to the maximum and minimum values. If you left the default, each chart would have a different scale, and so the charts would not be directly comparable.

■**Note** You could loop through all of the charts and find the maximum value and use that here, but then you would not be able to compare charts from different runs. With fixed values, you can take a chart from, say, a month ago and compare it with a current chart. Another problem with that approach is that when you fix the lower end as well, you enlarge the differences between values. The lowest is always scaled to be a very short line, whereas the largest always occupies the entire chart space. For example, if you had the values 54, 55, and 56 charted, 56 would appear to be twice as big as 55 and far bigger than 54.

Next, the code pulls out an average time for each event via a custom SQL statement and the find_by_sql method:

```
  sql = "SELECT event, AVG(time) as average_time
          FROM events AS e
                  INNER JOIN
                plays AS p
                  ON e.play_id=p.id
          WHERE p.game_id='#{game_id_to_analyze}'
                  AND
                p.player_id='#{player.id}'
          GROUP
              BY e.event DESC;"
  data = []
  Event.find_by_sql(sql).each do |row|
    bar_chart.data row.event, (row.average_time.to_i/1000)
  end
  bar_chart.labels = {0=>'Time'}
  bar_chart.write("#{pic_dir}/player_#{player.id}.png")
end
```

Each row contains an event description and an average time. You loop through these rows, and for each of those rows, you add a bar to your chart using the data method. After that, you set the column label and write your chart to a file.

As you can see, even though Listing 3-4 is more complex than Listing 3-1, it's still fairly simple.

Now let's try creating another type of chart with Gruff.

Creating a Line Chart

Suppose the management at Transmegtech Studios wants you to create a single chart containing the average build time for each event for all players. You can do that with a line chart. Listing 3-5 shows the code to create a single chart summarizing all of the players.

Listing 3-5. *Creating a Line Chart for All Player Events (all_players.rb)*

```
require 'gruff'
require 'active_record'

game_id_to_analyze = 5

ActiveRecord::Base.establish_connection(
  :adapter  => 'mysql',
  :host     => 'localhost',
```

```ruby
    :username => 'your_mysql_username_here',
    :password => 'your_mysql_password_here',
    :database => 'players_4')


class Player <  ActiveRecord::Base
  has_many :wins
end

class Game <  ActiveRecord::Base
  has_many :wins
end

class Play <  ActiveRecord::Base
  belongs_to :game
  belongs_to :player
end

class Event < ActiveRecord::Base
  belongs_to :play
end

def puts_underlined(text, underline_char="=")
  puts text
  puts underline_char * text.length
end

pic_dir='./all_players_graph_pics'
Dir.mkdir(pic_dir) unless File.exists?(pic_dir)

line_chart = Gruff::Line.new(1024)
index=0
columns = {}
Event.find(:all, :group=>'event DESC').each do |e|
  columns[index] = e.event
  index=index+1
end

line_chart.labels = columns
line_chart.legend_font_size = 10
```

```
line_chart.legend_box_size = 10
line_chart.title = "Chart of All Players"
line_chart.minimum_value = 0
line_chart.maximum_value = 110

Player.find(:all).each do |player|
  total_games = Play.count(:conditions=>['game_id = ? AND player_id = ?',
                          game_id_to_analyze, player.id]).to_f
  total_wins = Play.count(:conditions=>['game_id = ? AND player_id = ? AND won=1',
                          game_id_to_analyze, player.id]).to_f

 sql = "SELECT event, avg(time) as average_time

          FROM events as e
               INNER JOIN
               plays as p
                 ON e.play_id=p.id
        WHERE p.game_id='#{game_id_to_analyze}'
                AND
               p.player_id='#{player.id}'
        GROUP
            BY e.event DESC;"
  data = []
  Event.find_by_sql(sql).each do |row|
    data << (row.average_time.to_i/1000)
  end

  line_chart.data(player.name, data  )

end

line_chart.write("all_players.png")
```

Save this script as all_players.rb. You can run the script as follows:

```
ruby all_players.rb
```

The output from the script is shown in Figure 3-5. This example packs a lot of information into the chart for demonstration purposes. You can design your own charts to contain less information and be easier to read.

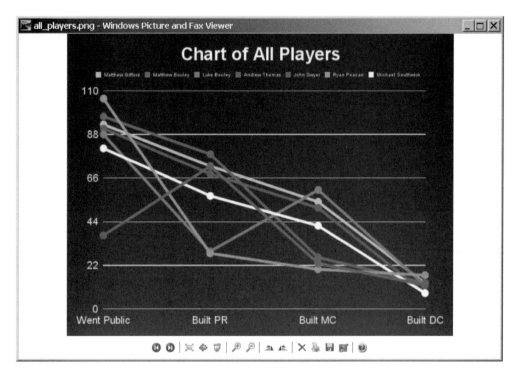

Figure 3-5. *Graph of data for all players*

Let's take a look at the code line by line.

Dissecting the Code

Most of the code in Listing 3-5 is identical to that in Listing 3-4; however, a few lines are different. For example, the object is a member of the Gruff::Line class, instead of the Gruff::Bar class:

```
line_chart = Gruff::Line.new(1024)
```

The parameter to the call to new is the horizontal size. You can also pass a string containing a full size parameter, such as 1024x768.

One of the noteworthy changes is inside the main loop, which iterates through all of the players. Instead of writing each chart to a different file, the data is aggregated into a single chart, as follows:

```
data = []
Event.find_by_sql(sql).each do |row|
  data << (row.average_time.to_i/1000)
end

line_chart.data(player.nickname, data)
```

This loop, like the one in Listing 3-4, goes through all of the event types and adds them into an array, and then adds that array to the chart.

Summary

In this chapter, you learned how you can create beautiful graphs in just a few lines of code with graphing libraries like Gruff and Scuffy. You saw how to use Active Record and Gruff to extract data from a database, and then create a graph from it with relatively simple code. The Transmegtech Studios examples demonstrated how to take business data, use Active Record to summarize the data into a useful form, and then use Gruff to present it. You created detailed reports on an entire staff of people in just 77 lines of code!

So far, you've learned how to perform calculations using Active Record and how to use Gruff to create attractive charts. However, these tasks are only part of a large project. Presenting the data to the users in a way they can use it is also important. The next chapter explains how you can let users view and manipulate data on their desktop.

■ ■ ■

## CHAPTER 4

Creating Reports on the Desktop

In the previous chapters, you've learned about creating reports using Active Record. However, it's not enough to simply create a report; you need to place the report in a context where it will be useful. Often, this means making the report accessible on the users' desktop in a format that's familiar to them. You can accomplish this in a number of ways, as you'll learn in this chapter.

Choosing a Desktop Format

One powerful way to deliver reports to your users is to create a stand-alone graphical user interface (GUI) application that they can run on their desktop. This application can blend in with native applications written in other languages, so it will be familiar to the users. Furthermore, it won't be subject to the security restrictions that apply to web applications, so it can even control other applications—launching them and so forth.

Of course, deploying desktop applications isn't an option for some applications. Many Ruby developers are restricted to deploying web applications only. If that's true for you, you'll need an alternate approach.

One alternative is to offer the users the ability to download a file that can be opened in a desktop application. A common example is a Microsoft Excel file, which is familiar to many businesspeople. This is a useful approach, since many office workers have been trained to do simple calculations on Excel spreadsheets. (Of course, Microsoft Excel files can be opened in OpenOffice.org as well, so it's something of a spreadsheet *lingua franca*.)

Note Currently, there aren't any open source solutions for creating Microsoft Word or PowerPoint documents; Microsoft's proprietary format can make interoperability difficult. Additionally, Word and PowerPoint are commonly used for presentation purposes, and they can often be supplanted by HTML and PDF versions. You've already done several HTML examples. Chapters 6, 8, and 10 have examples of PDF output.

In this chapter, you'll create a formatted spreadsheet for the end user, and then you'll see how to create a fully functional GUI application.

CONTROLLING QUICKTIME WITH A DESKTOP APPLICATION

An example of a useful desktop application is one that I created for The Casting Frontier, a digital casting services firm. This application uses FXRuby and the RubyOSA (rbosa) AppleScript library to control QuickTime Pro on Mac OS X.

The program automates the process of storing national commercial auditions online. Before this solution, the camera operators, who videotaped the auditions, needed to manually export each movie to a file, manually export the first frame of a movie as a thumbnail, make sure both files were named according to a convention, and then manually upload the file through FTP. (They also had a system to associate an actor's digital profile with a movie; if the users wanted to use this, the process became even more complicated.)

Using the new application, the users simply entered the actor's information, clicked Start, clicked Stop, and then clicked Upload. This sped up the process considerably.

If the solution were a web application, it would have been impossible to control QuickTime in order to export the movies and thumbnails. The camera operators would have needed to do it by hand, which would slow them down and cost money. The solution also reduced errors, since it ensured that all of the movie files and thumbnail files were correctly named and labeled. In fact, the time factor was very significant. Auditions are held in rented rooms, which cost extra if auditions run overtime. Also, if actors wait longer than a certain time, the casting director holding the audition must pay a large fee to the actors' union.

Exporting Data to Spreadsheets

Generally, clients love spreadsheets. Often, they don't have the expertise to manipulate data using SQL or a programming language like Ruby, but they do know how to perform calculations and analyze data using Microsoft Excel or a similar tool. If their data is directly delivered in their format of choice, they can skip a step and save time. (In fact, some less computer-savvy users may not realize that they can copy and paste data from a web page, so exporting to an Excel-compatible format may enable them to act on data in ways they could not before.)

Generating an Excel Spreadsheet

You can generate Excel spreadsheet documents—which, incidentally, can also be opened in the OpenOffice.org spreadsheet application—using the `spreadsheet-excel` gem. Install this gem by using the following command:

```
gem install spreadsheet-excel
```

■**Tip** If you want to generate Excel-compatible spreadsheets from HTML documents, see Chapter 16. The method described in that chapter is a bit of a hack, and you get less control over your output formatting, but it's extremely easy to implement. The method shown in this chapter offers greater control, such as the ability to arrange your Excel document into multiple sheets.

The following code creates a spreadsheet with "Hello, world!" in the upper-left corner:

```
require "spreadsheet/excel"
include Spreadsheet

workbook = Excel.new("test.xls")
worksheet = workbook.add_worksheet

worksheet.write(0, 0, 'Hello, world!')
workbook.close
```

This code is reasonably straightforward. You require the code (using the library file name spreadsheet/excel) and include the module, create a new workbook, and then add a sheet to it. Note that each spreadsheet (workbook) can have multiple worksheets, which behave similarly to tabs in a tabbed web browser, such as Mozilla Firefox or Opera. After that, you write the phrase "Hello, world!" to 0,0—the upper-left corner—and then close the workbook, which writes it to the indicated file. You can do other actions as well, such as format cells and columns, as we'll examine next.

Creating a Spreadsheet Report

Let's say that your manager at Transmegtech Studios, the fictional game development company we've used for the examples in previous chapters, wants a report on the game players' win/loss records per game in the form of a formatted spreadsheet. Listing 4-1 shows the script to create a simple Excel report.

Listing 4-1. *Player Win/Loss Spreadsheet (spreadsheet_team_performance.rb)*
```
require 'active_record'
require 'optparse'
require 'rubygems'
require 'active_record'
```

```ruby
ActiveRecord::Base.establish_connection(
  :adapter  => 'mysql',
  :host     => 'localhost',
  :username => 'insert_your_mysql_username_here',
  :password => 'insert_your_mysql_password_here',
  :database => 'players_4')

class Player <  ActiveRecord::Base
  has_many :plays
end
class Game <  ActiveRecord::Base
  has_many :plays
end
class Play <  ActiveRecord::Base
  belongs_to :game
  belongs_to :player
end

require 'spreadsheet/excel'
include Spreadsheet
spreadsheet_file = "spreadsheet_report.xls"
workbook = Excel.new(spreadsheet_file)
worksheet = workbook.add_worksheet


page_header_format = Format.new(:color=>'black', :bold=>true, :size=>30)
player_name_format = Format.new(:color=>'black', :bold=>true)
header_format      = Format.new(:color=>'gray',  :bold=>true)
data_format        = Format.new()

workbook.add_format(page_header_format)
workbook.add_format(player_name_format)
workbook.add_format(header_format)
workbook.add_format(data_format)

worksheet.format_column(0, 35, data_format)

current_row=0

worksheet.write(current_row, 0, 'Player Win/Loss Report', page_header_format)

current_row=current_row+1
```

```ruby
Player.find(:all).each do |player|

  worksheet.format_row(current_row, current_row==1 ? 20 : 33, player_name_format)
  worksheet.write(current_row, 0, player.name)
  current_row=current_row+1

  worksheet.write(current_row, 0, ['Game', 'Wins', 'Losses'], header_format)
  current_row=current_row+1


  Game.find(:all).each do |game|

    win_count = Play.count(:conditions=>[
                  "player_id = ? AND
                   game_id= ? AND
                   won=true",

                   player.id,
                   game.id])

    loss_count = Play.count(:conditions=>[
                  "player_id = ? AND
                   game_id= ? AND
                   won=false",

                   player.id,
                   game.id])

    worksheet.write(current_row, 0, [game.name, win_count, loss_count])
    current_row=current_row+1
  end

end

workbook.close
```

Save this code as spreadsheet_team_performance.rb. You can run it by issuing the following command:

```
ruby spreadsheet_team_perfomance.rb
```

The script creates a file called spreadsheet_report.xls. Open the file with Microsoft Excel or OpenOffice.org, as shown in Figure 4-1.

Figure 4-1. *Player win/loss spreadsheet in OpenOffice.org*

Tip You can use the `spreadsheet/excel` library to create spreadsheets dynamically in a Rails application, and then send them to the user. This lets you have a "Download this as Excel" link in your views, for example. You can see a scheme for quickly sending binary files in Rails at `http://wiki.rubyonrails.org/rails/pages/HowtoSendFilesFast`.

Dissecting the Code

The first few lines of Listing 4-1 create a connection to your database and set up your models, similar to the code in the previous examples. Next, you start creating the Excel report using the `spreadsheet-excel` gem:

```
require 'spreadsheet/excel'
include Spreadsheet

workbook = Excel.new("spreadsheet_report.xls")
worksheet = workbook.add_worksheet
```

The first line loads the `spreadsheet/excel` library, and the second line mixes the `spreadsheet/excel` code into your current module so you can use it. Next, you create a new Excel document, which is called a worksheet, and then add a new worksheet to the workbook. The worksheet will contain your report.

Note You can add more than one worksheet to a workbook if desired. Then your end users will be able to select between them using tabs at the bottom of their spreadsheet application.

Next, you set up some graphical formatting for your data:

```
page_header_format = Format.new(:color=>'black', :bold=>true, :size=>30)
player_name_format = Format.new(:color=>'black', :bold=>true)
header_format      = Format.new(:color=>'gray',  :bold=>true)
data_format        = Format.new(:color=>'black', :bold=>false)

workbook.add_format(page_header_format)
workbook.add_format(player_name_format)
workbook.add_format(header_format)
workbook.add_format(data_format)

worksheet.format_column(0, 35, data_format)
```

This code creates a number of formats and adds them to the workbook. You need to add them before you can use them later, because formats are specific to the entire document and then referenced when used. Next, you proceed to format the first column using the `format_column` method, passing three parameters:

- The first parameter specifies which column to format; in this case, column 0, or the first column.

- The second parameter specifies the width of the column; in this case, 35, which is wide enough to display all of the data in that column.

- The third parameter is a display format for the column; in this case, `data_format`.

An astute observer may notice that the `data_format` format contains no specific formatting, so it is not any different from an unformatted cell. This is intentional; the `format_column` method can, in theory, set just a column width without setting a format, but due to a bug, the library will crash if a format is not specified. (This will likely be fixed in a future release; as of this writing, the current version of the spreadsheet gem is 0.3.5.1.) However, by calling `format_column` with both a width and a dummy format, you can achieve the desired effect of widening the column without changing the display format.

Next, the script begins to write information to the spreadsheet. It begins with a header stating the title of the spreadsheet:

```
current_row=0

worksheet.write(current_row, 0, 'Player Win/Loss Report', page_header_format)
```

The first line initializes a variable, current_row, which will store the current row in the spreadsheet. The second line uses the write method of the worksheet object to write "Player Win/Loss Report" using the page_header_format format, which has a large, bold font. The worksheet.write method takes a row number, a column number, a value, and an optional format. (Note that the code uses the current_row variable only for consistency with later code, since it will always equal zero at this point.)

Next, you start looping through all of the players, first outputting a brief name and header for each player:

```
Player.find(:all).each do |player|

  worksheet.format_row(current_row, current_row==1 ? 20 : 33, player_name_format)
  worksheet.write(current_row, 0, player.name)
  current_row=current_row+1

  worksheet.write(current_row, 0, ['Game', 'Wins', 'Losses'], header_format)
  current_row=current_row+1
```

The second line uses the format_row method, which is much like the format_column method, except that it formats rows rather than columns. You format the first row, giving it a special format defined earlier, player_name_format, and giving it a variable height, depending on whether it's the second row or another row. The second row is the row immediately following the page header (which is in a font twice the size of the data rows), and it looks better with less vertical space.

Next, you write the player name to the first column of your current row and increment your current_row counter.

■Note The need to increment the current_row counter gets somewhat tedious. If it really irritates you, you could create an object that simulates a stream object fairly easily, which would let the object keep track of this for you. Whether this is helpful depends on your application, and such an approach would not necessarily help applications with a complicated layout.

After that, you write a brief header describing your data for each player. This call is interesting, since it passes an array to the `write` method of your `worksheet` object. This array is expanded into the cells to the right of the cell, so these two blocks of code are the same:

```
# This:

worksheet.write(current_row, 0, ['Game', 'Wins', 'Losses'], header_format)

# ... Is just like this:

worksheet.write(current_row, 0, 'Game', header_format)
worksheet.write(current_row, 1, 'Wins', header_format)
worksheet.write(current_row, 2, 'Losses', header_format)
```

Additionally, the `write` method can accept a format, just like the `format_column` and `format_row` methods. This can be used to highlight just one cell of a row or column. (In this particular case, you are formatting the entire row, so you could use the `format_row` method.)

Next, you loop through all of the games, tally the players' wins and losses for each game, and write them to the spreadsheet:

```
Game.find(:all).each do |game|

  win_count = Play.count(:conditions=>[
              "player_id = ? AND
               game_id= ? AND
               won=true",

               player.id,
               game.id])

  loss_count = Play.count(:conditions=>[
              "player_id = ? AND
               game_id= ? AND
               won=false",

               player.id,
               game.id])

  worksheet.write(current_row, 0, [game.name, win_count, loss_count])
  current_row=current_row+1
end
```

The two calls to the Active Record `count` method (discussed in Chapter 2) count the wins and losses, respectively. You then use the `worksheet` object's `write` method to put the information into the spreadsheet, and continue on to the next game. After all of the games have been reported, you continue on to the next player. After all of the players have been reported, you close the workbook, and you're finished:

```
workbook.close
```

As you can see, the spreadsheet/Excel interface is reasonably clean and easy to use. But if you need a more powerful, desktop GUI solution, there's a graphical interface library that is just as clean and easy to use.

Creating GUIs with Ruby

You have several options for creating GUIs with Ruby. Most of them are interfaces to well-established external libraries:

- Ruby-GNOME (`http://ruby-gnome2.sourceforge.jp/`) is a Ruby interface to GNOME.

- Korundum (`http://developer.kde.org/language-bindings/ruby/index.html`) offers access to KDE.

- RubyCocoa (`http://rubycocoa.sourceforge.net/HomePage`) offers an interface to the Mac OS X Cocoa framework.

- QtRuby is a binding to QT (`http://developer.kde.org/language-bindings/ruby/index.html`).

- JRuby (`http://jruby.codehaus.org/`), the Ruby implementation for the Java Virtual Machine, provides access to Java frameworks, like Swing.

Tip You can access Swing directly from JRuby, but Profligacy is a Ruby library designed to make Swing more Ruby-like. You can learn more about Profligacy at `http://ihate.rubyforge.org/profligacy/`.

- FXRuby (`http://www.fxruby.org/`) is an interface to the cross-platform FOX GUI library.

This book will focus on FXRuby. One of FXRuby's strengths is that it has a particularly strong Ruby feel to it. Many of the other libraries are quite clearly a bridge to a completely different programming paradigm. FXRuby makes GUI programming easy.

Using FXRuby

Install FXRuby as follows:

```
gem install fxruby
```

Additionally, you'll need an X11 server running under Linux or Mac OS X. Most Linux distributions come with an X11 server, and you can install it from the distribution CD if you don't have it currently loaded. Mac OS X is much the same—you can install an X11 server from the CD included with your computer. You'll need to explicitly launch the server under either operating system. To do so under Linux, use the startx command. On an OS X system, click the X11 icon.

Finally, you'll also need the FOX library installed. This library is included with the FXRuby gem under Windows, but you can install it fairly easily on other operating systems via your favorite software packaging method: MacPorts (port install rb-fxruby) or Apt (apt-get install fox fox-devel). You can also download and install it from http://www.fox-toolkit.org/.

After you've set up the prerequisites, you can try the simple example in FXRuby shown in Listing 4-2.

Listing 4-2. *Simple FXRuby Example (simple_fx_ruby_example.rb)*

```ruby
require 'fox16'

include Fox

myApp = FXApp.new

mainWindow=FXMainWindow.new(myApp, "Simple FXRuby Control Demo",
                                   :padding =>10, :vSpacing=>10)

my_first_button= FXButton.new(mainWindow, 'Example Button Control')
my_first_button.connect(SEL_COMMAND) do
  my_first_button.text="In a real-life situation, this would do something."
end

FXTextField.new(mainWindow, 30).text = 'Example Text Control'

FXRadioButton.new(mainWindow, "Example Radio Control")
FXCheckButton.new(mainWindow, "Example Check Control")

myApp.create
```

```
mainWindow.show( PLACEMENT_SCREEN )
```

```
myApp.run
```

You can run the example as follows:

```
ruby simple_fxruby_example.rb
```

Your application will look like Figure 4-2.

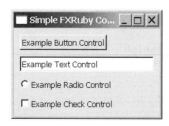

Figure 4-2. *A simple FXRuby example*

Let's take a look at the simple FXRuby demo in Listing 4-2.

Dissecting the Code

Listing 4-2 begins by creating an FXApp object, which represents your application, and then an FXMainWindow object, which holds all of the controls. The FXApp object handles application-wide tasks, like updating the mouse cursor and so forth.

```
myApp = FXApp.new
mainWindow=FXMainWindow.new(myApp, "Simple FXRuby Control Demo",
                                   :padding =>10, :vSpacing=>10)
```

Here, you set a couple properties. The padding property is set to 10, which gives 10 pixels of space on each side. The vSpacing property is also set to 10, for 10 pixels between each control. Taken together, these two properties make the controls evenly spaced out so that the application is visually attractive. By default, controls are arranged top to bottom; however, you can specify other arrangements, as you'll see in the next section.

After your FXApp and FXMainWindow objects are created, you can add your first control:

```
my_first_button= FXButton.new(mainWindow, 'Example Button Control')
my_first_button.connect(SEL_COMMAND) do
  puts "You've clicked the button!"
end
```

This is an FXButton control, which is designed to allow users to perform a specific action. The first line creates the control with the text "Example Button Control," and the following lines specify an action to take when the user clicks the button.

Next, you create a few more interface widgets:

```
FXTextField.new(mainWindow, 30).text = 'Example Text Control'
```

```
FXRadioButton.new(mainWindow, "Example Radio Control")
FXCheckButton.new(mainWindow, "Example Check Control")
```

The FXTextField object lets the user enter text. The text can be retrieved or preset using the text property, as in this example. You then create an FXRadioButton object, which lets the user select just one button from a group (of course, typically you would have more than one radio button). The last line creates an FXCheckButton control, which lets the user make an on/off choice.

Finally, having specified the elements for your interface, you then need to perform some actions. First, you call the create method on your application object. This calls the create method on all of your FXRuby objects, which uses the FOX GUI toolkit to actually create the objects and prepare them for display:

```
myApp.create
```

```
mainWindow.show( PLACEMENT_SCREEN )
```

The second line calls the show method, which, logically enough, shows the main window. The PLACEMENT_SCREEN constant specifies that the window should be centered on the screen.

As you can see, it's reasonably easy to create different types of controls: command buttons, text fields, radio (often called "option") buttons, check boxes, and so forth. (See the FXRuby documentation at http://www.fxruby.org/ for information about the other controls available and how they work.) Now let's apply the same basic techniques to a slightly more complicated example.

Graphing Team Performance on the Desktop

Let's say that Transmegtech Studios is reworking the artificial intelligence in its new strategy game using the graphs created in Chapter 3. However, the graphs were created as PNG files, and the chief executive officer (CEO) of the company does not know how to view PNGs. He wants to be able to click an icon on his desktop and launch an application that lets him view charts by clicking a player in a list. Fortunately, this is reasonably easy to do with FXRuby.

Before you can run this example, you'll need the database from Chapter 3 (shown partially in Listing 3-3). You can download the SQL from `http://rubyreporting.com/examples/player_4.sql` or from the Source/Downloads area of the Apress web site (`http://.www.apress.com`), and then import the data using the command `mysql -u my_mysql_user -p < player_4.sql`.

The code to create a simple desktop application for viewing graphs is shown in Listing 4-3.

Listing 4-3. *Desktop Team Performance Grapher (desktop_team_performance_graph.rb)*

```ruby
require 'fox16'
require 'active_record'
require 'optparse'
require 'rubygems'
require 'gruff'
require 'active_record'

ActiveRecord::Base.establish_connection(
   :adapter  => 'mysql',
   :host     => 'localhost',
   :username => 'insert_your_mysql_username_here',
   :password => 'insert_your_mysql_password_here',
   :database => 'players_4')

class Player <  ActiveRecord::Base
  has_many :plays
end
class Game <  ActiveRecord::Base
  has_many :plays
end
class Play <  ActiveRecord::Base
  belongs_to :game
  belongs_to :player
end
class Event < ActiveRecord::Base
  belongs_to :play
end


include Fox
```

```ruby
class TransmegtechGraphWindow
    def initialize

        @main_window=FXMainWindow.new(get_app,
                            "Transmegtech Studios Player Reporting Software",
                            nil, nil, DECOR_ALL )
        @main_window.width=640; @main_window.height=480

        control_matrix=FXMatrix.new(@main_window,4, MATRIX_BY_COLUMNS)

        FXLabel.new(control_matrix, 'Game:')
        @game_combobox = FXComboBox.new(control_matrix, 30, nil,
                                      COMBOBOX_STATIC | FRAME_SUNKEN  )
        @game_combobox.numVisible = 5
        @game_combobox.editable = false

        Game.find(:all).each do |game|
          @game_combobox.appendItem(game.name , game.id)
        end
        @game_combobox.connect(SEL_COMMAND) do
          update_display
        end

        FXLabel.new(control_matrix, 'Player:')

        @player_combobox = FXComboBox.new(control_matrix, 35, nil,
                                        COMBOBOX_STATIC | FRAME_SUNKEN  )
        @player_combobox.numVisible = 5
        @player_combobox.editable = false

        Player.find(:all).each do |player|
          @player_combobox.appendItem(player.name , player.id)
        end

        @player_combobox.connect(SEL_COMMAND) do
          update_display
        end

        @graph_picture_viewer = FXImageView.new(@main_window , nil, nil, 0,
                                          LAYOUT_FILL_X | LAYOUT_FILL_Y)
```

```ruby
    @graph_picture_viewer.connect( SEL_CONFIGURE ) do
      update_display
    end


    @main_window.show( PLACEMENT_SCREEN )
  end
  def update_display
    game_id_to_analyze = @game_combobox.getItemData(@game_combobox.currentItem)
    player = Player.find(@player_combobox.getItemData(
                                    @player_combobox.currentItem))
    bar_chart = Gruff::Bar.new("#{@graph_picture_viewer.width}x" <<
                              "#{@graph_picture_viewer.height}")
    bar_chart.legend_font_size = 12
    total_games = Play.count(:conditions=>['game_id = ? AND ' <<
                                          'player_id = ?',
                                          game_id_to_analyze, player.id]
                      ).to_f || 0
    total_wins = Play.count(:conditions=>['game_id = ? AND ' <<
                                          'player_id = ? AND won=1',
                                          game_id_to_analyze, player.id]
                      ).to_f || 0

    bar_chart.title = "#{player.name} (#{'%i' %
                                    (total_games==0 ? '0' :
                                    (total_wins/total_games * 100))
                                    }% won)"
    bar_chart.minimum_value = 0
    bar_chart.maximum_value = 110

    sql = "SELECT event, AVG(time) as average_time

      FROM events AS e
        INNER JOIN
        plays AS p
          ON e.play_id=p.id
      WHERE p.game_id='#{game_id_to_analyze}'
        AND
        p.player_id='#{player.id}'
      GROUP BY e.event DESC;"
```

```
      data = []
      Event.find_by_sql(sql).each do |row|
        bar_chart.data row.event, (row.average_time.to_i/1000)
      end
      bar_chart.labels = {0=>'Time'}
      chart_png_filename = "./player_#{player.id}.png"
      bar_chart.write(chart_png_filename)

      pic = FXPNGImage.new(FXApp.instance())

      FXFileStream.open(chart_png_filename,
                        FXStreamLoad) { |stream| pic.loadPixels(stream) }

      pic.create
      @graph_picture_viewer.image = pic
      File.unlink(chart_png_filename)

  end

end

fox_application=FXApp.new

TransmegtechGraphWindow.new

FXApp.instance().create # Note that getApp returns the same FXApp instance
                # as fox_application references.

FXApp.instance().run
```

Save this script as desktop_team_performance_graph.rb. You can run the script using the following command:

```
ruby desktop_team_performance_graph.rb
```

When you run this command, you will see a screen with the text "no data." You can then use the drop-down menus to select a game and a player. The sample database has data only for the Tech Website Baron game. Select that game to see a screen similar to Figure 4-3.

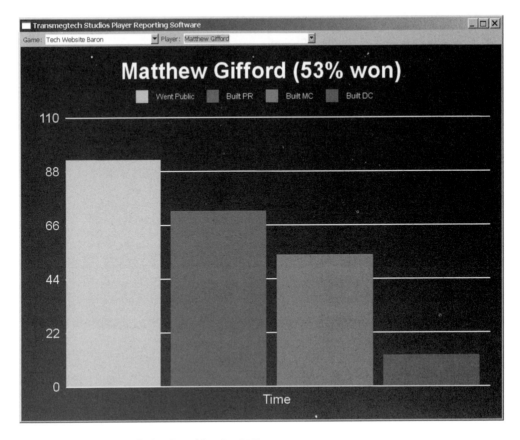

Figure 4-3. *Player graph displayed by the GUI*

Let's take a look at the important parts of the script.

Dissecting the Code

The first part of Listing 4-3 sets up the connection to MySQL, creates the various models, and so forth—nothing new there.

The bulk of the program is controlled by one class, TransmegtechGraphWindow, which is divided into two parts: update_display and initialize methods. update_display creates a graph for the selected player, writes it to a file, and then displays it in your application. Much of this graphing code is the same as the code from Listing 3-4 in Chapter 3. The initialize method creates a window and the user interface elements required: the drop-down lists to select the game and player to graph, the labels for those two drop-down lists, and the large display area that will be used to view the graph.

Whenever either of the drop-down entries is changed—that is, when the user selects a new game or a new player to graph—the update_display method will be called again.

```
def update_display
  game_id_to_analyze = @game_combobox.getItemData(@game_combobox.currentItem)
  player = Player.find(@player_combobox.getItemData(@player_combobox.currentItem))
  bar_chart = Gruff::Bar.new("#{@graph_picture_viewer.width}x" <<
                             "#{@graph_picture_viewer.height}")

  . . .

  bar_chart.write(chart_png_filename)

  pic = FXPNGImage.new(FXApp.instance())

  FXFileStream.open(chart_png_filename,
                    FXStreamLoad) { |stream| pic.loadPixels(stream) }

  pic.create
  @graph_picture_viewer.image = pic
  File.unlink(chart_png_filename)

  @graph_picture_viewer.image = pic

end
```

The first two lines of this method call the getItemData method of the two combo boxes. ItemData is where you can store an integer for each item in the list. Here, ItemData holds the game IDs and the player IDs. By calling the getItemData method with the currently selected item as the parameter, you can get the appropriate player and game IDs.

After that, you create a chart, just as in Listing 3-4. The chart is written to a file, and then loaded and displayed; however, unlike in the Chapter 3 example, you immediately unlink—or delete—the file after displaying it.

■**Note** You could use a Tempfile object, which automates the unlinking behavior, but you can't specify a Tempfile's extension, and FXRuby uses file extensions to determine the file format of a given image. This is an unfortunate approach, yet apparently fairly common—the Gruff and PDF writer gems both have a similar issue.

In order for the update_display method to do anything, you need a user interface element to call it. So, first you must create a window to contain that user interface:

```
fox_application=FXApp.new

@main_window=FXMainWindow.new(fox_application,
                                "Transmegtech Studios Player Reporting Software",
                                nil, nil, DECOR_ALL )
@main_window.width=640; @main_window.height=480
```

The first line creates a new FXApp object, which represents the entire application. FXApp handles application-wide tasks such as starting messaging loops, event timers, quitting the application, and so forth. The second line creates the main window as an instance of the FXMainWindow class. Note that you are using the default icon for this application, which is the nil, nil part of the call. The first of those two nil parameters sets the normal icon, and the second sets the minimized icon for your window. The third line sets the width and height. (You can actually set the height and width via optional parameters to the constructor, but this method is clearer, since the constructor already has a large number of parameters.)

Next, you need to place a strip of controls at the top of the window. These controls will be used to select the player and game for the report. Whenever these settings are changed, the graph should automatically update. Before you add the controls, you need to create a space to put them:

```
control_matrix=FXMatrix.new(@main_window,4, MATRIX_BY_COLUMNS)
```

This line creates a new FXMatrix called control_matrix, which is a FOX container in which you can place other controls. As noted earlier, by default, an FXMainWindow object places controls vertically. The MATRIX_BY_COLUMNS flag in the FXMatrix constructor makes it stack controls horizontally. The other alternative is MATRIX_BY_ROWS, which stacks controls vertically. The second parameter, 4, specifies how many controls should be placed inside the FXMatrix control before starting a new row. For example, you could set MATRIX_BY_ROWS with a parameter of 2 to make a long vertical row of labels next to a vertical row of text boxes.

After you have a place to put your report controls, you create them:

```
FXLabel.new(control_matrix, 'Game:')
@game_combobox = FXComboBox.new(control_matrix, 30,
                                nil, COMBOBOX_STATIC | FRAME_SUNKEN  )
@game_combobox.numVisible = 5
```

This code creates two controls: an FXLabel, which is a visual indicator of the purpose of the next control, and an FXComboBox, which is a list of elements that can be accessed by clicking a drop-down arrow. The second parameter to the FXComboBox constructor is the width. The third parameter is the message target. This parameter is a relic from the original FOX implementation in C, and you won't typically use it in an FXRuby application. (If you're interested, you can find out more at http://www.fxruby.org/doc/events. html.) The fourth parameter, COMBOBOX_STATIC | FRAME_SUNKEN, is a bit field consisting of various style bits. Specifically, it's two constants OR'd together: the COMBOBOX_STATIC constant makes the box static, so that users must pick from the list, and the FRAME_SUNKEN constant makes the box have a three-dimensional sunken effect.

Additionally, the numVisible attribute selects how many options are visible in the drop-down list at one time. Here, you set numVisible to 5 to let the user see all of the available elements without scrolling.

Next, you fill the FXComboBox with options:

```
Game.find(:all).each do |game|
  @game_combobox.appendItem(game.name, game.id)
end
```

This loop calls appendItem for each game in the database. The first parameter to the appendItem method is the text that represents the option in the drop-down list. The second parameter is the value the item has, which is stored in the itemData array in the @game_combobox object. The update_display method uses this value later in the code to retrieve the selected game ID.

Of course, you need to actually update the display when the user changes the FXComboBox. You use the connect method to do just that:

```
@game_combobox.connect(SEL_COMMAND) do
  update_display
end
```

The connect method attaches a block of code to a given FOX message on a given FOX object. In this case, you're specifying that whenever SEL_COMMAND is received by the object, the update_display method will be called. SEL_COMMAND is sent to FXComboBox objects when they change, so your update_display method will be called whenever someone selects a new game to analyze.

Tip Along with SEL_COMMAND, FOX has quite a few other trappable messages. You can use these to customize your users' experience with fine touches. You can get a complete list of all the FOX messages at http://www.fox-toolkit.org/ftp/FoxMessages.pdf.

After this, the script creates a player label and drop-down list in the same way as the game label and list.

Next, you need to create a place for the graphs to be displayed:

```
@graph_picture_viewer = FXImageView.new(main_window , nil, nil, 0,
                                         LAYOUT_FILL_X | LAYOUT_FILL_Y)

@graph_picture_viewer.connect( SEL_CONFIGURE ) do
  update_display
end
```

The first line creates an FXImageView object, which you will use to display the graphs. Note the use of the LAYOUT_FILL_X and LAYOUT_FILL_Y flags, which mean that the graph viewer will use all available space in the window.

Finally, outside your class, you need to actually display your window and let it run. The following three lines do just that:

```
FXApp.instance().create

main_window.show( PLACEMENT_SCREEN )

FXApp.instance().run
```

The first line creates the necessary objects, which are specific to the operating system (and, happily, the details are hidden from us). The second line displays your window on the screen, and the PLACEMENT_SCREEN flag means it will be centered. A call to FXApp.instance() returns your previously defined FXApp object, since FXApp is a singleton.

PACKAGING THE REPORTER DESKTOP APPLICATION

Simply creating a desktop application is not enough—users need to have the application running on their machine. If your application will be run by only a few users, or if your code will run only server side, this may not be an issue. However, if you need to install Ruby and associated libraries on users' machines for a wider distribution of your application, that can be a challenge.

Fortunately, a gem called RubyScript2Exe can help. This gem creates executable programs, and you can target Mac OS X, Windows, or Linux. (You'll need to be running the appropriate operating system to create an executable for it, however.) In fact, RubyScript2Exe can even copy Ruby library dependencies for you. It will run your program once as a "test run," and from there, determine which gems and other source code you've used. It will then copy the source into your finished executable, which will be transparently available to your finished program. Additionally, you can package binary or configuration files with your script, so that the entire program is one convenient package.

For the example in this chapter, you can create an executable with the following command:

```
rubyscript2exe desktop_team_performance_graph.rb
```

As you can see, this gem is very easy to use. Using various options, you can modify the output. You can find out more about `RubyScript2Exe` in my Apress book, *Practical Ruby Gems*, as well as from the `RubyScript2Exe` home page: `http://www.erikveenstra.nl/rubyscript2exe/index.html`.

Summary

This chapter covered how you can extend your applications directly onto users' desktops. You saw how to use the `spreadsheet-excel` gem to create an Excel spreadsheet report, which can be extremely helpful to end users. Then you created a desktop application that displays beautiful graphs using Gruff and Active Record.

As you can see, Ruby isn't a web-only or console-only language. It offers a great deal of flexibility for creating applications that extend directly to the user's desktop in familar formats, including thick-client and common office applications. However, there's no question that Ruby is best known for its usage on the Web. In the next chapter, you'll discover how all of the techniques you've learned so far can be used with Ruby on Rails, the popular web development framework.

## CHAPTER 5

Connecting Your Reports to the World

Reporting does not take place in a vacuum. Reports are written for a specific purpose for a given set of users. Technical choices like "what language do I use" and "how do I deliver the information" are heavily influenced by the users and by the purpose of the report. After all, your users must be able to access the report for it to be useful.

Perhaps the most powerful method to deliver reports to your user is via the World Wide Web. Users can access the information from virtually any Internet-connected device, and because of the Internet's ubiquity, you probably won't need to do any special configuration for their computers—just give users the web address, and they should be all set.

In this chapter, you'll learn how to make your reports accessible from the Web. Let's start with a quick look at your choices for accomplishing this.

Choosing a Web Framework

Many web frameworks and languages are available. Of course, since you bought this book, it's likely you're interested in Ruby web frameworks, and probably Ruby on Rails (typically referred to as simply *Rails*) in particular. In fact, Ruby itself has grown dramatically due to Rails' meteoric rise to prominence. (Incidentally, Active Record, which you've used in previous chapters, is part of Rails.)

However, you can use other Ruby web frameworks. Nitro (http://www.nitroproject.org/), for example, is a powerful alternative. Another is Merb (http://merb.rubyforge.org/), which is a framework similar to Rails, but with a much smaller footprint. Merb also lets you use alternate ORM frameworks, like Data Mapper, so it's more flexible.

Due to Rails' popularity and widespread community support, it's the framework you'll use for the web examples in this book. Rails, like Nitro and Merb, is a Model-View-Controller (MVC) framework. Following the MVC pattern, code is generally divided into three parts:

- The *model* represents the data used by the application.

- The *view* represents the actual presentation of the data.

- The *controller* controls the flow of the application. A controller often manipulates models to achieve an action requested by a user, and then presents the results with a view.

You can find out more about MVC frameworks at http://en.wikipedia.org/wiki/ Model-view-controller. You can find out more about Rails at its official home: http:// rubyonrails.org.

Now, let's take a look at how to create a Rails application to deliver a web report.

Live Intranet Web Reporting with Rails

Let's return to Transmegtech Studios, the fictional game development company we've used for the examples in the previous chapters. Transmegtech has decided to hire actors to do full-motion videos for its latest games. In order to save on costs, the studio is hiring several full-time actors and having them act in different games simultaneously. The various game sequences are filmed in different offices on different days.

Your manager wants you to create an application that tells actors where they need to appear for the day. The actors will check the schedule for the next day before they leave the office each day, but if they forget, they can use their cell phone to check the schedule in the morning. Of course, this means that the reporting application will need to be accessible via cell phone as well as the Web.

Before you get started, you need to install the Rails gem. You can do so as follows:

```
gem install rails -y
```

■**Note** The first example in this chapter is compatible with Rails versions 1.2 and later. The next example works with only versions 2.0 and later, so you'll need to upgrade your Rails installation with `gem update -y rails` if you have an older version.

Next, create a new Rails application called `actor_schedule`, as follows:

```
rails actor_schedule
```

```
create  app/controllers
create  app/helpers
create  app/models
create  app/views/layouts
create  config/environments
create  components
create  db
create  doc
create  lib
create  lib/tasks
create  log
create  public/images
create  public/javascripts
create  public/stylesheets
create  script/performance
create  script/process
create  test/fixtures
. . .
create  public/404.html
create  public/500.html
create  public/index.html
create  public/favicon.ico
create  public/robots.txt
create  public/images/rails.png
create  public/javascripts/prototype.js
create  public/javascripts/effects.js
create  public/javascripts/dragdrop.js
create  public/javascripts/controls.js
create  public/javascripts/application.js
create  doc/README_FOR_APP
create  log/server.log
create  log/production.log
create  log/development.log
create  log/test.log
```

Rails creates quite a few files and directories for you, in a directory structure that will hold the code that makes up our application. All of these directories and files are stored in a directory named after the project. In this case, the directory is actor_schedule, and so all of the paths in this example will be underneath the actor_schedule directory.

Setting Up the Database

Next, let's create the database to store the data:

```
mysqladmin create actor_schedule_development -u your_mysql_username -p
```

At this point, you've created a database for your application, but before you populate this database, let's connect the application to your database server. After that, you can use a Rails mechanism called *migrations* to create the database tables for you. Edit the config/database.yml file to read as shown in Listing 5-1.

Listing 5-1. *Database Configuration File for the Web Report (config/database.yml)*

```
development:
  adapter: mysql
  database: actor_schedule_development
  username: your_user_name
  password: your_password
  host: localhost
```

Note that Rails creates three database connection settings by default, but this example uses only the development environment to keep things simple. The other environments are testing, used for automated testing, and production, used for deployment. Additionally, the default file includes a number of comments, which I've removed from the listing for the sake of brevity.

Next, you need to create a new migration.

Creating a Migration

Migrations are bits of Ruby code that control the structure of a database. Each migration represents a set of changes to a database. The first migration usually specifies the initial structure of a database, and each successive version represents a change of some kind—adding a column, setting a default value, renaming a table, and so forth. Migrations are designed to be cross-platform, so you can usually run the same migration across multiple databases. (Of course, if you use any database-specific features, the migration won't be cross-platform.) Migrations are versioned, so you can upgrade and downgrade them as you see fit. Rails also keeps track of the current version of your database, so if you have a number of migrations, Rails will run only the new migrations.

Create a new migration by using the following command:

```
ruby script/generate migration initial_schema
```

```
create   db/migrate
create   db/migrate/001_initial_schema.rb
```

This creates a skeleton migration. The initial db/migrate/001_initial_schema.rb file looks like this:

```
class InitialSchema < ActiveRecord::Migration
  def self.up
  end

  def self.down
  end
end
```

As you can see, it's a single class that inherits from ActiveRecord::Migration, and it has two class methods: up and down, which upgrade and downgrade the version of the database structure, respectively, when the migration is run. Fortunately, Rails creates the skeleton containing the class definition and method names, so you only need to fill out the migration. Let's do that now. Listing 5-2 shows the full migration class.

Listing 5-2. *Application Schema (db/migrate/001_initial_schema.rb)*

```
class InitialSchema < ActiveRecord::Migration
  def self.up
    create_table :actors do |t|
      t.column :name, :string, :length=>45
      t.column :phone, :string, :length=>13
    end
    create_table :projects do |t|
      t.column :name, :string, :length=>25
    end
    create_table :rooms do |t|
      t.column :name, :string, :length=>25
    end
    create_table :bookings do |t|
      t.column :actor_id, :integer
      t.column :room_id, :integer
      t.column :project_id, :integer
      t.column :booked_at, :datetime
    end
  end
```

```
  def self.down
    drop_table :actors
    drop_table :projects
    drop_table :rooms
    drop_table :bookings
  end
end
```

Save this as db/migrate/001_initial_schema.rb.

Next, run the migration to create the database structure that the migration describes, using the following command:

```
rake db:migrate
```

```
(in /your_path/your_directory/actor_schedule)
== InitialSchema: migrating ===================================================
-- create_table(:actors)
   -> 0.0000s
-- create_table(:projects)
   -> 0.0160s
-- create_table(:rooms)
   -> 0.0000s
-- create_table(:bookings)
   -> 0.0000s
== InitialSchema: migrated (0.0160s) ==========================================
```

Note that this process also works in reverse. You can specify a version to migrate your database to using the VERSION=x option, and specifying 0 will revert your database. For example, the following command will undo the previous migration command:

```
rake db:migrate VERSION=0
```

```
(in /your_path/your_directory/actor_schedule)
== InitialSchema: reverting ===================================================
-- drop_table(:actors)
   -> 0.0000s
-- drop_table(:projects)
   -> 0.0000s
-- drop_table(:rooms)
   -> 0.0000s
-- drop_table(:bookings)
```

```
-> 0.0160s
== InitialSchema: reverted (0.0630s) =========================================
```

■Note The rake command has a whole host of other uses. It's similar to the make command, but it's written in pure Ruby and is used to perform various maintenance tasks for Rails applications. The particular rake task discussed here, db:migrate, uses migrations to either upgrade or downgrade a database. You can find a list of all of the tasks available for a Rails application by running the command rake -T.

Adding the Data

Now that you have a Rails application that can connect to your database and a database structure, you need to fill the database with some data. You can use the SQL code in Listing 5-3 to do just that.

Listing 5-3. *Sample Data for the Actor Scheduling Application (actor_schedule_data.sql)*

```
DELETE FROM actors;
DELETE FROM projects;
DELETE FROM rooms;
DELETE FROM bookings;

INSERT INTO actors (id, name) VALUES
                (1, 'Jim Thompson');
INSERT INTO actors (id, name) VALUES
                (2, 'Becky Leuser');
INSERT INTO actors (id, name) VALUES
                (3, 'Elizabeth Berube');
INSERT INTO actors (id, name) VALUES
                (4, 'Dave Guuseman');
INSERT INTO actors (id, name) VALUES
                (5, 'Tom Jimson');

INSERT INTO projects (id, name) VALUES
                (1, 'Turbo Bowling Intro Sequence');
INSERT INTO projects (id, name) VALUES
                (2, 'Seven for Dinner Win Game Sequence');
INSERT INTO projects (id, name) VALUES
                (3, 'Seven for Dinner Lost Game Sequence');
```

```
INSERT INTO rooms (id, name) VALUES
                  (1, 'L120, Little Hall');
INSERT INTO rooms (id, name) VALUES
                  (2, 'L112, Little Hall');
INSERT INTO rooms (id, name) VALUES
                  (3, 'M120, Tech Center');

INSERT INTO bookings (actor_id, room_id, project_id, booked_at) VALUES
                     (1,1,2, DATE_ADD( NOW(), INTERVAL 3 HOUR ));
INSERT INTO bookings (actor_id, room_id, project_id, booked_at) VALUES
                     (1,1,3, DATE_ADD( NOW(), INTERVAL 4 HOUR ));
INSERT INTO bookings (actor_id, room_id, project_id, booked_at) VALUES
                     (3,2,2, DATE_ADD( NOW(), INTERVAL 1 DAY ));
INSERT INTO bookings (actor_id, room_id, project_id, booked_at) VALUES
                     (2,3,1, DATE_ADD( NOW(), INTERVAL 5 HOUR ));
```

Save Listing 5-3 as `actor_schedule_data.sql`. In the listing, note the use of the `DATE_ADD` function to create relative times, rather than hard-coding them, so the times will always be in the future. Additionally, note the `DELETE FROM` statements at the beginning of Listing 5-3. These clear the database before the new data is inserted. For example, this lets you modify the data and then rerun this SQL script to have a fresh copy of your data.

■Tip You can also use migration to insert data, but the advantage of inserting your data in a separate SQL file is that it keeps the structure and the data separate. If you had two separate deployments, with two separate databases, you could use the same migrations on both.

You can run the SQL in Listing 5-3 and populate the database using the following command:

```
mysql -u my_mysql_username -p actor_schedule_development <  actor_schedule_data.sql
```

Now that your Rails application has been created, your database connection is ready, and your database structure and data are prepared, you need to create code that accesses this database. First, let's create the models.

Creating the Models for the Web Report

The models will represent your tables and the relationships between them. You can create the models using the following commands:

```
ruby script/generate model actor
```

```
      exists  app/models/
      exists  test/unit/
      exists  test/fixtures/
      create  app/models/actor.rb
      create  test/unit/actors_test.rb
      create  test/fixtures/actor.yml
      exists  db/migrate
      create  db/migrate/002_create_actors.rb
```

```
ruby script/generate model project
```

```
      exists  app/models/
      exists  test/unit/
      exists  test/fixtures/
      create  app/models/project.rb
      create  test/unit/project_test.rb
      create  test/fixtures/project.yml
      exists  db/migrate
      create  db/migrate/003_create_projects.rb
```

```
ruby script/generate model room
```

```
      exists  app/models/
      exists  test/unit/
      exists  test/fixtures/
      create  app/models/room.rb
      create  test/unit/room_test.rb
      create  test/fixtures/room.yml
      exists  db/migrate
      create  db/migrate/004_create_rooms.rb
```

```
ruby script/generate model booking
```

```
      exists  app/models/
      exists  test/unit/
      exists  test/fixtures/
```

```
create  app/models/booking.rb
create  test/unit/booking_test.rb
create  test/fixtures/booking.yml
exists  db/migrate
create  db/migrate/005_create_bookings.rb
```

Each of these commands creates a number of files. You now have files named after the tables in the app/models directory, and those are the files you will edit. The generate model command also creates unit tests and fixtures, as well as a migration for each table. You can safely delete the migrations, since you already created all of the tables in your initial migration. The unit test and fixture files are for unit testing; visit the Rails site (http://rubyonrails.org) for information about their use.

First, edit the app/models/actor.rb file so it looks like Listing 5-4.

Listing 5-4. *Actor Model (app/models/actor.rb)*

```
class Actor < ActiveRecord::Base
  has_many :bookings
end
```

Save the modified model file. Then edit app/models/booking.rb to look like Listing 5-5.

Listing 5-5. *Booking Model (app/models/booking.rb)*

```
class Booking < ActiveRecord::Base
  belongs_to :actor
  belongs_to :project
  belongs_to :room
end
```

The actor and booking models contain all of the relationships you will use in this example. The has_many relationship between the actor and booking tables lets you retrieve all of the booking objects for each actor, and the various belongs_to relationships in the booking model allow you to retrieve the details of each booking. You could also add has_many :bookings relationships to the room and project models, but since you won't use them in the controller, they are omitted.

At this point, you have a database with data in it and a Rails application with a few models. Of course, models are just one-third of an MVC application, so let's create a controller next.

Creating the Controller for the Web Report

The controller will respond to actions of the user by taking data from the model and presenting it via your views .The controller is named home, since you will have just one page. Create the app/controllers/home_controller.rb file with the code shown in Listing 5-6.

Listing 5-6. *Home Controller for the Web Report (app/controllers/home_controller.rb)*

```
class HomeController < ApplicationController
  def index
    @actors_today = []
    @actors_tomorrow = []
    Actor.find(:all).each do |actor|
      @actors_today << {:actor=>actor,
                        :bookings => actor.bookings.find(:all,
                                         :conditions => [
                                         'TO_DAYS(booked_at)=' <<
                                          'TO_DAYS(NOW())'])}
      @actors_tomorrow << {:actor=>actor,
                        :bookings => actor.bookings.find(:all,
                                         :conditions => [
                                         'TO_DAYS(booked_at)=' <<
                                          'TO_DAYS(NOW())+1'])}
    end
  end
end
```

This controller has just one action: index, which displays the bookings for today and tomorrow.

Creating the View for the Web Report

Next, let's create a view that actually displays this data, as shown in Listing 5-7.

Listing 5-7. *The Single View for the Actor Scheduling Application (app/views/home/index.rhtml)*

```
<style>
  body { font-family: sans-serif }
  h2 { margin-left: 10pt;}
  p { margin-left: 10pt; }
</style>
```

```
<h1>Today's Schedule:</h1>

<% @actors_today.each do |actor_today| %>
    <h2><%= actor_today[:actor].name %></h2>
    <p><%if actor_today[:bookings].length > 0 %>
              actor_today[:bookings].each do |b|
                        <%=b.booked_at.strftime('%I:%m%p') %>,
                        <%=b.room.name %>,
                        <%=b.project.name %><br>
              <%end%>
      <%else%>
                        Nothing for today!
      <%end%>
    </p>

<% end %>


  <h1>Tomorrow's Schedule:</h1>

<% @actors_tomorrow.each do |actor_tomorrow| %>
    <h2><%= actor_tomorrow[:actor].name %></h2>
    <p><%if actor_tomorrow[:bookings].length > 0 %>
              actor_tomorrow [:bookings].each do |b|
                        <%=b.booked_at.strftime('%I:%m%p') %>,
                        <%=b.room.name %>,
                        <%=b.project.name %><br>
              <%end%>
      <%else%>
                        Nothing for tomorrow!
      <%end%>


<% end %>
```

Save this file as app/views/home/index.rhtml.

Now you need just one more piece: a layout, which is used as a template. In other words, the view is displayed inside the layout. Listing 5-8 shows the layout.

Listing 5-8. *Layout for the Actor Schedule View (app/views/layouts/application.rhtml)*

```
<html>
  <head>
    <title>Actor Schedule Report</title>
  </head>
  <body>
    <%= yield %>
  </body>
</html>
```

Save this as `app/views/layouts/application.rhtml`. This layout will be used automatically for all pages in the application by default. You can set up a layout for just one controller, and you can also manually override layouts for a given action.

At this point, the application is complete.

Examining the Web Report Application

Let's launch the application using the built-in Rails test web server. You can do that by using the following command:

```
ruby script/server
```

```
=> Booting Mongrel (use 'script/server webrick' to force WEBrick)
=> Rails application starting on http://0.0.0.0:3000
=> Call with -d to detach
=> Ctrl-C to shutdown server
** Starting Mongrel listening at 0.0.0.0:3000
** Starting Rails with development environment ...
** Rails loaded.
** Loading any Rails specific GemPlugins
** Signals ready.  INT => stop (no restart).
** Mongrel available at 0.0.0.0:3000
** Use CTRL-C to stop.
```

Open a web browser and enter the address `http://localhost:3000/home` to see the application. You should see a result similar to Figure 5-1.

■**Note** The Rails test server can use one of two web servers: WEBrick, which is installed by default, and Mongrel, which is faster. It automatically uses Mongrel if it's installed. If Mongrel is not installed, it will use WEBrick, and your output will be slightly different than what is shown in the book. However, it won't make a difference for this example.

Figure 5-1. *Ruby on Rails actor schedule*

To view the report on a cell phone, you would need to run this application on a public server. If you did so, and then used your cell phone to navigate to port 3000 on the appropriate URL, you would see something similar to Figure 5-2 (of course, the exact view depends on the cell phone model). Additionally, you would likely add authentication and other real-world features before actually deploying this application. Nonetheless, as you can see, the approach of using simple semantic HTML can work well even on cell phones.

Figure 5-2. *Ruby on Rails actor schedule on a Samsung A900 cell phone*

Dissecting the Code

The bulk of the application is in the controller and the view, but before we get to that, let's take a brief look at the migration (Listing 5-2), which defines the database schema for the application:

```
class InitialSchema < ActiveRecord::Migration
  def self.up
    create_table :actors do |t|
      t.column :name, :text, :length=>45
      t.column :phone, :text, :length=>13
    end
    create_table :projects do |t|
      t.column :name, :text, :length=>25
    end
    create_table :rooms do |t|
      t.column :name, :text, :length=>25
    end
    create_table :bookings do |t|
      t.column :actor_id, :integer
      t.column :room_id, :integer
      t.column :project_id, :integer
      t.column :booked_at, :datetime
    end
  end
```

```
    def self.down
      drop_table :actors
      drop_table :projects
      drop_table :rooms
      drop_table :bookings
    end
end
```

This migration has two methods: up and down. The up method creates several tables using the Rails built-in column types, which are automatically mapped to database-specific types. The down method drops the tables and is used to undo a migration. Notice that these tables automatically have an artificial primary key column, id, added by default. If that is undesirable, you need to explicitly state you don't want an id column, by using the ;id=>false option in your create_table statement.

Next, let's look at the controller (Listing 5-6):

```
    def index
      @actors_today = []
      @actors_tomorrow = []
      Actor.find(:all).each do |actor|
        @actors_today << {:actor=>actor,
                          :bookings=>actor.booking.find(:all,
                                          :conditions=>[
                                          'TO_DAYS(booked_at)=' <<
                                          TO_DAYS(NOW())'])}
        @actors_tomorrow << {:actor=>actor,
                          :bookings=>actor.booking.find(:all,
                                          :conditions=>[
                                          'TO_DAYS(booked_at)=' <<
                                          TO_DAYS(NOW())+1'])}
      end
    end
```

The controller has just one action, which represents the main page people will see when they visit your page. This action prepares two lists of actors for the view: one for today's schedule and another for tomorrow's schedule. Each item in the list has two parts: an actor object representing the actor and a list of bookings for the appropriate time period.

After this controller is called, the view of the same name is automatically rendered to the screen by Rails. Specifically, it implicitly calls the render method for you; you can override this with your own call to the render method, which lets you render a view with a different name or that is associated with a different controller.

Let's take a look at that view (Listing 5-7) next. First, it prints out all of the actors and their schedule for the day, as follows:

```
<h1>Today's Schedule:</h1>

<% @actors_today.each do |actor_today| %>
    <h2><%= actor_today[:actor].name %></h2>
    <p><%if actor_today[:bookings].length > 0 %>
            actor_today[:bookings].each do |b|
                        <%=b.booked_at.strftime('%I:%m%p') %>,
                        <%=b.room.name %>,
                        <%=b.project.name %><br>
            <%end%>
    <%else%>
                        Nothing for today!
    <%end%>
    </p>

<%end %>
```

It loops through each of the actors, prints their name as an h2 element, and then prints the bookings. It formats the booked_at time for each and prints it, along with the room name and the project name. The stftime function formats the date into a nice, human-readable form (see http://ruby-doc.org/core/classes/Time.src/M000297.html for details).

Then you do a very similar loop for tomorrow's schedule. In fact, it's identical, except for the references to @actors_today being replaced with @actors_tomorrow and similar changes.

Note that you could easily display this data in a table, but using paragraphs and headers gives the browser more control over wrapping, which makes it display better on small screens, such as the cell phone display you saw in Figure 5-2.

Now that you've seen how easy it is to create a web application with Rails, let's take a look at a slightly more complicated example.

Graphical Reporting with Rails

Although a lot of web reporting is textual, as in the previous example, it's also possible to do graphical reporting with Rails. To demonstrate, let's re-create the team performance report presented at the end of Chapter 4. However, instead of using Gruff to create reports, you will use a Flash charting application. The advantage of using a Flash solution is that it allows for interactivity. For example, you can create tool tips that report exact values when users move their mouse over an area of the graph.

First, let's create a Rails project for the application:

```
rails team_performance_web
```

```
create
create  app/controllers
create  app/helpers
create  app/models
create  app/views/layouts
create  config/environments
create  components
create  db
create  doc
create  lib
create  lib/tasks
create  log
create  public/images
create  public/javascripts
...
```

For this example, you'll use a project called Open Flash Chart. It's open source, unlike many other Flash charting components, so you can use it on any size project without paying licensing fees. Obtain Open Flash Chart from `http://teethgrinder.co.uk/open-flash-chart/`. Unzip it into a temporary directory. Next, copy the `open-flash-chart.swf` file from the root of the ZIP file into a new directory into your Rails application: `public/flash`.

You'll also use the Flash Object plug-in, which helps you include Flash objects in your views. Install this plug-in using the following command:

```
ruby script/plugin install http://lipsiasoft.googlecode.com/svn/trunk/
flashobject_helper/
```

Now you can start generating your code.

Creating the Controller for the Graphical Report

Begin by generating a single controller, home, using the following command:

```
ruby script/generate controller home
```

```
exists  app/controllers/
exists  app/helpers/
create  app/views/home
exists  test/functional/
create  app/controllers/home_controller.rb
create  test/functional/home_controller_test.rb
create  app/helpers/home_helper.rb
```

For this example, you will use the `players_4` database from Chapter 3, so you will need to edit your `config/database.yml` file to look something like Listing 5-9.

Listing 5-9. *Database Configuration File for the Graphical Report (config/database.yml)*

```
development:
  adapter: mysql
  database: players_4
  username: your_mysql_username_here
  password: your_mysql_password_here
  host: localhost
```

As in the previous example, you're creating only a `development` environment at this point, so you can safely ignore the other two database connection settings for `testing` and `production`.

Place the code shown in Listing 5-10 in `config/routes.rb`.

Listing 5-10. *Application Routing Code (config/routes.rb)*

```
ActionController::Routing::Routes.draw do |map|
  map.connect 'performance/:game_id/:player_id',
              :controller=>'performance',
              :action=>'show'

  map.connect 'performance/:game_id/:player_id.:format',
              :controller=>'performance',
              :action=>'show'

  map.connect "/", :controller=>'home'

  map.connect ':controller/:action/:id'
  map.connect ':controller/:action/:id.:format'
end
```

Remove the `public/index.html` file, as it overrides your routing for `/`.

The code shown in Listing 5-11 goes in `app/controllers/home_controller.rb`.

Listing 5-11. *Home Controller for the Web Report (app/controllers/home_controller.rb)*

```ruby
class HomeController < ApplicationController
  def index
    @available_players =Player.find(:all)
    @available_games = Game.find(:all)
  end
end
```

The code shown in Listing 5-12 goes in `app/controllers/performance_controller.rb`.

Listing 5-12. *Web Performance Data Controller (app/controllers/performance_controller.rb)*

```ruby
class PerformanceController < ApplicationController
  def show
    @player = Player.find_by_id(params[:player_id])
    @game = Game.find_by_id(params[:game_id])

    @events = Event.find(:all,
                    :select=>'event, ' <<
                            'AVG(time)/1000 as average_time',
                    :group=>'events.event DESC',
                    :joins=>' INNER JOIN plays ON events.play_id=plays.id',
                    :conditions=>["plays.game_id = ? AND plays.player_id= ?",
                                @game.id, @player.id]
                      ).map { |event|
                        {:event=>event.event,
                         :average_time=>event.average_time.to_i}
                          }

      respond_to do |format|
        format.html { render :layout=>false if request.xhr? }
        format.text { render :layout=>false }
        format.xml  { render :xml=>{'player'=>@player,
                                   'game'=>@game,
                                   'events'=>@events
                                   }.to_xml(:root=>'player_performance_report',
```

```
                                          :skip_types=>true) }
    end

  end
end
```

Now you can create the models for the report.

Creating the Models for the Graphical Report

This example will use four models: event (app/models/event.rb), game (app/models/game.rb), play (app/models/play.rb), and player (app/models/player.rb). Their code is shown in Listings 5-13 through 5-16.

Listing 5-13. *Event Model (app/models/event.rb)*

```
class Event < ActiveRecord::Base
  belongs_to :play
end
```

Listing 5-14. *Game Model (app/models/game.rb)*

```
class Game <  ActiveRecord::Base
  has_many :plays
end
```

Listing 5-15. *Play Model (app/models/play.rb)*

```
class Play <  ActiveRecord::Base
  belongs_to :game
  belongs_to :player
end
```

Listing 5-16. *Player Model (app/models/player.rb)*

```
class Player <  ActiveRecord::Base
  has_many :plays
end
```

Creating the View for the Graphical Report

The final pieces are the views. Place the file shown in Listing 5-17 in app/views/home/
index.html.erb.

Listing 5-17. *View for the Team Performance Application (app/views/home/index.html.erb)*

```
<h1>Team Performance Reporting</h1>

<div id="top">
  <%=select 'player', 'id',
           [['Click here to select a player',""]] +
           @available_players.map { |p|
                                    [p.name, p.id] },
           {:include_blank=>false} %>
  <%=select 'game', 'id',
           [['Click here to select a game',""]] +
           @available_games.map { |g|
                                   [g.name, g.id] },
           {:include_blank=>false} %> </div>
<div id="chart">
</div>

<script>

  function show_report(){
    $('chart').hide();
    var player_id = $('player_id').value;
    var game_id = $('game_id').value
    if( player_id && game_id ) {
      new Ajax.Updater("chart",
                       '/performance'+
                       '/' + $('game_id').value +
                       '/' + $('player_id').value,

                       {evalScripts:true,
                        method:'get',
                        onComplete:function(){
                          setTimeout("$('chart').show();",
                                     400);   }
                       }
                     );
```

```
    }
  }
  Event.observe("player_id", "change", show_report);
  Event.observe("game_id", "change", show_report);
</script>
```

The code shown in Listing 5-18 goes in `app/views/performance/show.html.erb`.

Listing 5-18. *Performance Controller Show HTML View (app/views/performance/*
show.html.erb)

```
<%if @events.length>1%>

<div>
  <%      graph_params = { 'AllowScriptAccess'=>'SameDomain' } %>
<%=flashobject_tag   "/flash/open-flash-chart.swf",
                     :size=>"850x400",
                     :parameters=>graph_params,
                     :variables=>{'data'=>"/performance/#{@game.id}
                                        /#{@player.id}.text"} %>
  </div>

<%else%>
  <p>  <%=@player.name%> has no recorded data for <%=@game.name%>.</p>
<%end%>
```

The code shown in Listing 5-19 goes in `app/views/layouts/show.text.erb`.

Listing 5-19. *Performance Controller Show Text View (app/views/performance/show.text.erb)*

```
<%
    labels = @events.map { |e| e[:event] }
    values = @events.map { |e| e[:average_time] }
    min = 0
    max = values.max


    graph_variables = { "title"=>",{margin:10px;}",
                        "bar_3d"=>"60,#8E9BF0,#000000",
                        "values"=>"#{values.join(',')}",
                        "x_labels"=>"#{labels.join(',')}",
```

```
                        "y_max"=>max,
                        "y_min"=>min,

                        "x_axis_3d"=>"16",
                        "tool_tip"=>"#x_label#: #val#s Average Time",
                        "y_axis_colour"=>"#F0F0F0",
                        "y_grid_colour"=>"#E9E9E9",
                        "y_label_style"=>"12,#000000",
                        "x_axis_colour"=>"#6F6F7F",
                        "x_grid_colour"=>"#E9E9E9",
                        "x_label_style"=>"15,#000000",

                        "bg_colour"=>"#F8F8FF" }

    %>
&<%=graph_variables.to_a.map { |key,val| "#{key}=#{val}" }.join("& &") %>&
```

Finally, the code shown in Listing 5-20 goes in app/views/layouts/application.html.erb.

Listing 5-20. *Layout for the Team Performance View (app/views/layouts/application.html.erb)*

```
<html>
  <head>
    <title>Team Performance Web Analyzer</title>
    <style>
      body { font-family: verdana; }
      h1 { margin-bottom:0.5em; }
      #top { margin-bottom: 0; width:802px;
             background-color:#efefef; padding:10px 24px; }
    </style>
    <%=javascript_include_tag :defaults  %>
  </head>
  <body>
    <%=yield%>
  </body>
</html>
```

And that completes the graphical reporting application. Let's take a look at it.

Examining the Graphical Reporting Application

You can run the example by using the following command:

```
ruby script/server
```

Now open a web browser and browse to http://localhost:3000/. You'll see a screen showing the available players and games, just as in the example in Chapter 4. If you select Michael Southwick and Tech Website Baron from the drop-down lists, you will see a screen similar to Figure 5-3.

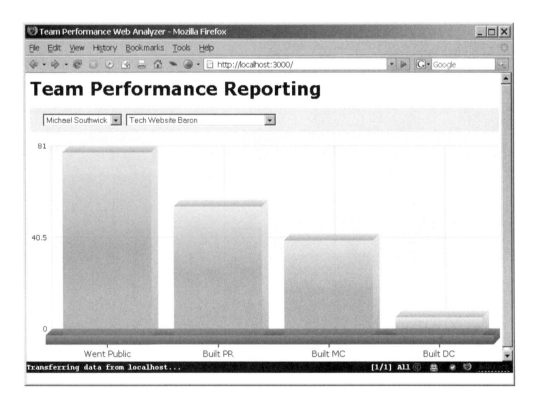

Figure 5-3. *Flash chart showing player statistics*

As you move your mouse over the various elements, you will see a tool tip with the details of each item; it should also highlight slightly.

Let's take a look at the code line by line.

Dissecting the Code

The models and application layout are fairly straightforward. The models are the same ones you used in Chapters 3 and 4. The application layout (Listing 5-20) is just a short wrapper for the application, which includes a bit of CSS to make the application more attractive. It does contain one important line:

```
<%=javascript_include_tag :defaults  %>
```

This includes the default list of JavaScript files, which includes Prototype by default. Because the Flash Object plug-in adds itself to the list of defaults, this line also includes the Flash Object plug-in for you.

■**Note** You need Prototype, as it's used later in this example. However, if you need to include Flash Object by itself, you can use this line of code: `<%= javascript_include_tag "flashobject" %>`.

Next, let's examine the `config/routes.rb` file (Listing 5-10), which controls the URLs for the entire application:

```
ActionController::Routing::Routes.draw do |map|
  map.connect 'performance/:game_id/:player_id',
              :controller=>'performance',
              :action=>'show'

  map.connect 'performance/:game_id/:player_id.:format',
              :controller=>'performance',
              :action=>'show'

  map.connect "/", :controller=>'home'

  map.connect ':controller/:action/:id'
  map.connect ':controller/:action/:id.:format'
end
```

The first route is a route that defines URLs of the form `performance/game_id/player_id`. The second route defines URLs that specifically set an output type, like `performance/game_id/player_id.xml` and `performance/game_id/player_id.html`. The next route specifies that / should map to the Home controller. The remaining routes are catchall routes. Although they are not used in the current version of this application, it's wise to include them so that you can easily add new controllers.

Let's examine the Home controller (Listing 5-11) next:

```
class HomeController < ApplicationController
  def index
    @available_players =Player.find(:all)
    @available_games = Game.find(:all)
  end
end
```

This code is pretty straightforward. It populates a list of available players and games, which is passed to your view. Let's take a look at that view next.

The first part of the view for the application (Listing 5-17) uses the @available_players and @available_games variables, and constructs two select boxes, which let users choose a player and game combination to view:

```
<h1>Team Performance Reporting</h1>

<div id="top">
  <%=select 'player', 'id',
            [['Click here to select a player',""]] +
            @available_players.map { |p|
                                    [p.name, p.id] },
            {:include_blank=>false} %>
  <%=select 'game', 'id',
            [['Click here to select a game',""]] +
            @available_games.map { |g|
                                    [g.name, g.id] },
            {:include_blank=>false} %> </div>


<div id="chart">
</div>
```

This code creates two drop-down lists from the data passed from the controller. You use the map method to turn each array of Active Record objects into the type of array that the select tag expects: an array of arrays, with the first element as the label and the second element as the value. This means that for the player Matthew Gifford, for example, the player's name will be displayed in the drop-down list, but the control will actually have the value 1 (the player's ID), which you'll use to display the appropriate chart. This code also puts a blank "Click here to select . . ." entry at the top of each drop-down list. This entry has a label but no value, and it serves to tell the user what to do.

The second div, which has the ID chart, will be used to store the chart. The following JavaScript makes that happen:

```
<script>

  function show_report(){
    $('chart').hide();
    var player_id = $('player_id').value;
    var game_id = $('game_id').value
    if( player_id && game_id ) {
      new Ajax.Updater("chart",
                        '/performance'+
                        '/' + $('game_id').value +
                        '/' + $('player_id').value,

                        {evalScripts:true,
                          method:'get',
                           onComplete:function(){
                             setTimeout("$('chart').show();",
                                         400);    }
                        }
                      );
    }
  }
  Event.observe("player_id", "change", show_report);
  Event.observe("game_id", "change", show_report);

</script>
```

This JavaScript code defines a new function, show_report, and then uses Prototype's Event.observe function to run the show_report function whenever either of the drop-down lists changes. The show_report button hides the existing chart, and then checks if both a player and game were selected. If neither or just one of them was selected, then the routine does nothing. If both are selected, then it uses Ajax.Updater to call the show method of the Performance controller, passing it both the ID of the selected game and the ID of the selected player. (Note that you don't need to specify explicitly that it's the show action, because you defined an appropriate route in your routes.rb file.)

The Ajax.Updater call has three important optional parameters passed to it:

- The first is evalScripts, which ensures that JavaScript code passed by the Performance controller is executed. By default, code retrieved by Ajax.Updater is not executed.

- The second is the method parameter. By default, Ajax.Updater uses a POST request, and since this is a read-only request that does not affect the state of the database, it should be a GET request.

- The third is a callback, onComplete, which will run when Ajax.Updater has finished updating the control. This is a small fix for a bug in the Flash Object plug-in, which results in a "You do not have Flash installed" message appearing while the page is loading. To avoid the problem, you wait 400 milliseconds to redisplay the chart component.

Next, let's take a look at the Performance controller (Listing 5-12):

```
class PerformanceController < ApplicationController
  def show
    @player = Player.find_by_id(params[:player_id])
    @game = Game.find_by_id(params[:game_id])

    @events = Event.find(:all,
                   :select=>'event, ' <<
                       'AVG(time)/1000 as average_time',
                   :group=>'events.event ASC',
                   :joins=>' INNER JOIN plays ON events.play_id=plays.id',
                   :conditions=>["plays.game_id = ? AND plays.player_id= ?",
                         @game.id, @player.id]
                       ).map { |event|
                         {:event=>event.event,
                          :average_time=>event.average_time.to_i}
                           }

    respond_to do |format|
      format.html { render :layout=>false if request.xhr? }
      format.text { render :layout=>false }
      format.xml { render :xml=>{'player'=>@player,
                                 'game'=>@game,
                                 'events'=>@events
                                }.to_xml(:root=>'player_performance_report',
                                         :skip_types=>true)  }
    end

  end
end
```

This code sets the @player and @game variables, which allow the view to know which player and game were selected and display the information, and then it prepares the data. It retrieves the performance data using SQL that is similar to the example at the end of Chapter 4, but it uses find to retrieve the values instead of find_by_sql. The routine then maps it into an array of hashes, with each hash having an event value and an average_time value.

■**Note** The reason the raw array of Event values isn't passed directly is that you need to call the to_i method on average_time, since Rails doesn't do that for you. This would require knowledge of the controller's internal structure to be embedded in the view, which violates MVC separation. By remapping it into a new data structure and calling to_i on the average_time method, you can have a controller-agnostic view. This has the benefit of letting you change the way this data is produced without affecting the view. As long as the data passed to the view is an array of hashes with the appropriate values, it should work.

Finally, a respond_to block is used to provide varying results depending on which format is called. For example, the URL http://localhost:3000/performance/5/1 will use the HTML format, since that's the default format specified in routes.rb.

The first format is HTML. This is the code that is called by the show_report JavaScript function in the Home controller. Note that it disables the layout if it's being called by an Ajax call. The request.xhr? method will return true during an XmlHttpRequest (XHR) request, and in that case, the layout is disabled.

The second format is text. This is the format that Open Flash Chart uses to store its data. The first format, HTML, calls this format to retrieve the data. This does mean that the SQL is executed twice. It is necessary because the chart component should not be rendered if there is no data for the player/game combination; instead, a message should be displayed. You can detect that by running the computation for the HTML format as well as the other formats.

The last format isn't used in the example, but it demonstrates how easy it is to add machine-readable formats to Rails 2.0 applications. The XML format can be read by an application written in almost any language, as well as a desktop application such as Microsoft Access. For example, the XML generated by this code for player Matthew Gifford and game Tech Website Baron can be seen at the URL http://localhost:3000/performance/5/1.xml and looks like this:

```
<player-performance-report>

  <game>
    <id>5</id>
    <name>Tech Website Baron</name>
  </game>

  <player>
    <drink>Moxie</drink>
    <id>1</id>
```

```
      <name>Matthew Gifford</name>
      <nickname>m_giff</nickname>
      <salary>89000.0</salary>
   </player>

   <events>

      <event>
        <event>Went Public</event>
        <average-time>93</average-time>
      </event>

      <event>
        <event>Built PR</event>
        <average-time>72</average-time>
      </event>

      <event>
        <event>Built MC</event>
        <average-time>54</average-time>
      </event>

      <event>
        <event>Built DC</event>
        <average-time>13</average-time>
      </event>
   </events>
</player-performance-report>
```

The exact appearance of the XML is controlled by two optional parameters passed to the to_xml method: :root=>'player_performance_report' and :skip_types=>true. The first, :root, sets the name of the root node to be easier to read; otherwise, it would simply be "hash," which isn't very descriptive. The second removes the type attributes, such as type="array" for the <events> element; those attributes clutter up the XML without adding much information.

Other optional parameters to to_xml are :include, which lets you specify exactly which elements to include, and :except, which lets you specifically exclude elements, such as password fields. You can find out more about to_xml at Ryan Daigle's blog: http://ryandaigle.com/articles/2007/4/13/what-s-new-in-edge-rails-a-more-flexible-to_xml.

Next, let's take a look at the view that contains the Flash container for the chart (Listing 5-18):

```
<%if @events.length>1%>

<div>
  <%      graph_params = { 'AllowScriptAccess'=>'SameDomain' } %>
<%=flashobject_tag    "/flash/open-flash-chart.swf",
                      :size=>"850x400",
                      :parameters=>graph_params,
                      :variables=>{'data'=>"/performance/#{@game.id}
                                      /#{@player.id}.text"} %>

</div>

<%else%>
  <p>  <%=@player.name%> has no recorded data for <%=@game.name%>.</p>
<%end%>
```

If the user/game combination has no data, the view displays a message to that effect. If the user has selected a player and game, the view will use flashobject_tag—provided by the Flash Object plug-in—to include a graph. The data for the graph comes from the path /performance/*game_id/player_id*.text.

Although it's possible to include Flash objects directly in your HTML views using EMBED tags, that's not a good idea. If the user doesn't have Flash installed, you should display a message stating that Flash is required to see the content. Additionally, if you use EMBED tags, Internet Explorer requires users to click Flash objects to activate them and display their content, which is annoying. The Flash Object plug-in will take care of both problems. It will check if Flash is installed, and if not, it will display the message. The plug-in also inserts the objects dynamically, which avoids the Internet Explorer click-to-activate issue.

Next, let's take a look at the last view, app/views/performance/show.text.erb (Listing 5-19):

```
<%
    labels = @events.map { |e| e[:event] }
    values = @events.map { |e| e[:average_time] }
    min = 0
    max = values.max
%>
```

First, you loop through the @events array and pull out the event and average_time from each element. The events are used as labels; the average time is used as values. Note that this code is in here and not in the controller to keep their concerns separate. You could pass the labels and values directly to the view, but that would require the controller code to embody knowledge of how Open Flash Chart works, which would violate MVC separation. It would also add code that is irrelevant to the three other output formats to the controller.

Next, the code sets a few view-specific options:

```
graph_variables = { "title"=>",{margin:10px;}",
                    "bar_3d"=>"60,#8E9BF0,#000000",
                    "values"=>"#{values.join(',')}",
                    "x_labels"=>"#{labels.join(',')}",
                    "y_max"=>max,
                    "y_min"=>min,
                    "x_axis_3d"=>"16",
                    "tool_tip"=>"#x_label#: #val#s Average Time",
                    "y_axis_colour"=>"#F0F0F0",
                    "y_grid_colour"=>"#E9E9E9",
                    "y_label_style"=>"12,#000000",
                    "x_axis_colour"=>"#6F6F7F",
                    "x_grid_colour"=>"#E9E9E9",
                    "x_label_style"=>"15,#000000",

                    "bg_colour"=>"#F8F8FF" }
    %>
&<%=graph_variables.to_a.map { |key,val| "#{key}=#{val}" }.join("& &") %>&
```

Many of these options are fairly self-explanatory. For example, x_axis_colour controls the color of the x axis lines. The y_ticks parameter is a comma-delimited list of three parameters, which control the ticks (the small lines that point to numeric labels) on the left side of the graph. The first y_ticks parameter is the distance from the ticks to the labels, the second is the distance from the labels to the chart itself, and the third is the total number of ticks. You can get a full list of parameters from http://teethgrinder.co.uk/open-flash-chart/.

The final line of the code converts the hash into *key=value* pairs surrounded by ampersands, which is the data format required by Open Flash Chart.

Summary

This chapter demonstrated how you can easily use Rails, along with the techniques you've already learned, to quickly create web applications that serve reports as textual HTML or as Flash charts. Rails is a fast and easy way to create reporting software. The Web is ubiquitous, which gives it implicit deployment advantages, and Rails is a great way to create web applications.

However, while Rails takes care of many of the problems inherent in web applications, it cannot address all software issues. You're still likely to encounter various application-specific problems. The rest of this book is dedicated to examples of how you can solve specific reporting problems with Ruby.

PART 2

■ ■ ■

Examples of Reporting with Ruby

CHAPTER 6

■ ■ ■

Tracking Auctions with eBay

Essentially, business is about money changing hands, and for that to happen, you need to have a buyer and a seller who need to connect somehow. Where they connect, of course, is a marketplace. Marketplaces come in many varieties, from a high-profile diamond market in London to a corner flea market in Wyoming. Of course, most businesses choose their marketplace according to the ability to reach their customers. eBay is perhaps the world's largest marketplace for many types of goods.

Unfortunately, it's not enough to simply sell your product on eBay. You need to intelligently price, describe, and promote it. This requires experimentation with all of the possible factors, as well as the ability to analyze which tactics increase sale price and volume. You also need to assess how cost efficient each factor is, since some factors are not free. For example, eBay allows sellers to place small icons next to a listing or to boldface the listing's title for a small fee. For a much larger fee, you can place your listing in a special "featured items" category, which appears at the top of every search. Any of these options may or may not be appropriate, and reporting can help you decide which options to use.

Of course, there are many other reasons why you might want to produce reports based on your eBay-driven initiatives. For example, you may have hired an intern to list a certain number of items per day, and you want to ensure that the intern is actually doing her job. Or you may not choose to sell on eBay at all, but rather want to make sure that no competitor is selling inferior goods on eBay and claiming they are yours.

Fortunately, the work of creating eBay reports does not have to be done by hand, as you'll learn in this chapter.

Using eBay APIs

eBay devotes an entire site to its various developer APIs. Although a Ruby example isn't available on eBay's site, it's reasonably easy to write Ruby code that accesses the APIs.

eBay offers several different APIs. This chapter focuses on one particular variant: the REST API.

The REST API is accessed using simple HTTP GET and POST requests, which return XML responses. As you'll learn in this chapter, both the request and response phases are easily handled by Ruby. The eBay REST API, although considerably easier to use than the full eBay API, is limited to retrieving information. You cannot post new items for sale using that API. Fortunately, read-only access is fine for reporting purposes. You can find out the full documentation for eBay's REST API at http://developer.ebay.com/developercenter/rest/eBayRESTAPIGuide.pdf.

Before you can do anything with the eBay API, you need to sign up and retrieve an authorization token. Visit http://developer.ebay.com/ to create an eBay developer account.

After you've created an account, you need to generate a set of authorization keys, which is fairly straightforward. As shown in Figure 6-1, you can create keys for either eBay's main site, called production, or for its test site, called sandbox. To follow the example in this chapter, you should create keys for the production site.

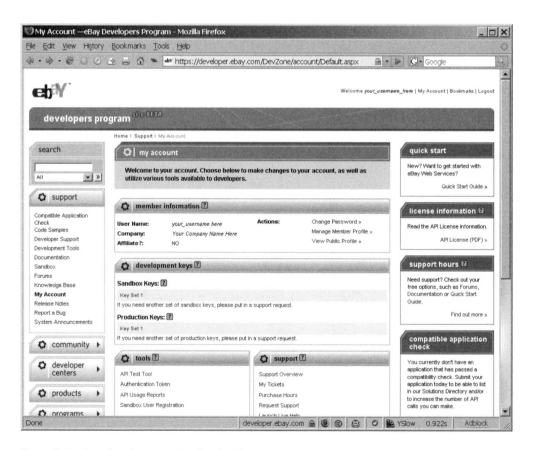

Figure 6-1. *eBay developer authorization key page*

Next, you'll be asked whether you want to create an authorization token, and you should select to do so. Authorization tokens are used to access the REST API, whereas authorization keys can be used to access eBay's full developer API. The authorization token is only slightly different from a set of authorization keys (and, truth be told, it's not really clear why eBay has two separate authorization systems). You'll need an eBay.com account in order to create an authorization token. Remember your eBay.com username, as you'll need to use it in conjunction with your authorization token.

Obtaining Competitive Intelligence via eBay Web Services

Suppose you own a business selling, say, musical instruments to the public, and you want to use eBay's web services to make sure your equipment is competitively priced. You would like to sell the instruments rapidly, so you don't want to price them too high, but you would also like to have as high a profit margin as possible, so you don't want to price them too low.

Of course, many people are selling instruments on eBay. You want to use eBay's REST API to perform searches on your various competitors, finding out how much they are getting for various items. Fortunately, it's easy to use Hpricot, a Ruby-based HTML and XML parsing library, to do just that. This chapter's example will use eBay's REST API and Hpricot to perform searches on multiple competitors, parse the result, and figure out the average price.

To present the report, you'll write the result to a PDF file, using the LaTeX document-preparation system. PDFs are particularly useful for a couple reasons. Unlike HTML, they appear almost identical in print as they do on the screen. Also, they can easily be e-mailed or saved on disk. (Modern web browsers permit HTML pages to be saved to disk with images, but most end users are not savvy enough to do this, and this facility will not work with complicated web pages.)

WHY LATEX?

There are many ways to produce PDFs using Ruby, so you might wonder why LaTeX is being used in this chapter. After all, LaTeX is an older technology that can be relatively hard to learn, particularly compared with Ruby. However, LaTeX has two large advantages over the alternatives: it's fast, and it's flexible. LaTeX can perform a huge array of PDF-formatting tasks—ranging from automatic page numbering, to footnotes, to mathematical formulas, to printing address labels—and it can create even very large PDF reports quickly.

On the othe hand, as mentioned, LaTeX is not the most user-friendly tool. If you're looking for another solution, you can try two other PDF-generation techniques demonstrated in this book:

- Converting HTML to PDF is an easy technique to use, as the source is HTML. However, you don't have detailed control over your formatting, since HTML is a very different format from PDF. This technique is demonstrated in Chapter 8.

- Using PDF::Writer is more flexible than HTML-to-PDF conversion, but slower and less flexible than LaTeX. However, PDF::Writer is written in pure Ruby, so if you pefer to use a pure Ruby library with no external dependencies, that's the way to go. An example of using PDF::Writer along with Gruff to create PDF graphs is presented in Chapter 10.

Installing Hpricot and LaTeX

For this example, you'll need both Hpricot and a LaTeX distribution installed. The LaTeX distribution you use depends on your operating system:

Windows: You can obtain MiKTeX, a TeX/LaTeX distribution for Windows, from `http://miktex.org`.

Mac OS X: You can obtain a TeX/LaTeX distribution for OS X at `http://tug.org/mactex/`. If you have a preferred ports manager for OS X, such as Fink or MacPorts, you can probably install LaTeX using that as well.

Linux: If you're running Linux, LaTeX may already be installed. If not, you should be able to install it easily using your system's package manager.

- The command for Debian Linux and related distributions (Ubuntu, for example) is `apt-get install texlive`.

- For Red Hat–based distributions, you should be able to use the command `sudo yum install tetex-latex`.

You'll also need to install Hpricot. You can install it using the following command:

```
gem install hpricot
```

You'll find that Hpricot is very easy to use. For example, you could parse a simple HTML document using Hpricot like this:

```
require 'hpricot'
html_document = "
<html>
```

```
  <body>
    <h1>Test Document</h1>

    <p>This is the first test paragraph.</p>
    <p>This is the second test paragraph.</li>
  </body>
</html>
END

parser=Hpricot.parse(html_document)

(parser/:p).each do |list_item|
      puts list_item.inner_html
end
```

If you ran this example, you would get these results:

```
This is the first test paragraph.
This is the second test paragraph.
```

This example simply divides your Hpricot parser document by :p (parser/:p). Because Hpricot interprets divide as "search by," it returns an array of all of the p tags. You then use the inner_html method, which returns the HTML code inside that element, to print out the contents of each of your test paragraphs. Of course, you can use Hpricot to search by other tags, and you can perform more complicated searches, such as finding all of the p tags inside a div of a certain class. You can find out more about using Hpricot at http://code.whytheluckystiff.net/hpricot/ or in my Apress book *Practical Ruby Gems.*

Coding the eBay Report

Now let's look at the code for the example. Since it's fairly complicated, I've divided it into parts. The first part, shown in Listing 6-1, includes the various libraries required and the setup code. Make sure you set your path to pdflatex.exe appropriately.

Listing 6-1. *Average Price Reporter, Part 1 (average_price_report.rb)*

```
require 'rexml/document'
require 'net/http'
require 'uri'
```

```
require 'hpricot'

(puts "usage: #{$0} keyword1,keyword2 seller1,seller2"; exit) unless ARGV.length>1

keywords=ARGV.shift.split(',')
sellers=ARGV.shift.split(',')
sellers << nil # This line adds an entry that displays all sellers;
               # note that you can delete this line if
               # you do not want your output to display
               # an average for all sellers.

path_to_pdflatex = '/somepath/pdflatex.exe'
            # Make sure you insert your path to pdflatex here.
```

Next is a class, eBaySearch, which the application will use to search eBay for prices, as shown in Listing 6-2.

Listing 6-2. *Average Price Reporter, Part 2 (average_price_report.rb)*

```
class EBaySearch
  @@ebay_config = {
    :ebay_address=> 'rest.api.ebay.com',
    :request_token => 'my_request_token',
    :user_id => 'my_ebay_user_id' }.freeze    # Insert your request token
                                              # and eBay user ID here.

  def self.get_average_price(keyword, seller_id=nil)

    params = {
    # Authorization information . . .
    'RequestToken'  => @@ebay_config[:request_token],
    'RequestUserId' => @@ebay_config[:user_id],

    # Function name
    'CallName' => 'GetSearchResults',

    # Search parameters
    'Query'=>URI.escape(keyword), # Note that only
            # some parameters are escaped.
            # This is because the RequestToken
            # is already escaped for URLs, so
            # re-URL encoding would cause
```

```ruby
          # problems; otherwise, we could just
          # run all of these values through a URI.escaping
          # loop.

  'ItemTypeFilter' => 3,   # Search all items,
                           # including fixed price items.
                           # If you change this to 2,
                           # you'll get fewer results,
                           # but it won't include in-progress
                           # auctions, which may make your
                           # results more accurate.

  'SearchInDescription'=>0, # Do not search inside of
                            # description, since it's easy to say
                            # "this item is like XYZ other item"
                            # in a description, thus throwing off our
                            # average.

  # Return data parameters
  'Schema' =>1, # Use eBay's new style XML schema instead of
                # of the old, deprecated one.
  'EntriesPerPage' =>100, # Return at most 100 entries.
                          # Note that for performance reasons,
                          # this code does not iterate through the pages,
                          # so it will calculate the average of
                          # only the first hundred items on eBay.
  'PageNumber' =>1

  }

if seller_id  # If the caller does not pass a seller id,
  # this function will search across all sellers.

  params['IncludeSellers'] = URI.escape(seller_id)

  # eBay usernames are currently limited to alphanumeric characters
  # and underscores, so this may not be necessary, but it's escaped
  # just in case.
end

url_path = "/restapi?" << params.map{|param, value| "#{param}=#{value}"}.join("&")
```

```ruby
    response_body = Net::HTTP.get($ebay_config[:ebay_address], url_path)
    hpricot_doc = Hpricot.XML(response_body)

    total_price = 0.0
    result_count = 0

    (hpricot_doc/:SearchResultItem).each do |item| # Iterate through
                                             # each SearchResultItem element.
      price_element = (item/:CurrentPrice)  # Find the CurrentPrice element
                                        # inside of each SearchResultItem element.
      if price_element # If it has a price . . .

        total_price = total_price +  price_element.first.innerHTML.to_f

                      #. . . then pull out the
                      # inside of the element,
                      # convert it to a float,
                      # and add it to the total.

                      # Note that the method is called innerHTML, but
                      # actually returns the inside of the element.
                      # This is because Hpricot was originally an HTML
                      # parsing library.

        result_count = result_count + 1

      end
    end

    if result_count > 0
      average_price = (total_price/result_count)
    else
      average_price = nil
    end

    [result_count, average_price] # Return the number of results and
                          # average price as an array.

  end

end
```

> **■Note** You'll need to replace the request token and eBay username with the appropriate values. They are marked with italics in Listing 6-2. See the "Using eBay APIs" section earlier in this chapter for instructions on how to sign up for an eBay developer account and create an authorization token.

Finally, the last part of the code, shown in Listing 6-3, will create the report in LaTeX and print out the results to a PDF file.

Listing 6-3. *Average Price Reporter, Part 3 (average_price_report.rb)*

```ruby
class String
  def latex_escape()

    replacements= {  '\\' =>'$\backslash$',
                     '$'=>'\$',
                     '%'=>'\%',
                     '&'=>'\&',
                     '_'=>'\_',
                     '~'=>'*~*',
                     '#'=>'\#',
                     '{'=>'$\{$',
                     '}'=>'$\}$',
                     }
    self.gsub(/[#{replacements.keys.join('|')}]/) do |match|
      replacements[match]
    end

  end
end


temporary_latex_file='average_price_report.tex' # This file name will also control
                                                # the output file name. The
                                                # file will be named
                                                # average_price_report.pdf.


latex_source='
\documentclass[8pt]{article}

\begin{document}
```

```
\huge                                    % Switch to huge size and
\textbf{Competitor Average Price Report} % print a header at the
                                         % top of the page.


\vspace{0.1in}                           % Add a small amount of
                                         % whitespace between the
                                         % header and the table.


\normalsize                              % Switch back to normal size.


\begin{tabular}{llll}                    % Start a table with four
                                         % left-aligned columns.


\textbf{Item}&                           % Four headers, each in bold,
\textbf{Seller}&                         % with labels for each column.
\textbf{Count}&
\textbf{Average Price}\\\\

'


keywords.each do |keyword|
  first=true
  sellers.each do |seller|
    total_items, average_price = *EBaySearch.get_average_price(keyword, seller)

    latex_source << "
    \\textbf{#{first ? keyword.latex_escape : ' '}} &
    #{seller ? seller.latex_escape : 'First 100 eBay Results'} &
    #{total_items} &
    \\#{average_price ? ('$%0.2f' % average_price) : ''}
    \\\\  "


  # Note that the character & is the marker for the end of a cell, and
  # that the sequence \\\\ is two escaped backslashes, which mark
  # the end of the row.


    first=false # This marker controls whether to redisplay the keyword.
                # For visual formatting reasons, each keyword is
                # shown only once.
  end
end
```

```
latex_source << '
\end{tabular}
\end{document}'

fh = File.open(temporary_latex_file, 'w')
fh.puts latex_source
fh.close

puts "Searched #{
            keywords.length} keywords and #{
            sellers.delete_if {|s| s.nil?}.length
          } sellers for a total of #{
            sellers.length*keywords.length
          } eBay searches."

puts `"#{path_to_pdflatex}" #{temporary_latex_file} --quiet` # Runs PDFLatex with
# the --quiet switch, which eliminates much of the chatter it usually displays.
# It will still display errors, however.

puts "Wrote report to average_price_report.pdf"
```

Save all the code as average_price_report.rb.

Note that I cannot include any specific eBay IDs in this book, but you can feel free to go to the eBay site, perform a random search, and insert a few user IDs and keywords into a command, like this one:

```
ruby average_price_report.rb "keyword1,keyword2" "seller_id1,seller_id2,seller_id3"
```

The results should look something like this:

```
Searched 2  keywords and 3 sellers for a total of 6 eBay searches.
entering expanded_mode . . .
Wrote report to average_price_report.pdf
```

This will create a file called average_price_report.pdf. If you open it, you should see something similar to Figure 6-2.

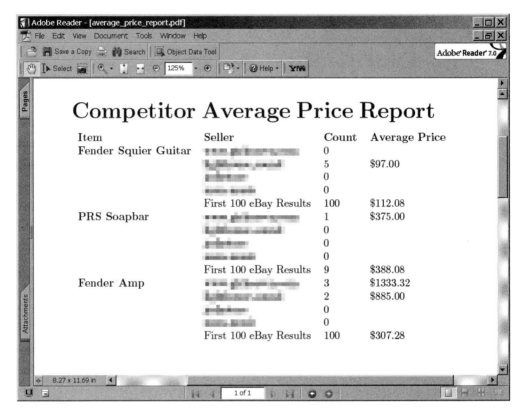

Figure 6-2. *Average price report output PDF in Adobe Reader*

Let's take a look at a few important lines from this example.

Dissecting the eBay Web Services Code

In Listing 6-2, the script first parses the arguments from the command line, which is fairly straightforward. After that, you define a class that can be used to get the average price of certain combinations of keywords and sellers:

```
class EBaySearch
  @@ebay_config = {
    :ebay_address=> 'rest.api.ebay.com',
    :request_token => 'my_request_token',
    :user_id => 'my_ebay_user_id' }.freeze   # Insert your request token
                                             # and eBay user ID here.
```

```ruby
def self.get_average_price(keyword, seller_id=nil)

  params = {
  # Authorization information . . .
  'RequestToken'  => @@ebay_config[:request_token],
  'RequestUserId' => @@ebay_config[:user_id],

  # Function name
  'CallName' => 'GetSearchResults',

  # Search parameters
  'Query'=>URI.escape(keyword), # Note that only
      # some parameters are escaped.
      # This is because the RequestToken
      # is already escaped for URLs, so
      # re-URL encoding would cause
      # problems; otherwise, we could just
      # run all of these values through a URI.escaping
      # loop.

  'ItemTypeFilter' => 3,    # Search all items,
                            # including fixed price items.
                            # If you change this to 2,
                            # you'll get fewer results,
                            # but it won't include in-progress
                            # auctions, which may make your
                            # results more accurate.

  'SearchInDescription'=>0, # Do not search inside of
                            # description, since it's easy to say
                            # "this item is like XYZ other item"
                            # in a description, thus throwing off our
                            # average.

  # Return data parameters
  'Schema' =>1,             # Use eBay's new style XML schema instead
                            # of the old, deprecated one.

  'EntriesPerPage' =>100,   # Return at most 100 entries.
                        # Note that for performance reasons,
                        # this code does not iterate through the pages,
```

```
                          # so it will calculate the average of
                          # only the first hundred items on eBay.
        'PageNumber' =>1


    }
```

As you can see, this class has just one method, and the first thing you do is create a hash that represents the parameters you'll pass to eBay's web services. The most important parameter is CallName, which controls which of the various available functions you call. In this case, you call GetSearchResults, which returns the result of an eBay search, logically enough. A number of other function calls are available, and each can be used in a manner similar to this one.

The second most important parameter is the Query parameter, which specifies the keywords to search by. However, you need to optionally search by seller as well, so the next chunk of code adds a second parameter if desired:

```
  if seller_id  # If the caller does not pass a seller id,
    # this function will search across all sellers.

    params['IncludeSellers'] = URI.escape(seller_id)

    # eBay usernames are currently limited to alphanumeric characters
    # and underscores, so this may not be necessary, but it's escaped
    # just in case.
  end
```

If the method is passed a seller_id that isn't false or nil, you add a new parameter to your call to GetSearchResults: IncludeSellers, which specifies which sellers to search for. If a call to GetSearchResults has both an IncludeSellers and a Query parameter, it will search for both; if the call has just an IncludeSellers value, it will return everything from that seller. (If it has just a Query parameter, it will search for that keyword without regard to who is selling the item.)

Next, since you've created an array of parameters to be passed to the eBay web services API, you need to begin constructing the actual URL you will send, as follows:

```
  url_path = "/restapi?" << params.map{|param, value| "#{param}=#{value}"}.join("&")

  response_body = Net::HTTP.get($ebay_config[:ebay_address], url_path)
```

The first line constructs the URL, turning the params hash into pairs of the form name=value. These pairs are then joined by & symbols, and the resulting string is the path you'll use to call the eBay REST API.

The second line actually calls the API, using the `Net::HTTP.get` method. This is a convenience method that skips several steps for you. Normally, you would need to open a connection to the server, request the document represented by `url_path`, and then close the connection. Fortunately, the `Net:HTTP.get` method does all that and returns a string, which represents the body of eBay's response to your request.

Next, you need to create an `Hpricot` object to parse the response. After that, you can use Hpricot to loop through the XML:

```
hpricot_doc = Hpricot.XML(response.body)
```

Incidentally, the XML you're parsing looks something like this:

```
<GetSearchResultsResponse xmlns="urn:ebay:apis:eBLBaseComponents">
  <Timestamp>2007-08-12T20:31:11.148Z</Timestamp>
  <Ack>Success</Ack>
  <Version>525</Version>
  <Build>e525_core_Bundled_5124914_R1</Build>
  <SearchResultItemArray>
    <SearchResultItem>
      <Item>
        <ItemID>120148832189</ItemID>
        <ListingDetails>
          <StartTime>2007-08-05T13:39:30.000Z</StartTime>
          ..snip...
          <CurrentPrice currencyID="USD">12.95</CurrentPrice>
          . . .
```

Essentially, you want to pull all of the `SearchResultItem` elements out of the document, and then retrieve the `CurrentPrice` elements from each of those. For each `SearchResultItem` element, you add the `CurrentPrice` of the object to the total. You also keep track of the total number of results.

```
total_price = 0.0
result_count = 0

(hpricot_doc/:SearchResultItem).each do |item| # Iterate through
                                        # each SearchResultItem element
    price_element = (item/:CurrentPrice)      # Find the CurrentPrice element
                                        # inside of each SearchResultItem element.
    if price_element # If it has a price . . .

      total_price = total_price +  price_element.first.innerHTML.to_f
```

```
                        #. . . then pull out the
                        # inside of the element,
                        # convert it to a float,
                        # and add it to the total.

                        # Note that the method is called innerHTML, but
                        # actually returns the inside of the element.
                        # This is because Hpricot was originally an HTML
                        # parsing library.
        result_count = result_count + 1
    end
  end
```

As you can see, Hpricot has a very simple interface. You use the divide operator (/) to extract all of the children of a certain type. The expression hpricot_doc/:SearchResultItem extracts all of the <SearchResultItem> elements and their children, and you then loop through them. For each of those items, you extract all of the <CurrentPrice> elements using the divide operator. Since the divide operator always returns an array—even when there's just one element—you then call the first method on that array, extracting the first element. Next, you call the innerHTML method, which returns the inside text of the element. Finally, you call to_f on the inside text, which converts it into a float, and then add the price to the total price.

Note that there is a bit of a trade-off here. eBay web services do not have a feature to search for listings in the past, so you are limited to searching among currently available listings. (The documentation does indicate that recently finished auctions may be included, though.) As a result, some auctions may not be finished, and you can retrieve only the current price. Since most of the auctions are likely to go higher, you can use this average as only a rough guide of an object's value. On the other hand, it's unlikely that the objects will drop in price, so the results are very useful as minimum prices.

Note Auctions occasionally drop in price. Bidders can cancel bids for a limited variety of reasons, and sellers can cancel bids for a similarly limited set of reasons. Both situations are uncommon, however.

MAKING THE PRICES MORE ACCURATE

You have a couple ways to make the prices obtained by the eBay report more accurate:

- Limit listings to fixed price eBay store listings, which you can do by changing the `ItemTypeFilter` parameter of your `params` hash to 2. Since this will not include regular auctions, it will limit the scope significantly, and if the goods you are searching for are uncommon, this could cause a problem.

- Search all auctions, but only to examine their Buy It Now price. Buy It Now prices are prices set by the seller, which the seller considers sufficient to stop the auction. If a user clicks Buy It Now, he agrees to pay that price regardless of the current auction price. Since that represents a static value set by the seller, you may consider it more accurate. You can easily check this instead of the current auction price by replacing `:CurrentPrice` with `:BuyItNowPrice`. (Note that if you do that, it won't count items without Buy It Now prices; this is because of the `if` statement checking for the existence of the price element.)

As you can see, the downside is that these approaches come at the expense of having less data to work with in your report.

Now you need to return the data to the caller of your method, as follows:

```
if result_count > 0
  average_price = (total_price/result_count)
else
  average_price = nil
end

[result_count, average_price] # Return the number of results and
                              # average price as an array.

  end

end
```

The first `if` statement checks if you have any results. If so, you calculate the average as the total divided by the number of results, and return the average and the total. If not, you return a zero total and `nil` as an average.

Next, let's take a look at the code that creates the PDF.

Dissecting the PDF Creation

The first thing that you do in the output routine in Listing 6-3 is define a new method called escape_latex. This will take arbitrary strings and make them safe to be included in a LaTeX script, so that characters that would usually have a special meaning will be included as text literals instead. This method is added to the String class, so that it can be called on any string. (This may seem very unusual to developers from nondynamic language backgrounds, but it's quite a common Ruby idiom.)

```
class String
  def latex_escape()

    replacements= {  '\\' =>'$\backslash$',
                     '$'=>'\$',
                     '%'=>'\%',
                     '&'=>'\&',
                     '_'=>'\_',
                     '~'=>'*~*',
                     '#'=>'\#',
                     '{'=>'$\{$',
                     '}'=>'$\}$'
                   }

    self.gsub(/[#{replacements.keys.join('|')}]/) do |match|
      replacements[match]
    end

  end
end
```

Note that many escape routines are simpler, but unfortunately, LaTeX has a fairly complex set of escape sequences. You cannot simply escape a list of strings with their backslashed counterparts, since they aren't all simple backslash substitutions, and substitutions contain earlier ones; the substitution for the backslash character contains dollar signs, for example. You therefore need to loop through the string using just a single regular expression, which you create using a character class consisting of each of the special characters, and you pass it to the gsub method. However, you don't pass a replacement string; instead, you pass a block, which lets you look up the appropriate substitution for each of the special characters.

Next, you start a string buffer, which will contain your document before it's written to a file:

```
temporary_latex_file='average_price_report.tex' # This file name will also control
                                                # the output file name. The
                                                # file will be named
                                                # average_price_report.pdf.

latex_source='
\documentclass{article}

\begin{document}

\huge                               % Switch to huge size and
\textbf{Competitor Average Price Report} % print a header at the
                                    % top of the page.

\vspace{0.1in}                      % Add a small amount of
                                    % whitespace between the
                                    % header and the table.

\normalsize                         % Switch back to normal size.

\begin{tabular}{llll}               % Start a table with four
                                    % left aligned columns.

\textbf{Item}&                      % Four headers, each in bold,
\textbf{Seller}&                    % with labels for each column.
\textbf{Count}&
\textbf{Average Price}\\\\

'
```

The string in this code is a header for the LaTeX file. It contains a header with big text, a vertical space, and then a table with four columns. You can see a brief explanation of each element in the code comments. (The % symbol is a comment character in LaTeX, which is why each comment begins with a %.)

Next, you loop through each keyword and seller and print out a single row for each keyword/seller combination, as follows:

```
keywords.each do |keyword|
  first=true
  sellers.each do |seller|
    total_items, average_price = *EBaySearch.get_average_price(keyword, seller)
```

```
    latex_source << "
    \\textbf{#{first ? keyword.latex_escape : ' '}} &
    #{seller ? seller.latex_escape : 'First 100 eBay Results'} &
    #{total_items} &
    \\#{average_price ? ('$%0.2f' % average_price) : ''}
    \\\\  "

  # Note that the character & is the marker for the end of a cell, and
  # that the sequence \\\\ is two escaped backslashes, which marks
  # the end of the row.

    first=false # This marker controls whether to redisplay the keyword.
                # For visual formatting reasons, each keyword is
                # shown only once.
  end
end
```

This code loops through each seller/keyword combination, searches eBay using the get_average_price class, and prints out a single line of LaTeX for each combination. For the first line for each keyword, it displays the keyword in bold; otherwise, you would have a repeated cell value for every seller, which would be visually repetitive.

Note that the cells in your LaTeX row are separated by & characters, and that there's a special case to handle sellers with a value of nil. The argument-handling part of the script adds a nil to the end of the sellers array, so that for every keyword, an average value of the first 100 eBay results—regardless of who is selling the items—will be displayed. The code detects that and prints out "First 100 eBay Results" when seller is nil.

The average price is formatted using the % operator and a format string of '$%0.2f'. This will cause the value of 5 to be formatted as $5.00, for example.

Finally, you need to add the footer to your LaTeX document, write it, and then run pdflatex on your LaTeX source file:

```
latex_source << '
\end{tabular}
\end{document}'

fh = File.open(temporary_latex_file, 'w')
fh.puts latex_source
fh.close

puts "Searched #{keywords.length} keywords and #{sellers.length} sellers for a total
of #{sellers.length*keywords.length} eBay searches."
```

```
puts `"#{path_to_pdflatex}" #{temporary_latex_file} --quiet` # Runs PDFLatex with
# the --quiet switch, which eliminates much of the chatter it usually displays.
# It will still display errors, however.

puts "Wrote report to average_price_report.pdf"
```

As you can see, you simply end your tabular and document elements, write the report to a file, and pass it to pdflatex. pdflatex then creates a .pdf file, and you write the name to the screen.

■Tip If you don't want to write to a file with the same name as your input file, you can use the --job-name switch to specify another file name. For example, adding --job-name my_report to the pdflatex command would make pdflatex write to my_report.pdf.

Summary

eBay is a vast world marketplace with a rich set of developer APIs. In this chapter, you used eBay's REST API. You saw how you can use Ruby and Hpricot to easily perform searches on eBay's vast selection of goods and then package the results into a report generated as a PDF file by LaTeX.

The next chapter's example shows how you can take data from PayPal and use MySQL and Markaby to create an HTML report detailing your spending habits.

CHAPTER 7

■■■

Tracking Expenditures with PayPal

PayPal is an e-commerce service that facilitates the electronic transfer of monies via the Internet. Often, PayPal is used by merchants as an easy way to accept credit cards without a merchant account. Additionally, PayPal accounts can be linked to special debit cards, which allows purchases to be made at brick-and-mortar stores using the money in a PayPal account. You can learn more about PayPal at `http://www.paypal.com/`.

Individuals who do a great deal of business online frequently use PayPal as a convenient way to spend and receive money. In those cases, reporting on data from PayPal can provide important information about financial transactions, as demonstrated in the example in this chapter.

Gathering Data from PayPal

You can take a couple approaches to gathering PayPal data for analysis. One is to use PayPal's web API to download transaction information. Unfortunately, results from searches via the PayPal web API are limited to 100 transactions, which makes it implausible to analyze any significant amount of data.

■**Tip** This chapter covers reporting on PayPal transactions. If you would like your application to be able to accept payments via PayPal, you can do that with the `paypal` gem, available from `http://dist.leetsoft.com/api/paypal/`.

Another approach is to download data in CSV format through PayPal's web site. If you have a business PayPal account, you can use the following procedure to download your own PayPal data for this chapter's example. If you don't have a business PayPal account, or you don't have any activity to analyze, you can download sample data from the Source/Downloads area of the Apress web site (`http://www.apress.com`) or from `http://rubyreporting.com/examples/paypal_example.csv`. (The reason you need a business account is that its data includes a number of additional fields that are not in the personal account data.)

1. Log in to your PayPal account at `http://www.paypal.com/`.

2. Click the History tab, as shown in Figure 7-1.

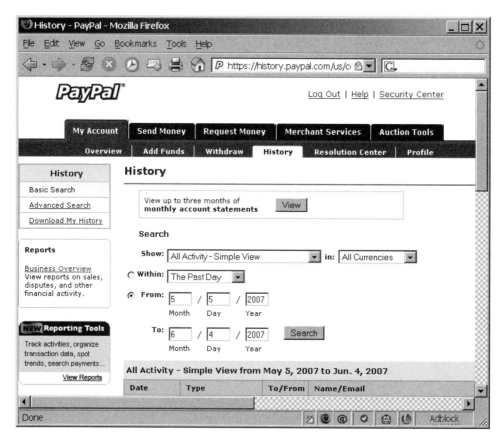

Figure 7-1. *PayPal History screen*

3. Click Download My History to see a screen similar to Figure 7-2.

■**Tip** If you have a large volume of data, PayPal will put your report in a queue and e-mail you when it is ready for download.

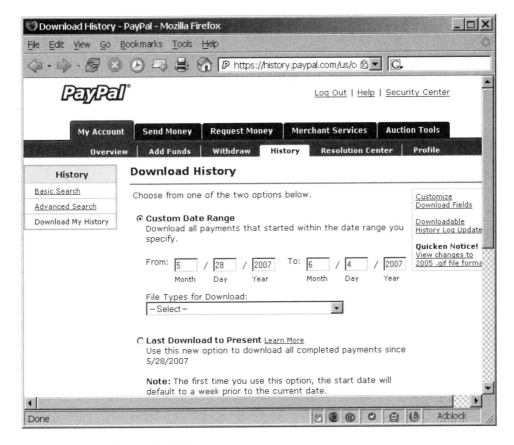

Figure 7-2. *PayPal Download History screen*

4. Select a date range. It doesn't matter which range you pick for this example, as long as it reflects some activity on your PayPal account.

5. From the File Types for Download drop-down list, select Comma Delimited - All Activity.

6. Click Download History.

7. When prompted to save the file, do so. Remember the location, as you'll use this file in this chapter's example.

■**Note** Why aren't we automating the download? Unfortunately, it's because there's no web service available to download it programmatically. It's possible to script the download using, say, the Ruby `net/http.rb` download library and an HTML parsing library like Hpricot, but unless you have explicit permission from the web site in question, that's typically not a good idea. Potentially, you could be blocked from PayPal or, in an extreme situation, get sued. However, if you do decide to take that route, you might want to employ a library that is easier to use than Ruby's built-in libraries, such as scRUBYt! (`http://scrubyt.org/`).

Now that you have a CSV file, you can analyze it. It's possible to analyze the data file directly in Ruby, but you might not want to write your own statistical code. Instead, you can load the data into MySQL, and then use MySQL's built-in aggregation functions to analyze it in detail.

Many companies use CSV files to transfer financial, inventory, and other data, so this approach can work with data from organizations other than PayPal.

Reporting PayPal Expenses

Suppose you and a business partner share a PayPal business account, and you have a disagreement about the dispensation of funds. Your partner claims that expenses are too high, and that you routinely spend money from the business account on the weekends when you are not working. Conversely, you claim that the expenses occur mostly during the week, and that they are a necessary part of doing business. To see who is correct, you want to create a program that analyzes the data from the PayPal account and produces a report on when expenses occur. Specifically, you'll create a chart that will graphically display the amount of weekend expenses compared to weekday expenses.

Note that once the data has been loaded into MySQL, you could easily modify your script to perform other calculations, such as to determine where you spend the most money.

For this example, you'll need FasterCSV, Active Record, and Markaby installed. You can install the required gems with the following commands:

```
gem install fastercsv active_record markaby
```

To read data from the CSV file, you'll use FasterCSV, which is a fast CSV parsing library for Ruby. We'll take a closer look at FasterCSV next, before beginning the example. Markaby is a markup library for Ruby. It lets you represent HTML using Ruby code. You can find more information about Markaby at `http://markaby.rubyforge.org/`.

■**Tip** If you don't want to have an additional dependency, you can also parse CSV using Ruby's built-in CSV module, although it will be slower. See the Ruby documentation at `http://www.ruby-doc.org/stdlib/libdoc/csv/rdoc/index.html` for details.

Also, you need to create a MySQL database to store the data. You can do so by using the following command:

```
mysqladmin -u mysql_username -p paypal
```

Using FasterCSV

To give you an idea of how FasterCSV works, let's look at the simplest use of FasterCSV: when you have a string consisting of CSV and you would like to parse it one row at a time. Here's an example:

```
require "fastercsv"

csvdata = "moonrock,10000,safe\n"
csvdata << "collectible spoon,10,cupboard\n"
csvdata << "scratched Billy Joel CD,1,desk\n"

FasterCSV.parse(csvdata) do |row|
  item, value, location = *row
  puts "I own a #{item}, it's worth $#{value}, and I keep it in my #{location}."
end
```

The result is as follows:

```
I own a moonrock, it's worth $10000, and I keep it in my safe.
I own a collectible spoon, it's worth $10, and I keep it in my cupboard.
I own a scratched Billy Joel CD, it's worth $1, and I keep it in my desk.
```

This example uses the `parse` method of FasterCSV to loop through each row. It returns each row as an array, and uses the * operator to split those arrays into three individual variables. As you can imagine, you can also use this same technique on data read from a file, as in the upcoming script in Listing 7-1.

FasterCSV can also create CSV from a Ruby array. Here's an example of that usage:

```
require "fastercsv"

secrecy_levels_array = [['SUPERSECRET', 'Supersecret Data', "Tell No One"],
                        ['SEMISECRET', 'Semisecret Data', 'Tell Some People'],
                        ['UNSECRET', 'Unsecret Data', 'Tell Everyone']]

secrecy_levels_array.each do    |line|
  puts line.to_csv
end
```

This example has the following output:

```
SUPERSECRET,Supersecret Data,Tell No One
SEMISECRET,Semisecret Data,Tell Some People
UNSECRET,Unsecret Data,Tell Everyone
```

This code loops through each element of the array, calls the to_csv method (provided by FasterCSV) on it, and prints the result. You cannot simply call to_csv on the entire array because to_csv expects just one row of data at a time. If you tried that, FasterCSV would treat your entire array as one long row of data.

You can use techniques like those described here to create files people can easily import into programs like Microsoft Excel, Microsoft Access, OpenOffice.org, and File-Maker Pro.

Converting PayPal CSV Data

Listing 7-1 shows the script that uses FasterCSV to read data from the CSV file and then uses Active Record to load it into your MySQL database.

Listing 7-1. *Using ActiveRecord to Load PayPal Data from CSV (paypal_load_data.rb)*

```
require 'active_record'
require 'fastercsv'

(puts "usage: #{$0} csv_filename";
      exit) unless ARGV.length==1
```

```ruby
paypal_source_file = ARGV.shift

ActiveRecord::Base.establish_connection(
  :adapter  => 'mysql',
  :host     => 'insert_your_mysql_hostname_here',
  :username => 'insert_your_mysql_username_here',
  :password => 'insert_your_mysql_password_here',
  :database => 'paypal')


class PaypalTransaction <  ActiveRecord::Base
end

class String
  def columnize
    self.strip.downcase.gsub(/[^a-z0-9_]/, '_')
  end
end

max_gross=0
date_fields = ['Date' ]
float_fields = ['Gross', 'Fee', 'Net']
cols = {}
weeks = []

first = true

FasterCSV.foreach(paypal_source_file) do |line|

  if first
    first=false
    line.each_with_index do |field_name, field_position|
      next if field_name.strip ==''

      cols[field_name.columnize] = field_position
    end

    unless PaypalTransaction.table_exists?
      ActiveRecord::Schema.define do
        create_table PaypalTransaction.table_name do |t|
          cols.each do |col, col_index|
```

```ruby
                if date_fields.include?(col)
                  t.column col, :date
                elsif float_fields.include?(col)
                  t.column col, :float
                else
                  t.column col, :string
                end
              end
            end
          end
        end

    else
      if PaypalTransaction.count_by_sql("SELECT COUNT(*)
                                  FROM paypal_transactions
                                  WHERE transaction_id
                                        ='" <<
                                          line[cols[
                                            'Transaction ID'.columnize
                                              ]   ] <<
                                        "';")==0
        PaypalTransaction.new do |transaction|
          cols.each do |field_name, field_position|

            transaction .send("#{field_name }=", line[field_position])

          end
          transaction .save
        end
      end
    end
  end
end
```

Save this script as paypal_load_data.rb.

You can run the script using the following command:

```
ruby paypal_load_data.rb /path/to/paypal_file.csv
```

Of course, replace the italicized parts with the appropriate values for your system.
Next, let's examine the code.

Dissecting the Code

The first few lines of Listing 7-1 pull the arguments from the command line and assign them to variables:

```
(puts "usage: #{$0} csv_filename";
      exit) unless ARGV.length==1

paypal_source_file = ARGV.first
```

This code ensures that you have only one value passed to the command line. If you have more or less than one argument, the program exits with an explanation of how the program should be called. ($0 is a special variable referring to the name of the current program.) You then take the single entry in your array of arguments and assign its value to the paypal_source_file variable. This single variable specifies from which file to load the data.

Next, you create a connection to your database:

```
ActiveRecord::Base.establish_connection(
  :adapter  => "mysql",
  :host     => 'insert_your_mysql_hostname_here',
  :username => 'insert_your_mysql_username_here',
  :password => 'insert_your_mysql_password_here',
  :database => 'paypal')
```

This creates a connection for use by Active Record, so all of your later code will use this connection. If you wanted to connect to a different database, such as PostgreSQL or SQLite, you could change the adapter parameter to use a different adapter. (Note that these parameters are similar to those that you'll find in a Rails application's database.yml file.)

Next, the following line creates a very simple model, called PaypalTransaction:

```
class PaypalTransaction <  ActiveRecord::Base
end
```

Because the class inherits from ActiveRecord::Base, it automatically gets a number of methods based on the characteristics of the paypal_transactions table. See Chapter 1 for more information about Active Record models.

You also extend the String class:

```
class String
  def columnize
    self.strip.downcase.gsub(/[^a-z0-9_]/, '_')
  end
end
```

This adds a method, `columnize`, to all strings. The `columnize` method removes white-space from the string, lowercases it, and replaces everything that is not a letter, a number, or an underscore with an underscore. In most languages, this would be implemented as a method that takes a string as an argument, but in Ruby, it's customary to simply extend an existing class. (Of course, in most languages, you cannot extend an existing class by adding methods to it, so you don't get a choice.) For example, you could use the `columnize` method like this:

```
puts "A column name".columnize
```

And get the following result:

```
a_column_name
```

In other words, `columnize` converts strings into names that can easily be used as MySQL column names.

> **■Note** Active Support, which is part of Rails, also has a method named `columnize`, which works similarly to the one discussed here. So, you wouldn't need to define this method if you were inside a Rails application. See `http://wiki.rubyonrails.org/rails/pages/ActiveSupport` for more information. (You could include Active Support in a script like this, but it's a large library, so using it here would be overkill.)

After that, the code loops through each line of the CSV file using FasterCSV. FasterCSV handles the parsing and passes just one array per line to the code, as follows:

```
first = true

FasterCSV.foreach(paypal_source_file) do |line|
```

Inside this loop, the code is split into two parts. The first handles the first line of the CSV file, which contains a list of column labels.

```
if first
  first=false
  line.each_with_index do |field_name, field_position|
    next if field_name.strip ==''

    cols[field_name.columnize] = field_position
  end
```

This loop creates a list of columns, along with their positions in the index.

The second part of the loop uses this list of column names to create a table to store the data in if it does not already exist.

```
unless PaypalTransaction.table_exists?
  ActiveRecord::Schema.define do
    create_table PaypalTransaction.table_name do |t|
      cols.each do |col, col_index|

        if date_fields.include?(col)
          t.column col, :date
        elsif float_fields.include?(col)
          t.column col, :float
        else
          t.column col, :string
        end
      end
    end
  end
end
```

This code uses the column definitions from the first line of the CSV file to create the table column definitions and determine the order of the fields. This way, you won't need to rely on fixed CSV file layouts or fixed table definitions.

Specifically, the `ActiveRecord::Schema.define` method is used to create a schema definition. The program has a hard-coded list of date, float, and string fields, but they aren't exhaustive, since PayPal can change the format at any time. In a production environment, you would likely use a fixed schema. However, this approach is very flexible and will work through simple format changes. In fact, the loading portion contains very little code that is specific to the PayPal format, so you could fairly easily use it on another CSV file; the code would create a simple schema to represent it.

Next, the remaining lines of the CSV file contain data, so each line following the first should be entered into the database, assuming it hasn't already been entered:

```
else
  if PaypalTransaction.count_by_sql("SELECT COUNT(*)
                          FROM paypal_transactions
                          WHERE transaction_id
                            ='" <<
                              line[cols[
                                'Transaction ID'.columnize
                                  ]   ] <<
```

```
                                         "';")==0
      PaypalTransaction.new do |transaction|
        cols.each do |field_name, field_position|

           transaction.send("#{field_name }=", line[field_position])

        end
        transaction.save
      end
    end
  end
end
```

The call to count_by_sql checks if a given transaction_id has already been entered; if it has, then the transaction won't be reentered. (Of course, in theory, the same file won't be entered twice, but if the user does enter the same file twice, you won't get any duplicate results.)

The PaypalTransaction.new method creates a new transaction, and then the code loops through each column, and uses the send method to set each column to its appropriate value. send is a Ruby method that allows you to dynamically call methods on a given object. It takes a string with the method name and some arguments, and calls that method with the specified arguments. In other words, the following two lines are identical:

```
some_object.some_method(some_value)
some.object.send('some_method', some_value)
```

By using the send method, you can loop through the array and set the appropriate value for each field; otherwise, you would need to hard-code which methods to use, which would be much longer and also defeat the purpose of dynamically generating a schema.

Finally, the save method of the new PaypalTransaction object is called. It saves your object into the database.

Analyzing the Data

Once the data has been entered into the database, you need a way to analyze it. In this case, you are going to use an HTML graph of the various weeks, which will show the weekend vs. weekday spending. The weekend spending will be colored red, and the weekday spending will be shown in green. The code in Listing 7-2 does just that, using Markaby.

Listing 7-2. *Using Markaby to Create an Expense Report (paypal_expense_report.rb)*

```ruby
require 'active_record'
require 'fastercsv'
require 'yaml'
require 'markaby'

(puts "usage: #{$0} mysql_hostname mysql_username " <<
     "mysql_password database_name"; exit) unless ARGV.length==4

mysql_hostname,
mysql_username,
mysql_password,
mysql_database= *ARGV

ActiveRecord::Base.establish_connection(
  :adapter  => "mysql",
  :host     => mysql_hostname,
  :username => mysql_username,
  :password => mysql_password,
  :database => mysql_database)  # Establish a connection to the database.


class PaypalTransaction <  ActiveRecord::Base
end

first = true
c = {}


sql = "
SELECT  WEEK(p1.date) + 1 as week_number,
    YEAR(p1.date) as year,
    COALESCE((SELECT SUM(ABS(p2.gross))
          FROM paypal_transactions as p2
        WHERE (WEEK(p2.date) = WEEK(p1.date)
          AND YEAR(p2.date) = YEAR(p1.date)
          AND WEEKDAY(p2.date) IN (5,6)
          AND p2.gross<0
          AND p2.status='Completed')
    ),0) as weekend_amount,
```

```
      COALESCE((SELECT SUM(abs(p3.gross))
            FROM paypal_transactions as p3
          WHERE (WEEK(p3.date) = WEEK(p1.date)
            AND YEAR(p3.date) = YEAR(p1.date)
            AND WEEKDAY(p3.date) NOT IN (5,6)
            AND p3.gross<0
            AND p3.status='Completed')
    ),0) as weekday_amount

    FROM paypal_transactions as p1

    GROUP BY YEAR(date) ASC,  WEEK(date) ASC;
"


weeks = []

max_gross=0.0

PaypalTransaction.find_by_sql(sql).each do |week|
  # First, if the weekday is the highest total spending we've seen so far,
  # we'll keep that value to calibrate the size of the graph . . .

  max_gross = week.weekday_amount.to_f  if week.weekday_amount.to_f > max_gross

  # . . . and if the weekend spending is the highest, we'll use that:

  max_gross = week.weekend_amount.to_f  if week.weekend_amount.to_f > max_gross

  # We'll add a hash with the week number, the year,
  # the weekday spending, and the weekend spending to the weeks array:

  weeks << {   :week_number=>week.week_number.to_i,
               :year=>week.year.to_i,
               :weekday_amount=>week.weekday_amount.to_f,
               :weekend_amount=>week.weekend_amount.to_f
        }
end

mab =  Markaby::Builder.new() do
  html do
    head do
      title 'PayPal Spending Report'
```

```ruby
      style  :type => "text/css" do %[
              .weekday_bar { display:block; background-color: blue; }
              .weekend_bar { display:block; background-color: red; }
             %]
      end
    end
    body do
      h1 ''
      table do
        weeks.each do |week|
          tr do
            th :style=>"vertical-align:top;" do
              p "Week \##{week[:week_number]}, #{week[:year]}"
            end
            td do
              div :class=>:weekday_bar,
                          :style=>"width:" << ((week[:weekday_amount] /
                                  max_gross * 199 ) + 1).to_s  do
                " "
              end
              span "Week - $#{'%0.2f' % week[:weekday_amount]}"
            end
          end
          tr do
            td ""
            td do
              div :class=>:weekend_bar,
                          :style=>"width: " << ((week[:weekend_amount] /
                                  max_gross * 199) + 1 ).to_s  do
                ' '
              end
              span "Weekend - $#{'%0.2f' % week[:weekend_amount]}"
            end
          end
        end
      end
    end
  end
end

puts mab
```

Save the code as `paypal_expense_report.rb`. You can run the code as follows:

```
ruby paypal_paypal_expense_report.rb mysql_hostname mysql_username mysql_password
paypal > report.html
```

As before, replace the italicized arguments with the appropriate values for your system.

At this point, `report.html` should contain a neatly formatted report, showing a graph of weekend vs. weekday spending for each day in the report. If you open it in a web browser, you should see a result similar to Figure 7-3.

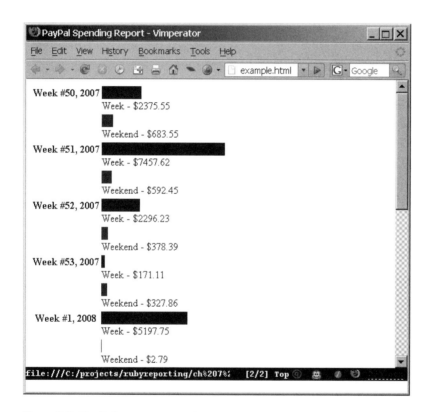

Figure 7-3. *PayPal expense report output*

Now, let's examine the code in more detail.

Dissecting the Code

The first part of the code in Listing 7-2 connects to the database and creates a model for your transaction table. Most of the code in this book uses hard-coded values, but that's not necessary. This particular listing lets you specify your connection details on the command line:

```
(puts "usage: #{$0} mysql_hostname mysql_username " <<
     "mysql_password database_name"; exit) unless ARGV.length==4
```

```
mysql_hostname,
mysql_username,
mysql_password,
mysql_database= *ARGV
```

```
ActiveRecord::Base.establish_connection(
  :adapter  => "mysql",
  :host     => mysql_hostname,
  :username => mysql_username,
  :password => mysql_password,
  :database => mysql_database)  # Establish a connection to the database.
```

First, the line checks if the proper number of arguments have been passed. If not, it tells the user what the program expects and exits. It uses the construct *ARGV to take the four arguments and put them in four separate variables. Then you create the connection to the database.

Next is the SQL query that pulls the report from the database:

```
SELECT  WEEK(p1.date) as week_number,
    YEAR(p1.date) as year,
    COALESCE((SELECT SUM(ABS(p2.gross))
         FROM paypal_transactions as p2
        WHERE (WEEK(p2.date) = WEEK(p1.date)
          AND YEAR(p2.date) = YEAR(p1.date)
          AND WEEKDAY(p2.date) IN (5,6)
          AND p2.gross<0
          AND p2.status='Completed')
    ),0) as weekend_amount,

    COALESCE((SELECT SUM(abs(p3.gross))
         FROM paypal_transactions as p3
        WHERE (WEEK(p3.date) = WEEK(p1.date)
          AND YEAR(p3.date) = YEAR(p1.date)
          AND WEEKDAY(p3.date) NOT IN (5,6)
          AND p3.gross<0
          AND p3.status='Completed')
    ),0) as weekday_amount
```

```
    FROM paypal_transactions as p1

GROUP BY YEAR(date) ASC,  WEEK(date) ASC;
```

This query groups the transactions by year and by date. This means that you'll get one row for every week/year combination. From there, the query uses two correlated subqueries to locate the total amount of money that was spent during the week and during the weekend.

Subqueries are queries inside a larger query. Their results are evaluated first, and then used as either single values or, if they return a number of values, as a set. (Since tables are sets, and since subqueries return sets, you can use subqueries anyhwere you could use a table.) The two examples here both return a single value. There are two principal types of subqueries:

Simple subquery: This type of subquery is not dependent on the outer query. Simple subqueries are faster. Since their value does not change for each row of the outer query, they are evaluated only once.

Correlated subquery: The subqueries in the example are the more complicated varieties, called correlated subqueries. The subqueries are called for each row of the outer query because their value depends on the outer query. As a result, they are calculated again for each row of the outer query.

Both subqueries search for rows that occur in the same week and year as the outer query, whose gross is negative (in other words, which are purchases and not income), and that are completed transactions (as opposed to expired transactions or temporary authorizations). The code then sums all of those transactions and returns the value to the outer query.

The WEEKDAY function is used to determine whether a given transaction occurs on a weekend or a weekday. If the WEEKDAY function returns a 6 or a 7—that is, Saturday or Sunday—it's a weekend transaction.

The COALESCE function returns its first non-null argument. It is used to ensure you return a zero rather than a null if there was no spending.

DETERMINING A WEEKEND DATE IN RUBY

If you need to determine whether a given date is a weekend in Ruby, you can use the following code to do just that:

```
class Date
  def is_weekend?
    self.cwday == 6 or self.cwday == 7 # If it's a Saturday or a Sunday,
                                       # it's a weekend.
  end
end
```

This code extends the Date class to have an additional method, is_weekend?, which returns true if the given date is on a weekend and false otherwise.

Next, you loop through your results and convert them into an array of data suitable for graphing:

```
weeks = []

max_gross=0.0

PaypalTransaction.find_by_sql(sql).each do |week|

  max_gross = week.weekday_amount.to_f  if week.weekday_amount.to_f > max_gross
  max_gross = week.weekend_amount.to_f  if week.weekend_amount.to_f > max_gross
  weeks << {   :week_number=>week.week_number.to_i,
             :year=>week.year.to_i,
             :weekday_amount=>week.weekday_amount.to_f,
             :weekend_amount=>week.weekend_amount.to_f
         }
end
```

This loop handles two issues: first, you can track the highest value, which will be used to scale your graph. Next, an element is appended to the weeks array, which contains your data cast to an appropriate type: integer or float. (Without this cast, the variables would be returned as strings.) This array will be used next to produce an HTML page with a list of weeks and a graph.

The HTML page is produced using Markaby. The first part of the code that uses Markaby is as follows:

```
mab =  Markaby::Builder.new() do
  html do
    head do
      title 'PayPal Spending Report'
      style  :type => "text/css" do %[
                .weekday_bar { display:block; background-color: blue; }
                .weekend_bar { display:block; background-color: red; }
                            %]
    end
  end
```

Essentially, the code creates a Markaby::Builder object. You pass it a block. Inside that block, you can use methods named after HTML tags—html, head, tr, td, p, and so on—and these methods will produce corresponding HTML code.

The first part of the code here sets up your document, adding a head and a title. It also adds a style element, which sets up your two CSS classes: weekday_bar and weekend_bar, used for the weekday and weekend bar portions of the graph, respectively.

Next, let's take a look at the heart of the Markaby code:

```
body do
  table do
    weeks.each do |week|
      tr do
        th :style=>"vertical-align:top;" do
          p "Week \##{week[:week_number]}, #{week[:year]}"
        end
        td do
          div :class=>:weekday_bar,
                      :style=>"width:" <<
                              ((week[:weekday_amount] /
                                max_gross * 199 ) + 1).to_s  do
            " "
          end
          span "Week - $#{'%0.2f' % week[:weekday_amount]}"
        end
      end
      tr do
        td ""
        td do
          div :class=>:weekend_bar,
```

```
                        :style=>"width: " <<
                            ((week[:weekend_amount] /
                              max_gross * 199) + 1 ).to_s  do
              ' '
          end
          span "Weekend - $#{'%0.2f' % week[:weekend_amount]}".
        end
      end
. . ..
end

puts mab
```

This code loops through all of the weeks. For each week, you create a label, showing the week number and year. You also create a row for the weekend spending and a row for the weekday spending, each with a label and a colored bar. Each bar is sized proportionally to the others, so that the biggest spending weekend or weekday gets a bar that is 200 pixels wide. The other bars are a percentage of that size, such as 50% (the minimum size is 1%).

After you have finished building the HTML page, the code will be stored in the `Markaby::Builder` object, and then you print it using the `puts` method.

Summary

PayPal lets you easily download financial information in CSV format, and you can quickly and efficiently use FasterCSV and Markaby to process that information. In this chapter's example, you used both of these tools to dynamically create a database structure, load data into it, use Active Record and MySQL to pull data from it, and then quickly create a custom, attractive CSS graph. You can use similar techniques anywhere you need to load CSV data into MySQL or when you need to create lightweight CSS graphs from CSV data.

The next chapter covers how to do reporting using SugarCRM, a popular customer relationship management (CRM) system.

CHAPTER 8

■ ■ ■

Creating Sales Performance Reports with SugarCRM

According to Peter Drucker, the famous management consultant, "the purpose of business is to create a customer." The way to create customers is with sales, and when you have a large and active sales force, your salespeople will generate a huge, and often intimidating, amount of customer data. Systems that manage customer data are called customer relationship management (CRM) systems. An excellent choice is an open source product called SugarCRM (http://www.sugarcrm.com/), which is freely available for download and use but also offers paid technical support services.

The example in this chapter demonstrates how to produce a sales performance report with SugarCRM, as well as how to use two open source utilities—html2ps and Ghostscript—to create PDFs from HTML documents.

Installing SugarCRM

To run the examples in this chapter, you'll need to install SugarCRM. You can download SugarCRM from the following site:

```
http://www.sugarcrm.com/crm/download/sugar-suite.html
```

At the download site, you'll find two types of installers: the first includes just the SugarCRM source code, which is ideal if you've already installed the Apache/MySQL/PHP stack. If not, installers that combine all of the required components (along with SugarCRM, of course) are available for Linux, Mac OS X, and Windows. Choose the appropriate installer for your system.

After you've downloaded the SugarCRM installer, follow the installation instructions to install SugarCRM. You can download the instructions from this site:

```
http://www.sugarcrm.com/crm/index.php?option=com_docs&edition=OS&Itemid=375
```

The installer also adds sample data, which you'll use in this chapter's example. Of course, if you already have a SugarCRM database, you can use that data instead.

Sales Force Reporting

Let's suppose your boss has experienced productivity problems with the sales force. In an effort to boost output, he wants to reward productive employees with a gift based on their number of meetings with clients and potential clients. The more meetings a salesperson has, the better the gift.

He would like to keep tabs on this effort, and wants you to produce a report that lists each salesperson and the gift that person has earned. Your boss wants the report to be made available in a format that is easy to print and e-mail. Therefore, you've decided to create the report as a PDF file.

Fortunately, it should be fairly easy to create a Ruby report that pulls this data from the SugarCRM database. First, though, you'll need to modify the database to include the extra gift information.

Updating the Database

You can use the SQL in Listing 8-1 to add some sample data to your database.

Listing 8-1. *Sample Data for the Sales Force Reporting Application (rewards_data.sql)*

```
CREATE TABLE rewards (
  reward_id INT(11) NOT NULL AUTO_INCREMENT PRIMARY KEY,
  meeting_count INT(11) NOT NULL,
  description VARCHAR(255));

INSERT into rewards (meeting_count, description)
          VALUES (50, "'You Are Number One!' Pen");

INSERT into rewards (meeting_count, description)
          VALUES (100, "'Super Salesman' Coffee Mug");

INSERT into rewards (meeting_count, description)
          VALUES (150, "'You Make Our Company Great' Sweatshirt");

INSERT into rewards (meeting_count, description)
          VALUES (200, "Granite 'Rock Hard Sales' Paperweight");
```

Save the SQL as `rewards_data.sql`. You can create the table and insert the data as follows:

```
mysql -u your_mysql_username sugarcrm < rewards_data.sql
```

The `rewards` table has just four rows and three fields: an artificial primary key, a number of meetings that must be exceeded before the salesperson gets the reward, and a description of the reward itself.

Now that you have a table populated with various rewards, let's take a look at how to create a PDF report for it. For simplicity's sake, you'll use the data in Listing 8-1 coupled with the sample data added during SugarCRM installation.

Tip The rewards data is stored in the database and not hard-coded into your script so that it's easy to change. In fact, if your boss decides to change the rewards, you can just change the data and use the code as is. You could even create a Rails application using a scaffolding framework like ActiveScaffold (`http://activescaffold.com/`) to let him change the data himself, and you would need to write only a few lines of code. (ActiveScaffold is designed to make administrative tasks like this—simple create/read/update/delete (CRUD) activities—easy and require almost no code.) Incidentally, if you're worried about modifying another application's database, don't be. Most applications are well behaved enough not to touch tables they don't recognize. (You could store the table in a different database or in an external file, but that, in my opinion, is additional work for little or no gain.)

Creating PDFs from HTML Documents

For this example, you will use the open source utilities html2ps and Ghostscript to create PDFs from HTML documents. This approach has the advantage of being very easy to learn. However, html2ps is slower than using LaTeX, which was demonstrated in Chapter 6. LaTeX also has more powerful control over the output, since html2ps is limited to a subset of HTML's formatting capabilities. However, when you don't need LaTeX's additional power, you can quickly create PDF reports using the html2ps/Ghostscript combination.

html2ps generates only PostScript files, so you'll need another tool, ps2pdf, to convert those PostScript files into PDF files. ps2pdf is included with Ghostscript, which is available for most popular operating systems, including Windows, Linux, and Mac OS X. Note that html2ps is a Perl script, so you'll need Perl installed to run it. (Linux and OS X typically include Perl by default, but you can get a free Perl distribution at `http://activeperl.com`.)

You can download html2ps from here:

```
http://user.it.uu.se/~jan/html2ps.html
```

You can get Ghostscript from the following site:

```
http://pages.cs.wisc.edu/~ghost/
```

Finally, since html2ps needs HTML to work with, you'll use Erubis to create your HTML document using Rails-like RHTML templates. You can install Erubis using the following command:

```
gem install erubis
```

Tip Erubis is an eRuby implementation. *eRuby* is a generic term for Ruby embedded in HTML, just as you would use in a Rails application. However, Erubis is faster than the ERB library used by Rails and has more features. You can learn more about Erubis in my Apress book, *Practical Ruby Gems*, as well as from the Erubis web site (`http://www.kuwata-lab.com/erubis/`).

The script to create the PDF report is shown in Listing 8-2.

Listing 8-2. *Salesperson Reward Report (calculate_rewards.rb)*

```ruby
require 'active_record'
require 'erubis'

ActiveRecord::Base.establish_connection(
  :adapter  => 'mysql',
  :host     => 'localhost',
  :username => 'your_mysql_user_name',
  :password => 'your_mysql_password',
  :database => 'sugarcrm')

path_to_ps2pdf = '/some/path/to/ps2pdf'    # Insert your path to ps2pdf here.
                                           # Note that ps2pdf should be included
                                           # with your Ghostscript distribution.


path_to_html2ps = '/some/path/to/html2ps'  # Insert your path to html2ps here.


# Windows can't run Perl scripts directly,
# so Windows users should preface their html2ps
# path with their Perl path, so that it looks
# something like this:
# path_to_html2ps = 'C:\perl\bin\perl.exe" "c:\path\to\html2ps'
```

```
#
# Note the double quotes after perl.exe and before the script file name.
# This ensures that the string is interpolated like this:
# "c:\perl\bin\perl.exe" "c:\path\to\html2ps"
#
# Without the extra double quotes, Windows will look for a program
# named "C:\perl\bin\perl c:\path\to\html2ps", and since that
# does not exist, it will cause problems.


class User < ActiveRecord::Base
  has_many :meetings, :foreign_key=>:assigned_user_id
  def reward
    Reward.find(:first,
         :conditions=>['meeting_count < ? ',
                            self.meetings.count],
          :order=>'meeting_count DESC',
          :limit=>1)
  end
end

class Meeting < ActiveRecord::Base
  belongs_to :users, :foreign_key=>:assigned_user_id
end

class Reward < ActiveRecord::Base
end

html = '<html>
<body>
<h1>Salesperson Reward Report</h1>
<table>
  <tr>
    <th>Name</th>
    <th>Meetings</th>
    <th>Reward</th>
  </tr>
    '



users = User.find(:all,
               :conditions=>['not is_admin'],
```

```
                       :order=>'last_name ASC, first_name ASC'
          )

html = Erubis::Eruby.new(File.read('rewards_report_template.rhtml')
                    ).evaluate({ :users=>users })

open('|"'+path_to_html2ps+'"', 'wb+') do |process_handle|
    process_handle.puts html
    process_handle.close_write
    ps_source = process_handle.read
end

pdf_source = ''

open('|"' + path_to_ps2pdf +'" - -', 'wb+') do |process_handle|
    process_handle.puts ps_source
    process_handle.close_write
    pdf_source = process_handle.read
end

File.open('report.pdf','wb+') do |pdf_file_handle|
    pdf_file_handle.puts pdf_source
end
```

Save this file as `calculate_rewards.rb`. Next, create the HTML template, as shown in Listing 8-3.

Listing 8-3. *HTML Template for the Salesperson Reward Report (rewards_report_template.rhtml)*

```
<html>
<body>
<h1>Salesperson Reward Report</h1>
<table>
  <tr>
    <th>Name</th>
    <th>Meetings</th>
    <th>Reward</th>
  </tr>

<%@users.each do |user|%>
<%  meeting_count = user.meetings.count
```

```
    next if meeting_count==0 or !user.reward%>
    <tr><td><%=user.last_name%>, <%=user.first_name%></td>
        <td><%=meeting_count%></td>
        <td><%=user.reward.description%></td></tr>

<%end%>
</table>
</body>
</html>
```

Save this file as `rewards_report_template.rhtml`.
You can run this script using the following command:

```
ruby calculate_rewards.rb
```

Now open the file `report.pdf` (you'll need a PDF viewer, such as Adobe Acrobat or GSview). You should see a screen similar to Figure 8-1. (Since you're using the sample data, which is randomly generated by SugarCRM when you install it, your exact results will vary.)

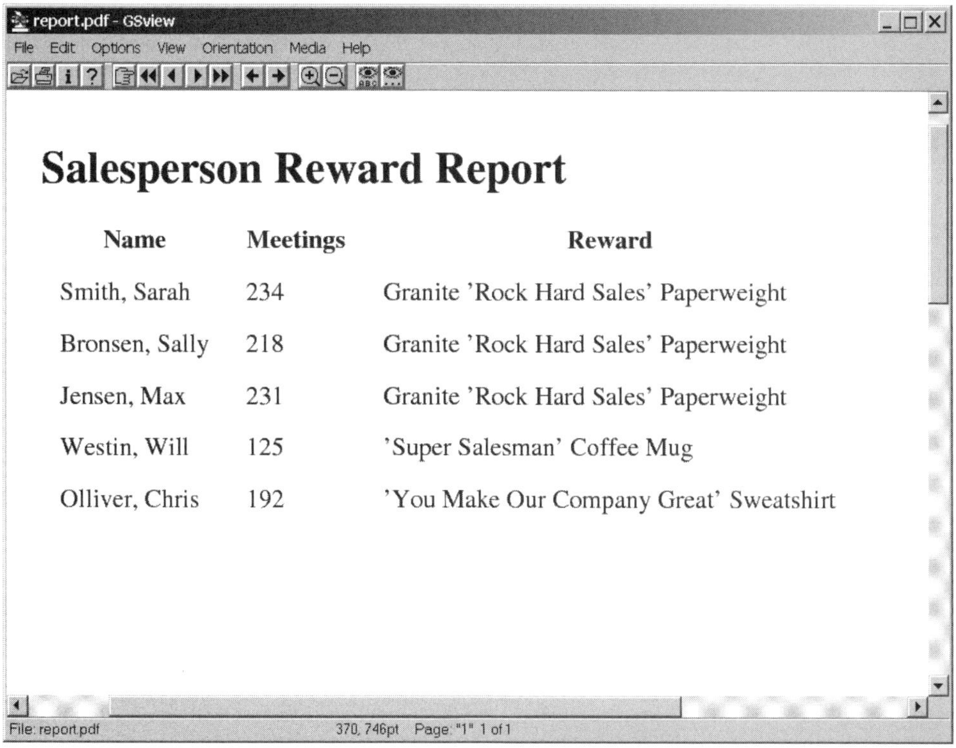

Figure 8-1. *PDF salesperson rewards report*

Now, let's take a look at this example line by line.

Dissecting the Code

For the report (Listing 8-2), first you create a connection to the database, as follows:

```
ActiveRecord::Base.establish_connection(
  :adapter  => 'mysql',
  :host     => 'localhost',
  :username => 'someuser',
  :password => 'password',
  :database => 'sugarcrm')
```

This sets a base connection used by Active Record for all models by default, as discussed in Chapter 1 and used in previous examples. Of course, you'll need to replace the italicized values with appropriate values for your system. That's also true of the code's next section, which specifies the path to your helper utilities:

```
path_to_ps2pdf = '/some/path/to/ps2pdf'    #Insert your path to ps2pdf here.
                                           #Note that ps2pdf should be included
                                           #with your Ghostscript distribution.
path_to_html2ps = '/some/path/to/html2ps' #Insert your path to html2ps here.
```

The paths for ps2pdf and html2ps vary depending on your operating system.

Next, you create the Active Record models that represent the tables you're using:

```
class User < ActiveRecord::Base
  has_many :meetings, :foreign_key=>:assigned_user_id
  def reward
    Reward.find(:first,
          :conditions=>['meeting_count < ? ',
                             self.meetings.count],
             :order=>'meeting_count DESC',
             :limit=>1)
  end
end

class Meeting < ActiveRecord::Base
  belongs_to :users, :foreign_key=>:assigned_user_id
end

class Reward < ActiveRecord::Base
end
```

You create the models by deriving from `ActiveRecord::Base` (as discussed in Chapter 1). The `User` model also has a custom method, `reward`, which returns a `reward` object—one whose meeting count is lower than the number of `meetings` a salesperson has. Note, though, that the possible rewards are sorted by a descending `meeting_count`; in other words, the first `reward` listed, and thus the `reward` returned, will be the `reward` with the highest `meeting_count` field. Therefore, salespeople will receive the highest reward for which they are eligible.

The last model, `Reward`, refers to the table that you created earlier in this chapter. The first two models refer to two tables defined by SugarCRM: `users` and `meetings`. The `users` table looks like this:

```
CREATE TABLE `users` (
  `id` char(36) NOT NULL,
  `user_name` varchar(60) default NULL,
  `user_hash` varchar(32) default NULL,
  `authenticate_id` varchar(100) default NULL,
  `sugar_login` tinyint(1) default '1',
  `first_name` varchar(30) default NULL,
  `last_name` varchar(30) default NULL,
  . . .
  KEY `user_name_idx` (`user_name`)
) ENGINE= MyISAM DEFAULT CHARSET=utf8;
```

The `meetings` table looks like this:

```
CREATE TABLE `meetings` (
  `id` char(36) NOT NULL,
  `date_entered` datetime NOT NULL,
  `date_modified` datetime NOT NULL,
  `assigned_user_id` char(36) default NULL,
  . . .
  PRIMARY KEY  (`id`),
  KEY `idx_mtg_name` (`name`),
  KEY `idx_meet_par_del` (`parent_id`,`parent_type`,`deleted`)
) ENGINE=MyISAM DEFAULT CHARSET=utf8;
```

As you can see, the two tables are related by a foreign key named `assigned_user_id` in the `meetings` table. Since the default name for a foreign key in the `meetings` table refering to the `user` table would be `user_id`, you manually specify it in your `has_many` relationship.

Next, you use these models to create an HTML report, which you can use later to turn your report into a PDF:

```
users = User.find(:all,
                  :conditions=>['not is_admin'],
                  :order=>'last_name ASC, first_name ASC'
        )

html =  Erubis::Eruby.new(File.read('rewards_report_template.rhtml')
                         ).evaluate({ :users=>users })
```

You use an Erubis template to create your report HTML gradually. You create a new
`Erubis::Eruby` object using the Erubis source from the file `rewards_report_template.rhtml`,
and then call the `evaluate` method on it. The `evaluate` method takes a single argument,
which is a list of variables that are accessible to the Eruby template.

■**Note** You can use other options to create your HTML. For example, you can use Markaby to create the
output. Markaby uses Ruby methods to represent HTML elements. Chapter 7 includes an example of using
Markaby. Of course, you may find that entering HTML directly in your code is easier to understand.

The single variable you pass to your view is an array of `users`. You pass it to your
`eruby_object` variable, and it becomes a class variable `@users` for your view, in the same
way that Rails views work.

The `users` variable is created by using the `User.find` method to loop through all of
your users. You add a `not is_admin` condition, which means that only non-admin users
will be included in your report. (This is assuming that admin users are used to adminis-
trate the system and not to do sales work; if that's not true, you can easily remove this
condition.) The order is set through the option `:order=>'last_name ASC, first_name ASC'`,
which means that you sort first by the last name, and second by the first name, both in
alphabetic, A–Z order. The second sort order kicks in only if two people have the same
last name. If you replaced `ASC` with `DESC`, it would sort in Z–A order.

Let's take a look at the actual view (Listing 8-3):

```
<html>
<body>
<h1>Salesperson Reward Report</h1>
  <table>
    <tr>
      <th>Name</th>
      <th>Meetings</th>
      <th>Reward</th>
    </tr>
```

```
<%@users.each do |user|%>
<%  meeting_count = user.meetings.count
    next if meeting_count==0 or !user.reward %>
    <tr><td><%=user.last_name%>, <%=user.first_name%></td>
        <td><%=meeting_count%></td>
        <td><%=user.reward.description%></td></tr>

<%end%>
</table>
</body>
</html>
```

For each user, you add a row to the table that contains the name of the user, the total amount of meetings that salesperson had, and the name of the reward, if any. The loop calls `meetings.count` for each row and skips the users without any meetings. You might want to include users without any meetings; in which case, you can easily delete the `next if meeting_count==0` line.

INCREASING DATABASE QUERY PERFORMANCE

For this chapter's example, you'll probably find that the database queries do not take nearly as long to run as the html2ps and ps2pdf calls, so further optimization is probably unnecessary. However, this won't always be the case. If either the `meetings` or the `users` table were much larger, or if you had a more complicated query with more relationships, you might need to make the queries go faster. You can speed up the queries in a few ways.

For example, the call to `user.meetings.count` means that you have one extra SQL query per user. This could be a problem when you need to count a large number of records. Fortunately, Rails can automatically cache the count of relationships for you. In the example, this approach won't work. That's because SugarCRM won't update the cache for you, and since it will be updating the table, that would leave you with an invalid cache. However, in situations where only your Rails application accesses the database, adding a counter cache could speed up your report's performance significantly.

Counter caching has a few caveats. One is that the counter may be invalid if your database is accessed outside your Rails applications. Also, it won't work if you manually set association IDs instead of using association proxies. You can find out more about using counter caches at `http://wiki.rubyonrails.org/rails/pages/MagicFieldNames`.

You can create a counter cache by adding a column called `meetings_count`, with a default value of 0, to the `users` table. You also need to add a `:counter_cache=>true` option to the relationship in the `Meetings` model. The `Meetings` model would then look like this:

```
belongs_to :users, :foreign_key=>:assigned_user_id, :counter_cache=>true
```

Some databases, like PostgreSQL and MySQL 5, support triggers. In that case, you may also be able to use triggers to automatically update your counter cache whenever the associated table is changed, even if it's changed by SugarCRM or another non-Rails application. For details, consult your database documentation. You can also see a simple example of using MySQL triggers at http://www. phpied.com/mysql-triggers/.

Also notice that this example does not have one large, custom SQL query, which is unlike many of the other examples in this book. Calculating using custom SQL queries, rather than by using Active Record methods, has two advantages: you can use the database to extract complicated information, which would be harder to code in Ruby, and you can often make custom SQL queries that are faster than the autogenerated queries that Active Record creates behind the scenes. Sometimes, you can squeeze multiple calls by Active Record into just one SQL query. It's possible to turn this example into a custom SQL query. You can do that in a few ways, but they all require either subqueries or temporary tables. Here's a replacement query loop that uses custom SQL:

```
users = User.find_by_sql("

SELECT  users_meetings.*,
        COALESCE(rewards_1.description, '') as reward_description
   FROM
       (SELECT users.*,
               COUNT(meetings.id) as meeting_count
         FROM  (users
                   RIGHT OUTER JOIN
                 meetings
                   ON meetings.assigned_user_id=
                     users.id)
                 GROUP BY
                   meetings.assigned_user_id
               ) as users_meetings
        INNER JOIN
            rewards as rewards_1
        ON rewards_1.meeting_count <
           users_meetings.meeting_count
           AND NOT EXISTS (
               SELECT *
                 FROM rewards as rewards_2
                 WHERE (rewards_2.meeting_count <
                        users_meetings.meeting_count)
                             AND
                        (rewards_2.meeting_count >
                         rewards_1.meeting_count))
```

```
    ORDER BY last_name ASC, first_name ASC
        ;

")
end
```

It's definitely more complicated, but it works. Notice that, unlike the previous approach, this query excludes users who are not eligible for a reward. The reason this query is so complicated is because the relationship between the `rewards` table and the `users` table has a grouping function in it, which cannot appear in a join condition. If you could use counter caching, you could do a simpler version of this query. The counter-caching version would look something like this:

```
users = User.find_by_sql("

    SELECT users.*
        COALESCE(rewards_1.description, '') as reward_description
    FROM users
        INNER JOIN
      rewards as rewards_1
        ON rewards_1.meeting_count <
          users.meeting_count
          AND NOT EXISTS (
              SELECT *
                FROM rewards as rewards_2
              WHERE (rewards_2.meeting_count <
                    users.meeting_count)
                  AND
                  (rewards_2.meeting_count >
                    rewards_1.meeting_count))
    ORDER BY last_name ASC, first_name ASC
        ;")
```

After you have finished creating your HTML, you need to run it through two successive programs. First, you put it through html2ps, as follows:

```
ps_source = ''

open('|"'+path_to_html2ps+'"', 'wb+') do |process_handle|
    process_handle.puts html
    process_handle.close_write
```

```
        ps_source = process_handle.read
end

pdf_source = ''

open('|"' + path_to_ps2pdf +'" - -', 'wb+') do |process_handle|
        process_handle.puts ps_source
        process_handle.close_write
        pdf_source = process_handle.read
end
```

This code does not use temporary files, which are the most obvious way to communicate with an outside process; instead, the block of code uses pipes. Specifically, the open call lets you open an arbitrary file, a URI, or a pipe to a process, and the pipe at the beginning of the argument to open lets Ruby know that you intend to open a process. You can then use the pipe to that process to read and write to it as if it were a file, but instead of writing to a file, you send input to the program as if it were typed into the program by the user. Conversely, when you read, the output from the program is read into your program instead of being displayed on the screen. This process lets you eliminate the temporary files, and read and write directly from the program.

Note that your temporary variables are created outside the open block. This is so that they are scoped appropriately, as opposed to being local variables of the block, and can be accessed outside the block.

Additionally, you might notice that the call to ps2pdf is preceded by two dashes. The first dash tells the program that instead of reading from a file, it should read its input from STDIN, which is normally the keyboard but, in this case, is your program.

Finally, note that the calls have the flags wb+. In fact, so do your previous two open calls, which open the pipes to the html2ps and ps2pdf utilities. This is a three-part flag:

- The w means write, so it can be written to.

- The + means that you can read from it as well.

- The b affects only calls on Windows, and means it's binary mode. This affects the way \n characters are handled. Without the b flag, \n is transparently converted into \r\n, and since binary files often contain \n elements, they can be corrupted easily. Note that, strictly speaking, the first call to html2ps might be okay without the b flag, but there is no point in taking chances.

You can find out more about open at http://www.ruby-doc.org/core/classes/Kernel.html# M005969.

After this, the variable `pdf_source` contains your PDF file. All that's left to do is print it:

```
File.open('report.pdf','wb+') do |pdf_file_handle|
    pdf_file_handle.puts pdf_source
end
```

Of course, you can change the `report.pdf` string literal to some other file name if you want to use a different file name for your report.

Summary

SugarCRM is a powerful open source alternative to expensive CRM software, and its architecture lets you quickly and easily create reports using Ruby and Active Record. In this chapter, you used html2ps and Ghostscript to extend SugarCRM with reporting for sales goals, and that combination let you create PDFs without using a special-purpose language. Plus, you used Erubis to keep the HTML clean and separate from your source code, even though the script isn't a Rails application.

In the next chapter, you'll see how to create reports from Apache logs, so you can generate reports that pull data from the traffic logs of any web site that runs Apache.

■■■

## CHAPTER 9

Investment Tracking with Fidelity

It's easier to invest money than ever before. You can invest in companies around the globe with just a phone call or a few clicks of your mouse. You can put your money in a seemingly infinite number of vehicles for those same companies, such as mutual funds (which contain a selection of companies in the same stock) or index funds (which mirror the movement of entire industries' worth of stock). You can even invest in extremely complicated derivatives, which are related to the underlying stock (or, for that matter, other security) and minimize risk for one party while increasing the potential reward for the other.

Along with the increased number of investment options, the pace of the economy continues to get faster. So, it becomes harder and harder to keep up with the status of all of your current and future investments. Yet, you need to be able to take rapid action to respond to changing marketplace conditions, which means you want to be able to follow those changing conditions quickly and easily.

Of course, you can keep track of the marketplace using traditional tools—like the newspaper and television reports—as well as through investment sites like Yahoo! Finance or various online stock brokerage sites. However, if you want to accomplish a specific, custom reporting goal, you need to write some custom code. This chapter's example demonstrates how to create such a report, tracking investments with Fidelity Investments (http://www.fidelity.com).

Writing a Small Server to Get Report Data

For this chapter's example, you will create a small web server to feed data to your reporting system. This approach can be useful in several situations.

For example, if you have mixed Linux and Windows servers, often you'll find that some tasks, such as controlling Component Object Model (COM) objects or communicating with a Microsoft SQL Server, are better performed directly on the Windows system.

(COM is a way for Windows applications to access the software components of other Windows applications.)

To handle these tasks, you can often write a tiny server that uses proprietary extensions directly on the Windows server and then serve it up in an open, easy-to-use format, such as XML. This lets the work of accessing proprietary Windows libraries stay on the Windows machine, so you don't need to use potentially buggy open source drivers designed to access proprietary code. (Of course, some open source drivers designed to access proprietary code are very good, and in those cases, you might not need an intermediary.)

Tip At times, the opposite approach works well. For example, you could write an XML feed on your Linux server that is read by a client-side Windows application, which then uses COM to automatically open Microsoft Word or Microsoft Access to insert the data. This way, you don't need to generate Word or Access documents by hand, which is problematic when it's even possible at all. You get the entire benefit of Microsoft Office without writing any custom Word or Access output code, and your clients get data in a familiar format that they can manipulate.

Mongrel is a popular web server that works with Ruby. Mongrel is typically used to serve Rails applications, but it can also be used to host small web servers directly. You can find more information about Mongrel at `http://mongrel.rubyforge.org/rdoc/files/README.html`. You'll use Mongrel as a simple XML server in this chapter's example.

Of course, you could write a Rails application to serve XML data. But for a simple server, such as one that has only a single URL, that might be overkill. Consider that an empty Rails application on my FreeBSD machine uses 3MB of memory, and, in my experience, Rails applications of any complexity rarely use less than 10MB of memory per process (and often more).

For example, if you need a chat server with one connection per user, and you're using a Rails application consuming 10MB or more of memory per user, that memory consumption can add up very quickly. If you have hundreds of users, that becomes a very serious problem. Alternatively, you can often handle your chat connection with a simple server. Using a server like Mongrel will be much faster than using a full-featured Rails server, and you'll be able to serve more clients in the given amount of memory.

Of course, Rails takes up memory for a reason: it does numerous great things for you automatically. So if you need features such as sessions or complex templating, you're probably better off creating a Rails application.

Nonetheless, for conceptually simple and lightweight purposes, writing a small Mongrel web server is a great way to make your application have less code, take less memory, and run faster.

Tracking a Stock Portfolio

Suppose you are a technology executive who has a large portfolio of personal investments, which you actively manage and trade. You want a tool that lets you easily track your investments on your desktop, and you aren't happy with the existing utilities. You do a little digging, and discover that your online stock broker, Fidelity Investments, allows you to download your stock portfolio in CSV format. So you decide to write a tool to extract the data and display it in a ticker format on your desktop.

You routinely download your portfolio into a CSV file on your computer at home, which allows you to import the data into various tools, such as your financial planning application. However, you would also like to track your stock's progress at work, and you don't want your IT staff to know the details of your portfolio. Since the IT staff routinely monitors traffic, you don't want to log in directly to your Fidelity account or, for that matter, any of the other financial trackers you might use. You don't mind that the stock symbols themselves are available, since they say nothing about the total size of your investment.

To meet your needs, you'll create a simple XML server to get the data and a graphical stock ticker to display updates.

For this example, you'll need a Fidelity CSV file. If you have a Fidelity account, you can get a Fidelity CSV file by logging in, clicking an appropriate account, and clicking Download. If you don't have a Fidelity account or would prefer to use other data, you can download a sample file from the Source/Downloads area of the Apress web site (`http://www.apress.com`) or `http://rubyreporting.com/examples/example_fidelity.csv`.

Creating an XML Server with Mongrel

To create the server, you need three gems installed: `mongrel`, `fastercsv`, and `remarkably`. FasterCSV, introduced in Chapter 7, is a fast CSV-parsing library for Ruby. Remarkably is a library designed to help you output XML using Ruby code. It's loosely based on the Markaby library, which was also introduced in Chapter 7. You can install the gems as follows:

```
gem install -y mongrel fastercsv remarkably
```

Then create the XML server script shown in Listing 9-1.

Listing 9-1. *Fidelity Investments XML Loader and Server (xml_server.rb)*

```
require 'mongrel'
require 'fastercsv'
require 'remarkably/engines/xml'
```

```ruby
(puts "usage: #{$0} csv_file_1 csv_file_2..."; exit) unless ARGV.length >=1

class StocksList
  def initialize
    @symbols = []    # Holds our list of symbols
  end

  def load_csv(files)
    valid_symbol_labels = ['Symbol']
    files.each do |file|
      rows = FasterCSV.parse(open(file))
      first_row= rows.shift
      symbol_index = nil

      first_row.each_with_index do |label, index|
        if(valid_symbol_labels.include?(label))
          symbol_index = index
          break
        end
      end
      if symbol_index.nil?
        puts "Can't find symbol index on first row in file #{file}."
      else
        @symbols = @symbols + rows.map { |r| r[symbol_index]
                             }.delete_if { |s| s.nil? or s ==''  }
      end
    end
  end

  include Remarkably::Common
  def to_xml # Output our stocks list as XML
      xml do
        symbols do
        @symbols.each do |s|
          symbol s
        end
        end
      end.to_s
  end
end
```

```ruby
class StocksListHandler < Mongrel::HttpHandler
  def initialize(stocks_list)
    @stocks_list = stocks_list
    super()
  end
  def process(request, response)
    response.start(200) do |headers, output_stream|
      headers["Content-Type"] = "text/xml"

      output_stream.write(@stocks_list.to_xml)
    end
  end
end


stocks_list = StocksList.new
stocks_list.load_csv(ARGV)

interface = '127.0.0.1'
port = '3000'

mongrel_server = Mongrel::HttpServer.new( interface, port)
mongrel_server.register("/", StocksListHandler.new(stocks_list))
puts "** Fidelity XML server started on #{interface}:#{port}!"
mongrel_server.run.join
```

Save this file as xml_server.rb.
You can run the example as follows:

```ruby
ruby xml_server.rb example_fidelity.csv
```

Note that if you have multiple accounts with Fidelity, you can run this script with multiple files, as follows:

```ruby
ruby xml_server.rb first_csv_file.csv second_csv_file.csv ...
```

This script is meant to be used in conjunction with the graphical ticker (shown later in Listing 9-2), but for now, you can see the output in a web browser by visiting the following URL:

```
http://127.0.0.1:3000/
```

You should see output similar to that shown in Figure 9-1.

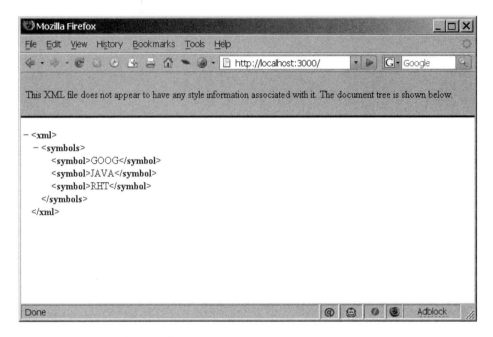

Figure 9-1. *XML stock symbol server in action*

Let's take a look at a few lines from this example.

Dissecting the Code

The code in Listing 9-1 has two classes:

- StocksList: This class maintains the list of stock symbols that you will serve as XML. It handles the loading of the symbols and then the list of symbols.

- StocksListHandler: This class is a Mongrel handler. It processes requests from the ticker, and then serves them as XML. The ticker then uses those symbols.

The code for the StocksList class has three methods. The first method, initialize, sets up the array holding the list of symbols:

```
def initialize
  @symbols = []    # Holds our list of symbols
end
```

initialize is the constructor—a special method called by Ruby when a class is instantiated into an object. The constructor has just a single line of code, which initializes your @symbols array.

The next `StocksList` method is `load_csv`, which is used to load the CSV data into the object:

```ruby
def load_csv(files)
  @symbols = []
  valid_symbol_labels = ['Symbol']
  files.each do |file|
    rows = FasterCSV.parse(open(file))
    first_row= rows.shift
    symbol_index = nil

    first_row.each_with_index do |label, index|
      if(valid_symbol_labels.include?(label))
        symbol_index = index
        break
      end
    end
    if symbol_index.nil?
      puts "Can't find symbol index on first row in file #{file}."
    else
      @symbols = @symbols + rows.map { |r| r[symbol_index]
                      }.delete_if { |s| s.nil? or s =='' }
    end
  end
end
```

This method loops through each of the CSV files and loads them. It does this by assuming that the first row of each file is a header, and it loops through it looking for a column named `Symbol`. This has the advantage of working with any CSV file whose first line is a header row and that has a `Symbol` column. If your CSV files have symbol columns labeled something else, you can add support for them by adding to the `valid_symbol_labels` array.

The end result of this is a `@symbols` array full of symbols, which you use next. You expose a single method, `to_xml`, which converts it into XML:

```ruby
include Remarkably::Common
def to_xml
  xml do
    symbols do
      @symbols.each do |s|
        symbol s
      end
```

```
      end
    end.to_s
  end
```

The `to_xml` method uses Remarkably's `xml` method to create a simple XML document. (You can use the `xml` method because you mixed in the `Remarkably::Common` framework using `include`.) You create a `symbols` node, and then a `symbol` node for each of your symbols. When you call a method that's not defined inside a call to the `xml` function, Remarkably uses it as a node name, so you can use the `symbols` and `symbol` methods to create nodes named `symbols` and `symbol`, respectively. (This approach is very similar to Markaby, and while it appears strange at first, it rapidly becomes more familiar.) Undefined methods are caught using Ruby's `method_missing` technique, and they are converted into XML tags.

■**Tip** You could replace the `to_xml` method with a `to_json` or a `to_s` method if your application needed the output as JSON or as a string, respectively.

The `StocksListHandler` class is the Mongrel handler that responds to the request for the XML list of stocks:

```
class StocksListHandler < Mongrel::HttpHandler
  def initialize(stocks_list)
      @stocks_list = stocks_list
      super()
  end
  def process(request, response)
    response.start(200) do |headers, output_stream|
      headers["Content-Type"] = "text/plain"

      output_stream.write(@stocks_list.to_xml)
    end
  end
end
```

The `StocksListHandler` class inherits from `Mongrel::HttpHandler`, so you need to define only two methods. The rest of the functionality relating to the web server is handled by Mongrel. The first, `initialize`, is a constructor used to set your `@stocks_list` instance variable. Note the call to `super`, which calls the `Mongrel::HttpHandler`'s initialize method so that it can do any Mongrel-specific initialization. The call to `super` has empty parentheses after it. In this case, because no arguments are specified, `super` calls the overridden constructor with the original arguments. Because `Mongrel::HttpHandler`'s constructor takes no arguments, it will raise an error if you do not explicitly indicate to super that you do not wish to pass your arguments to Mongrel::HttpHandler's constructor.

The second method defined in StocksListHandler is process, which handles a request from a web browser or other HTTP client, such as the stock ticker you will create next (Listing 9-2). You use Mongrel's response method to respond with a 200 status code, which means success. You could return other error codes if necessary, of course, such as 404 if a file isn't found or 501 if an internal server error occurs. Next, you set the Content-Type header, which specifies the type of content you're sending, to text/xml. If your page is viewed with a web browser, this will affect how the page is displayed. Finally, it calls the to_xml method of your StocksList instance to render your list of stocks as XML, and then writes that to the output stream, which, in turn, sends it to the client requesting the information.

■Tip A Mongrel handler like the one in Listing 9-1 can be used as a very simple, operating system-independent way to perform interprocess communication. For example, you could have a graphical interface that processed large audio files. You could use a shell script to actually process the files, and then use wget or curl (both of which download files or web pages from web servers) to trigger a refresh of the graphical display. This allows you to easily have many background processes running asynchronously without having threads piling up in the host program, which can affect performance. If you need more complex communication than a simple triggering of some action, then using a more sophisticated communications method, such as is provided by your operating system or programming language, is a good idea. (Conceivably, you could embed an entire RESTful web application inside your desktop application, but that may be overkill.)

After you define the two classes that make up the bulk of your functionality, you start the server running:

```
stocks_list = StocksList.new
stocks_list.load_csv(ARGV)

interface = '127.0.0.1'
port = '3000'

mongrel_server = Mongrel::HttpServer.new( interface, port)
mongrel_server.register("/", StocksListHandler.new(stocks_list))
puts "** Fidelity XML server started on #{interface}:#{port}!"

mongrel_server.run.join
```

The first line grabs a list of files from the command line and creates a new StocksList object. Then you call the load_csv method, which causes the list of symbols to be loaded from the CSV files.

Next, you create a new `Mongrel::HttpServer` instance on a hard-coded interface and port number. Note that, by default, it serves files on only your loopback interface, so once you're finished testing it and you're happy that it won't leak any details of your portfolio, you need to change the `interface` variable to `0.0.0.0`.

After that, you register your handler class. Note the string, which indicates the path for which each handler will receive requests. The handlers receive everything starting with the indicated path, unless there's a more specific handler; in other words, the following URLs will all be handled by `StocksHandler`:

```
http://127.0.0.1/
http://127.0.0.1/random_path
http://127.0.0.1/test
```

These handlers ignore path information, so if they receive a request, they treat it in the same way, no matter what the exact path is. If you want to ignore nonstandard requests, you can parse the URLs and throw errors in your Mongrel handler.

■Note If you're communicating complex information in your URLs, you may be better off using a more powerful framework—such as Merb, Sinatra, or Ruby on Rails—rather than parsing the URLs yourself.

Creating the Graphical XML Ticker

The ticker you'll create will scroll across the screen, displaying constantly updated data on all of the stocks in your portfolio.

To run this example, you'll need a few gems installed: `yahoofinance`, `fxruby`, and `xml-simple` gems. The `YahooFinance` module provides the quotes (you can refer to `http://transparentech.com/projects/yahoofinance` and my Apress book, *Practical Ruby Gems*, for more information about `YahooFinance`). FXRuby, introduced in Chapter 4, is an interface to the cross-platform FOX GUI library. XmlSimple reads XML documents into hashes. It's based on the Perl module of a similar name, `XML::Simple`. It is, as the name implies, simpler than other methods of reading XML documents, so it's well suited for reading the relatively simple array of symbols from the server.

■Note XmlSimple is a fantastic choice for simple documents, since it is easy to understand and use. For more complex requirements, you can choose from a number of more sophisticated parsers, such as REXML, which is included with Ruby, and Hpricot, which is demonstrated in Chapters 6 and 13.

You can install the necessary gems as follows:

```
gem install -y yahoofinance fxruby xml-simple
```

Listing 9-2 shows the code for the graphical XML ticker.

Listing 9-2. *Scrolling Chart Prices with FXRuby (xml_ticker.rb)*

```ruby
require 'net/http'
require 'yahoofinance'
require 'fox16'
require 'xmlsimple'

(puts 'Usage: ruby xml_ticker.rb HOSTNAME PORT_NUMBER'; exit) unless ARGV.length==2

class FXTickerApp
  include Fox
  def initialize(hostname, port_number,
              font_size = 100, quote_frequency=1)

    # Quote_frequency is in minutes

    @hostname = hostname
    @port_number = port_number
    @quote_frequency = quote_frequency

    load_symbols_from_server

    @fox_application=FXApp.new
    @main_window=FXMainWindow.new(@fox_application, "Stock Ticker ",
                              nil, nil, DECOR_ALL | LAYOUT_EXPLICIT)
    @tickerlabel = FXLabel.new(@main_window, get_label_text,
                              nil, 0,  LAYOUT_EXPLICIT)

    @tickerlabel.font.setFont "helvetica [bitstream],#{font_size}"

    def scroll_timer(sender, sel, ptr)
      self.scroll_label
      @fox_application.addTimeout(50, method(:scroll_timer))
    end
    @fox_application.addTimeout(50, method(:scroll_timer))
```

```ruby
  def update_label_timer(sender, sel, ptr)
    @tickerlabel.text = self.get_label_text
    @fox_application.addTimeout(1000*60*@quote_frequency,
                                    method(:update_label_timer))
  end
  @fox_application.addTimeout(1000*60*@quote_frequency,
                                  method(:update_label_timer))


  @fox_application.create
end
def load_symbols_from_server

  xml_body = Net::HTTP.new(@hostname, @port_number).get('/').body

  xml = XmlSimple.xml_in(xml_body)

  @symbols = xml['symbols'][0]['symbol']
end

def scroll_label
  if(@tickerlabel.x < -@tickerlabel.width)
    @tickerlabel.move(@main_window.width , @tickerlabel.y)
  else
    @tickerlabel.move(@tickerlabel.x - 3, @tickerlabel.y)
  end
end

def get_label_text
  label_text = ''
  YahooFinance::get_standard_quotes( @symbols ).each do |symbol, quote|
    label_text << "#{symbol}: #{quote.lastTrade} ... "
  end
  label_text
end

def go

  @main_window.show( PLACEMENT_SCREEN )
```

```
    @fox_application.run
  end
end

hostname = ARGV.shift
port_number = ARGV.shift

my_app = FXTickerApp.new(hostname, port_number, 240)
my_app.go
```

Save this script as xml_ticker.rb.

You can run the script using a command like the following:

```
ruby xml_ticker.rb localhost 3000
```

Note that under Mac OS X and Linux, you'll need to launch the X11 server in order to see anything. X11 is available from the Mac OS X installation media. X11 comes standard with most Linux distributions. To launch X11 under Linux, use the startx command. On an OS X system, click the X11 icon.

You should see a screen similar to Figure 9-2.

Figure 9-2. *XML stock ticker*

Let's examine the code line by line.

Dissecting the Code

The code in Listing 9-2 has a single class, FXTickerApp, which has a number of methods. The first is the initialize method, which creates the user interface elements you need. However, before you start creating user interface elements, you need to initialize the settings and load the stock symbols from the server:

```
class FXTickerApp
  include Fox
  def initialize(hostname, port_number,
               font_size = 100, quote_frequency=1,
               reload_csv_frequency=60)
    # Quote_frequency and reload_csv_frequency are in minutes
```

```
@hostname = hostname
@port_number = port_number
@quote_frequency = quote_frequency
@reload_csv_frequency = reload_csv_frequency

load_symbols_from_server
```

The first few lines set appropriate instance variables. Then you call `load_symbols_from_server`, which loads the symbols from the indicated XML server. Next, the code begins to create user interface objects:

```
@fox_application=FXApp.new
@main_window=FXMainWindow.new(@fox_application, "Stock Ticker ",
                             nil, nil, DECOR_ALL | LAYOUT_EXPLICIT)
@tickerlabel = FXLabel.new(@main_window, get_label_text,
                           nil, 0,  LAYOUT_EXPLICIT)

@tickerlabel.font.setFont "helvetica [bitstream],#{font_size}"
```

The first line creates an `FXApp` object, which is a FOX object that represents the entire application and handles application-wide tasks, such as setting timers. The second line creates a window object, which represents your only window. After that, the code creates the single control in your window, which is a label that occupies the entire window. The call to `get_label_text` returns a label with all of the stock names and prices.

Next, you create a timer that automatically scrolls the ticker every 50 milliseconds:

```
def scroll_timer(sender, sel, ptr)
  self.scroll_label
  @fox_application.addTimeout(50, method(:scroll_timer))
end
@fox_application.addTimeout(50, method(:scroll_timer))
```

The `addTimeout` method will call the `scroll_timer` method after 50 milliseconds. Note that this doesn't recur, so you need to add a new timeout after each execution of the method. You call the `method` function to get a `Method` object to use with the `scroll_timer` method. The `method` function takes a symbol and returns a `Method` object representing the method with that symbol name.

The actual scrolling of the label from right to left is done by the `scroll_label` class method defined later in the class. This is in order to separate the code that manages the timer from the code that scrolls the label.

Next, you set up one more timer, which will update the text of the label once a minute:

```
  def update_label_timer(sender, sel, ptr)
    @tickerlabel.text = self.get_label_text
    @fox_application.addTimeout(1000*60*@quote_frequency,
                                method(:update_label_timer))
  end
  @fox_application.addTimeout(1000*60*@quote_frequency,
                              method(:update_label_timer))

  @fox_application.create
end
```

By default, the stock prices are loaded from Yahoo! Finance once a minute. The timer calls class functions that implement the actual functionality. The first one loads the stock symbols:

```
def load_symbols_from_server

  xml_body = Net::HTTP.new(@hostname, @port_number).get('/').body

  xml = XmlSimple.xml_in(xml_body)

  @symbols = xml['symbols'][0]['symbol']
end
```

First, you request the XML using the Ruby built-in library `Net::HTTP`, and then you parse it using XmlSimple. The XML document you are trying to parse looks like this:

```
<xml>
  <symbols>
    <symbol>GOOG</symbol>
    <symbol>JAVA</symbol>
    <symbol>RHT</symbol>
  </symbols>
</xml>
```

The call `xml['symbols'][0]['symbol']` returns an array of `symbol` nodes inside the first `symbols` node. There is only one `symbols` node, but XmlSimple returns all elements of a given name as arrays, even if there's just one. Because the symbol objects are nodes with a text element (in other words, elements with text inside them) and no attributes or child nodes, they are returned as strings in an array. You retrieve them using the final `['symbol']` reference.

Next, the `scroll_label` method scrolls the ticker label containing the stock symbols and prices across the screen:

```
def scroll_label
  if(@tickerlabel.x < -@tickerlabel.width)
    @tickerlabel.move(@main_window.width , @tickerlabel.y)
  else
    @tickerlabel.move(@tickerlabel.x - 3, @tickerlabel.y)
  end
end
```

This function scrolls the label from right to left. Once the ticker has completely scrolled off the left edge, the function resets it back to the right side of the screen. The 3-pixel-per-call move is arbitrary, so feel free to change that amount if you would like a faster or slower ticker. You can also change the frequency of the timer call in the `initialize` function, which would result in the `scroll_label` function being called less often. However, if the function is called too infrequently, the scrolling motion will be jerky.

The ticker will scroll completely off the screen before being reset to the right side of the screen. This means that there will be a short period when only a relatively small percentage of the label is visible. If you would like, you can modify the ticker to constantly fill the screen by using two labels (for the sake of this example, that's more complexity for relatively little gain). And if you would prefer a right-to-left scrolling ticker, the following replacement method does just that:

```
def scroll_label
  if(@tickerlabel.x > @main_window.width)
    @tickerlabel.move(-@tickerlabel.width , @tickerlabel.y)
  else
    @tickerlabel.move(@tickerlabel.x + 3, @tickerlabel.y)
  end
end
```

Next, the `get_label_text` function takes the list of stock symbols and gets a price for each of them:

```
def get_label_text
  label_text = ''
  YahooFinance::get_standard_quotes( @symbols ).each do |symbol, quote|
    label_text << "#{symbol}: #{quote.lastTrade} ... "
  end
  label_text
end
```

This function calls the `YahooFinance::get_standard_quotes` function, which takes an array of stock symbols, downloads the current prices from the web site, and returns a hash where the keys are the stock symbols and the values are the quotes.

The last method in the class actually starts the application running:

```
def go

  @main_window.show( PLACEMENT_SCREEN )

  @fox_application.run
end
end
```

The `go` method simply shows the main screen and starts the application. The constant `PLACEMENT_SCREEN` indicates that your main window should be shown centered in the screen. There are a few other options, which you can see in the documentation at `http://www.fxruby.org/doc/api/classes/Fox/FXTopWindow.html`.

Finally, let's take a look at the initialization code:

```
hostname = ARGV.shift
port_number = ARGV.shift

my_app = FXTickerApp.new(hostname, port_number, 240)
my_app.go
```

This code simply takes the server hostname and port number from the command line and passes them to the `FXTickerApp` class. The call to `new` also includes an optional parameter specifying the font size. This parameter is in tenths of a point, so the value 240 produces a 24-point font.

Summary

Financial applications can be complicated and involve transferring rapidly changing data across multiple machines. In some cases, you can make this easier and faster by writing custom servers with Mongrel, as in this chapter's example. Additionally, you can easily create graphical interfaces for financial applications by using FXRuby to create a portable and easy-to-use interface, and Remarkably and XmlSimple can make the graphical interface and the server communicate easily.

In the next chapter, you'll see how you can analyze large amounts of data from an Apache web server to get valuable cost/sale information about advertising campaigns.

CHAPTER 10

■ ■ ■

Calculating Costs by Analyzing Apache Web Logs

At the time of this writing, the Web is less than 20 years old. While that may seem like a lifetime in software terms, in business terms, the Web is still an infant, with countless new ventures being built around it.

Because the Web is such a new business concept, we're still developing benchmarks for measuring the success of new approaches. Therefore, it can be difficult to determine exactly how well a fledgling startup is doing, particularly if it's in a prerevenue phase. Of course, one way to measure success is through advertising revenues gained by traffic. However, many startups have not defined a plan to monetize their traffic. Rather, they hope to create a massive source of traffic and sell out to a large company, which will then devise a plan for deriving revenue from the traffic. As a result, the essential value of those startups is their web traffic, and analyzing that traffic—not to mention finding ways to increase it—is vitally important.

Logically, traffic plays a significant role beyond advertising results. For businesses selling a product or service, traffic is extremely important, because web-based sales are a function of traffic. Accordingly, it makes sense for these businesses to analyze traffic much in the same way brick-and-mortar stores analyze customer visitation and purchase patterns. While some of these questions can be answered by prepackaged tools like AWStats (http://awstats.sourceforge.net/), analyzing complex questions sometimes calls for custom reporting software.

In this chapter, you'll see how to create a custom report to analyze web site traffic and sales, based on a high volume of data in Apache logs. For this example, you will use Gruff, which was introduced in Chapter 3, plus two new tools: ActiveRecord::Extensions and PDF::Writer. Let's begin by looking at what these two tools can do for you.

Speeding Up Insertions with ActiveRecord::Extensions

ActiveRecord::Extensions is, as the name implies, a collection of extensions for Active Record. These are generally performance extensions. The extension you'll use in this chapter's example allows you to insert multiple rows of data at a time into a single table. This will speed up performance significantly and can reduce memory use, since you won't need to create large numbers of objects. Since the example calls for inserting large numbers of records into a database from the Apache log, this performance boost will be significant.

ActiveRecord::Extensions is very easy to use. Let's take a look at a brief example to see how it works. Suppose you want to insert some data into a table named webhosts, which has two columns: domain and description. You could use the following Active Record code:

```
Webhost.new(:domain=>'www.somecompany.example',
            :description=>'Some Company Site').save
Webhost.new(:domain=>'www.teststore.example',
            :description=>'A Test Store').save
Webhost.new(:domain=>'www.smallblog.example',
            :description=>'A Small Blog').save
```

You could also use the following ActiveRecord::Extensions code:

```
Webhost.import([:domain, :description],
                [['www.somecompany.example, 'Some Company Site'],
                 ['www.teststore.example', 'A Test Store'],
                 ['www.smallblog.example', 'A Small Blog']]
```

This method saves the time required to create the Active Record object, which can be very significant. It also runs just one query rather than three. In other words, the first Active Record example produces queries like this:

```
INSERT INTO webhosts (domain, description) ('www.somecompany.example',
                                            'Some Company Site');
INSERT INTO webhosts (domain, description) ('www.teststore.example',
                                            'A Test Store');
INSERT INTO webhosts (domain, description) ('www.smallblog.example',
                                            'A Small Blog');
```

On the other hand, the ActiveRecord::Extensions code produces a query like this:

```
INSERT INTO webhosts (domain, description) ('www.somecompany.example',
                                    'Some Company Site'),
                                    ('www.teststore.example',
                                    'A Test Store'),
                                    ('www.smallblog.example',
                                    'A Small Blog');
```

As you can see, the same data is inserted in three queries in the first example but in just one query in the second example. It won't take very long to insert three records no matter what you do. However, in cases where you need to scale, and even more so when you need to insert large amounts of data at once, the time savings can be quite valuable.

You might initially think that a database like MySQL or PostgreSQL would take the same amount of time to insert a given number of rows, without regard to how many queries are used, but that's not true. Significant overhead is associated with each additional query. In fact, as you'll see when we examine the completed solution later in this chapter, the code that inserts Apache log data using this extension will perform at triple the speed of Active Record alone. If you have a more complex situation—with a number of keys or with a large amount of data being read at a time, for example—it will speed up processing even more.

For more details on ActiveRecord::Extensions, see `http://www.continuousthinking.com/are/activerecord-extensions-0-0-5`.

▪Tip Actually, the fastest way to do MySQL inserts is by using the `LOAD DATA INFILE` statement. This requires your data to be on disk in CSV format, however. In some cases, you can convert data from another format, write it as CSV, and then load it with `LOAD DATA INFILE`. This will still be faster than using separate `INSERT` statements, but the additional complexity may not be worth it, particularly if you're dealing with dynamic data from, say, a user filling out a form on a web site. Also, `LOAD DATA INFILE` has the disadvantage of being MySQL-specific, and you need to place the CSV file on the server or else deal with some security issues. You can find more information about `LOAD DATA INFILE`, as well as on speeding up `INSERT` statements (including the relatively obscure `INSERT DELAYED` statement) at `http://dev.mysql.com/doc/refman/5.0/en/insert-speed.html`.

Creating PDFs with PDF::Writer

PDF::Writer is a pure Ruby PDF-creation library. This has the advantage of not requiring any outside libraries installed on the host operating system, which is unlike the LaTeX solution discussed in Chapter 6 or the html2ps solution discussed in Chapter 8. PDF::Writer is less flexible and slower than LaTeX, but it's also easier to learn and more Ruby-like. The html2ps solution is easy to learn, but slow, since it runs through multiple passes, and it's inflexible. HTML alone does not support all of the formatting features PDF does, so the conversion is imprecise, and html2ps does not support all possible types of HTML formatting.

For example, the following code creates a PDF containing only the text `Hello world!`:

```
require 'pdf/writer'

pdf_document = PDF::Writer.new

pdf_document.select_font "Times-Roman"
pdf_document.text "Hello world!"
pdf_document.save_as "out.pdf"
```

The Rails PDF plug-in (rpdf), works with PDF::Writer to make writing PDF views in Rails easy. It allows you to access a new type of Rails view: an `.rpdf` view. For example, if you needed to write the preceding example as a Rails view, you could do it like this:

```
pdf.select_font "Times-Roman"
pdf.text "Hello world!"
```

As you can see, you get an implicit PDF::Writer object, `pdf`, and the results of your PDF view are automatically sent to the user's browser.

You can get the full details on PDF::Writer at its home page: `http://ruby-pdf.rubyforge.org/pdf-writer/`.

Now that you have an idea of what ActiveRecord::Extensions and PDF::Writer can do, let's take a look at how to use them.

Cost-Per-Sale Reporting

Suppose you operate an online store that sells digital books in PDF format. The books are marketed through a variety of online advertising sources. Each source referral comes at a certain cost per click, and each source provides a different amount of traffic each month. Additionally, each source provides a different response rate, since visitors from sites whose topic is closely linked to the e-books being sold are more likely to buy an e-book, as are visitors from sites whose median income is higher. As a result, it's difficult to analyze the sales from the different sources.

You would like to use Ruby to analyze your web logs and determine exactly how many sales are being derived from each source, as well as exactly how much each sale costs. If the average sale cost from an advertiser is more than the value of each sale, then the advertiser should be dropped. On the other hand, spending should be increased on an advertiser whose cost per sale is particularly low. You want to create a report that has nice, attractive graphs with this data, and you want to be able to easily update the reports with a web interface. Additionally, these reports should be easy to redistribute, so that you can send them to your less technically savvy business partners.

However, there's a catch: the site has an extremely large amount of traffic, so whatever method is used to analyze the data will need to be extremely fast; otherwise, it might take hours or days to import all of the data. You would like to use a small set of test data to compare different approaches to see which is fastest.

Let's cover exactly how you can accomplish these goals with Rails. To begin, you'll need to install the `ar-extensions`, `gruff`, and `pdf-writer` gems, as follows:

```
gem install -y ar-extensions gruff pdf-writer
```

Next, create a new project with the following command:

```
rails apache_sales_tracker
```

Then enter the `apache_sales_tracker` directory and install the rpdf plug-in, as follows:

```
ruby script/plugin install svn://rubyforge.org//var/svn/railspdfplugin/railspdf/
```

Now, let's start creating the files that make up the application.

Creating the Controllers

First, create the controller for the main page, as shown in Listing 10-1.

Listing 10-1. *Home Page Controller (app/controllers/home_controller.rb)*

```
class HomeController < ApplicationController
end
```

Save this as `app/controllers/home_controller.rb`.
Next, create a controller for uploading Apache log files, as shown in Listing 10-2.

Listing 10-2. *Log Controller (app/controllers/logs_controller.rb)*

```
require 'benchmark'
require 'tempfile'
require 'ar-extensions'

# Note that some developers would prefer to put the above
# require statements in the config/environment.rb file.
```

```ruby
class LogsController < ApplicationController
  def upload

    flash[:notice] = "Uploaded new file... \n"
    count=0

    if params[:upload_with_active_record_extensions]

      # If the user chose the Active Record extensions
      # button, we'll use that and measure the time
      # it took.

      real_time_elapsed = Benchmark.realtime  do
        columns = [:user_agent, :path_info, :remote_addr,
                   :http_referrer, :status, :visited_at]
        values = []
        LogParser.new.parse_io_stream(params[:log][:file]) do |l|
          values <<
                   [ l['HTTP_USER_AGENT'],
                     l['PATH_INFO'],
                     l['REMOTE_ADDR'],
                     l['HTTP_REFERER'],
                     l['STATUS'],
                     Date.parse(l['DATETIME']) ]
          count = count + 1
        end
        Hit.import columns, values, :validate=>false if values.length>0
      end
    else
      # If the user chose the "Upload with Active Record" button,
      # then use regular Active Record to upload the records and
      # measure the time it takes.

      real_time_elapsed = Benchmark.realtime  do
        LogParser.new.parse_io_stream(params[:log][:file]) do |l|
          Hit.create(
            :user_agent => l['HTTP_USER_AGENT'],
            :path_info => l['PATH_INFO'],
            :remote_addr => l['REMOTE_ADDR'],
            :http_referrer => l['HTTP_REFERER'],
            :status => l['STATUS'],
            :visited_at => l['DATETIME'] )
```

```
            count = count + 1
        end
      end
    end

    flash[:notice] << " #{count} uploaded, #{Hit.count} total\n"
    flash[:notice] << " #{'%0.2f' %  real_time_elapsed} elapsed, " <<
                      "#{'%0.2f' % (count.to_f /
                                    real_time_elapsed)*60
                         }  records per minute ."

    redirect_to :controller=>:home, :action=>:index

  end

  def clear_all
    Hit.delete_all
    flash[:notice] = 'Logs cleared!'
    redirect_to :controller=>:home, :action=>:index
  end
end
```

Save this as app/controllers/logs_controller.rb.

Now, define a controller that creates your reports, as shown in Listing 10-3.

Listing 10-3. *Report Controller (app/controllers/report_controller.rb)*

```
require 'tempfile'
require 'gruff'

class ReportController < ApplicationController

  def combined
    @rails_pdf_inline  = true

    @graph_files = {
            'Graph of per-sale costs'=>
                  get_sale_graph_tempfile,
            'Graph of total visitors from each advertiser'=>
                  get_visitor_graph_tempfile
                  }
    # Note that the key is the label and the value is the
```

```ruby
    # graph filename. Note you could easily add more graphs in
    # here if you'd like.

    render:layout=>nil

    # At this point, the images have already been embedded in the PDF,
    # so we can safely delete them.
    @graph_files.each do |label, filename|
      File.unlink filename
    end
  end


  protected # Protected functions are for internal use only and
            # don't correspond to a URL.

  # This function is used by the two graph functions to create a
  # temporary filename.

  def get_tempfile_name(prefix)
    File.join(RAILS_ROOT, "tmp/#{prefix}_#{request.env['REMOTE_ADDR']
                                  }_#{Time.now.to_f
                                  }_#{rand(10000)}.jpg")
  end

  def get_visitor_graph_tempfile # Graph of visitor and purchasing visitors
    graph_tempfile_name = get_tempfile_name('visitor_graph')

    advertisers = Advertiser.find(:all)

    g = Gruff::Bar.new(1000)
    g.title = "Advertising Traffic Report"
    g.legend_font_size = 16
    advertisers.each do |a|
      visitor_addresses  = Hit.find(:all,
                  :group=>'remote_addr',
                  :conditions=>['http_referrer= ? ',
                  a.referrer_url]
                  ).map { |h| h.remote_addr }

      sale_count = Hit.count('remote_addr',
                  :conditions=>['remote_addr IN (?)
```

```
                             AND
                             path_info LIKE "/cart/checkout%"',

                          visitor_addresses])

    g.data(a.company_name, [ visitor_addresses.length, sale_count ] )
  end

  g.labels = {0 => 'Visitors', 1 => 'Visitors With One or More Purchases' }

  g.write(graph_tempfile_name)
  graph_tempfile_name
end

def get_sale_graph_tempfile # Graph of per-click and per-sale costs

  graph_tempfile_name = get_tempfile_name('sale_graph_tempfile')

  advertisers = Advertiser.find(:all)

  g = Gruff::Bar.new(1000)

  g.title = "Cost Per Sale Report"
  g.legend_font_size = 16
  g.y_axis_label = 'Cost (USD)'

  advertisers.each do |a|
    visitor_addresses  = Hit.find(:all,
                  :group=>'remote_addr',
                  :conditions=>['http_referrer= ? ',
                  a.referrer_url]
                  ).map { |h| h.remote_addr }

    sale_count = Hit.count('remote_addr',
                  :conditions=>['remote_addr IN (?)
                     AND
                     path_info LIKE "/cart/checkout%"',
                       visitor_addresses])

    total_cost = visitor_addresses.length*a.cost_per_click
    cost_per_sale = total_cost / sale_count
```

```ruby
      g.data(a.company_name, [a.cost_per_click, cost_per_sale ] )
    end


    g.labels = {0 => 'Cost Per Click', 1 => 'Cost Per Sale' }
    g.minimum_value = 0


    g.write(graph_tempfile_name)
    graph_tempfile_name
  end


  # These two methods will display errors as HTML, as per
  # the rpdf documentation at http://railspdfplugin.rubyforge.org/wiki/wiki.pl


  def rescue_action_in_public(exception)
   headers.delete("Content-Disposition")
   super
  end


  def rescue_action_locally(exception)
   headers.delete("Content-Disposition")
   super
  end

end
```

Save this as app/controllers/report_controller.rb.

Creating the Layout and Views

Next up is the layout for the report, as shown in Listing 10-4.

Listing 10-4. *Report HTML Layout (app/views/layouts/application.html.erb)*

```html
<!DOCTYPE html PUBLIC "-//W3C//DTD XHTML 1.0 Transitional//EN"
"http://www.w3.org/TR/xhtml1/ DTD/xhtml1-transitional.dtd">
<html xmlns="http://www.w3.org/1999/xhtml">
<head>
  <meta http-equiv="Content-Type" content="text/html; charset=UTF-8" />
  <title><%= @page_title || 'Apache Log Tracker'%></title>
  <%= stylesheet_link_tag 'apachetracker' %>
  <%= javascript_include_tag 'prototype', 'scriptacolous', 'effects'%>
</head>
```

```
<body>
  <%flash.each do |key, text|%>
    <div id="flash_<%=key%>">
      <%=text.gsub("\n", "\n<br>")%>
    </div>
    <script>new Effect.Highlight('flash_<%=key%>'); </script>
  <%end%>
  <%= @content_for_layout %>
</body>
</html>
```

Save this as `app/views/layouts/application.html.erb`.

Of course, you need a CSS style sheet for the home page, as shown in Listing 10-5.

Listing 10-5. *Home Page CSS Style Sheet (public/stylesheets/apachetracker.css)*

```
body { font-family: franklin gothic book,
                    helvetica,
                    verdana,
                    sans-serif;
       padding-left:1em;
     }

h1, h2 { font-family: franklin gothic heavy,
                      arial black, sans-serif;
         font-weight: normal;   }

h3 { font-family: franklin gothic medium;
     font-weight: normal; }

a:visited { color:black }
a:hover { text-decoration: none; }
a { }
h3 { padding-left:2em;}
form {
  padding-left: 4em;
}
#flash_notice, #flash_error {
  padding:1em; margin:1em;
  border: 3px dashed #cecece;
  }
```

Save this as public/stylesheets/apachetracker.css.

Next, let's take a look at the views. The first is the main home page view from which the various actions can be accessed, shown in Listing 10-6.

Listing 10-6. *Home Page RHTML View (app/views/home/index.html.erb)*

```
<h1>Apache Log Analyzer</h1>

<h2>Would you like to...</h2>
<h3>... upload a New Apache Log? </h2>
<%  form_tag( { :controller => :logs,
                 :action => :upload } , {:multipart => true} )do %>
  <%=file_field 'log', 'file' %>
    <%=submit_tag 'Upload with Active Record',
            :name=>:upload_with_active_record%>
    <%=submit_tag 'Upload with Active Record Extensions',
            :name=>:upload_with_active_record_extensions%>
<%end%>
<h3>... <%=link_to 'clear your old logs?',
            :controller=>:logs, :action=>:clear_all%></h3>
<h3>... <%=link_to 'view the cost per sale report?',
            :controller=>:report, :action=>:combined, :format=>'pdf'%></h3>
```

Save this as app/views/home/index.html.erb.

Next, Listing 10-7 shows the .rpdf view that will create the report.

Listing 10-7. *Report .rpdf View (app/views/report/combined.pdf.rpdf)*

```
pdf.select_font "Times-Roman"

figure_number = 1
@graph_files.each do |title, graph|
  pdf.image graph
  pdf.text "<i>Figure #{figure_number
                    } of #{@graph_files.length
                        }- #{title}</i>", :left=>6, :font_size=>12
  figure_number = figure_number  + 1
end
```

Save this as app/views/report/combined.pdf.rpdf.

Downloading a Parser Library

The `log_parser.rb` library is part of the Mint plug-in for Rails. Mint (http://haveamint.com) is commercial software used to analyze web sites, and the Mint plug-in helps you to connect your Rails application to Mint. However, you can use the `log_parser.rb` library from the Mint plug-in for other purposes, as you will here. You can find out more about the Mint plug-in at http://nubyonrails.com/articles/2006/02/16/activerecord-model-for-mint,

For this example, you'll use the `log_parser.rb` library to provide an easy means to parse the Apache logs in a variety of common formats. Also, the `logs` controller will use it to load the data into the database.

Download the `log_parser.rb` library from the following URL:

```
http://topfunky.net/svn/plugins/mint/lib/log_parser.rb
```

Save it as `lib/log_parser.rb`.

Creating the Routing File

Next, you'll need a `config/routes.rb` file. Add a line that lets you set the default home page for the user, as shown in Listing 10-8.

Listing 10-8. *Routes File (config/routes.rb)*

```
ActionController::Routing::Routes.draw do |map|
  map.root :controller=>'home'

  map.connect ':controller/:action/:id.:format' # These two routes are
  map.connect ':controller/:action/:id'         # created by Rails.
end
```

This code connects /— the root of the server—to the `home` controller. Since you didn't specify an action, it uses the `index` action. Note that the `public/index.html` file overrides this route, though, so delete the `public/index.html` file now.

Setting Up the Database and Schema

Next, let's create a database for this application:

```
mysqladmin -u root -p create apache_sales_tracker
```

At this point, you need to modify `config/database.yml` to reflect your database connection parameters. Edit it and replace the default values with the correct values for your machine.

The next step is to build a schema for the application, as shown in Listing 10-9.

Listing 10-9. *Database Initial Schema Migration (db/migrate/001_initial_schema.rb)*

```ruby
class InitialSchema < ActiveRecord::Migration
  def self.up
    create_table :hits do |t|
        t.column :user_agent, :string
        t.column :path_info,:string
        t.column :remote_addr, :string
        t.column :http_referrer, :string
        t.column :status, :string
        t.column :visited_at, :datetime
    end
    create_table :advertisers do |t|
        t.column :company_name, :string
        t.column :referrer_url, :string
        t.column :cost_per_click, :decimal,
                 :precision => 9, :scale => 2
    end
  end

  def self.down
    drop_table :hits
    drop_table :advertisers
  end
end
```

Save this as db/migrate/001_initial_schema.rb. You can run the migration as follows:

```
rake db:migrate
```

```
== 1 InitialSchema: migrating =================================================
-- create_table(:hits)
   -> 0.1570s
-- create_table(:advertisers)
   -> 0.1250s
== 1 InitialSchema: migrated (0.2820s) ========================================
```

Defining the Models

This example uses two models: `Advertiser` and `Hit`, as shown in Listings 10-10 and 10-11.

Listing 10-10. *Advertiser Model (app/models/advertiser.rb)*

```
class Advertiser < ActiveRecord::Base
end
```

Listing 10-11. *Hit Model (app/models/hit.rb)*

```
class Hit < ActiveRecord::Base
end
```

Save these as `app/models/advertiser.rb` and `app/models/hit.rb`, respectively.

Examining the Log Analyzer and Cost-Per-Sale Report

To see the solution in action, you'll need some data. Download the sample advertiser list from the Source/Downloads area of the Apress web site (`http://www.apress.com`) or from `http://rubyreporting.com/examples/apachetracker_sample_advertisers.sql`.
    You can import the data as follows:

```
mysql -u your_mysql_username_here -p apache_sales_tracker <
                 apachetracker_sample_advertisers.sql
```

You can run the server with the following command from the root of your Rails application:

```
ruby script/server
```

Open a web browser and surf to `http://localhost:3000`. You should see a page similar to Figure 10-1. To upload an Apache log, click Browse, and then click the Upload with Active Record button. You can grab a sample Apache log from either the Apress web site or `http://rubyreporting.com/examples/test_output.rb.apache.log.small`. You should see a message indicating how long the upload took.

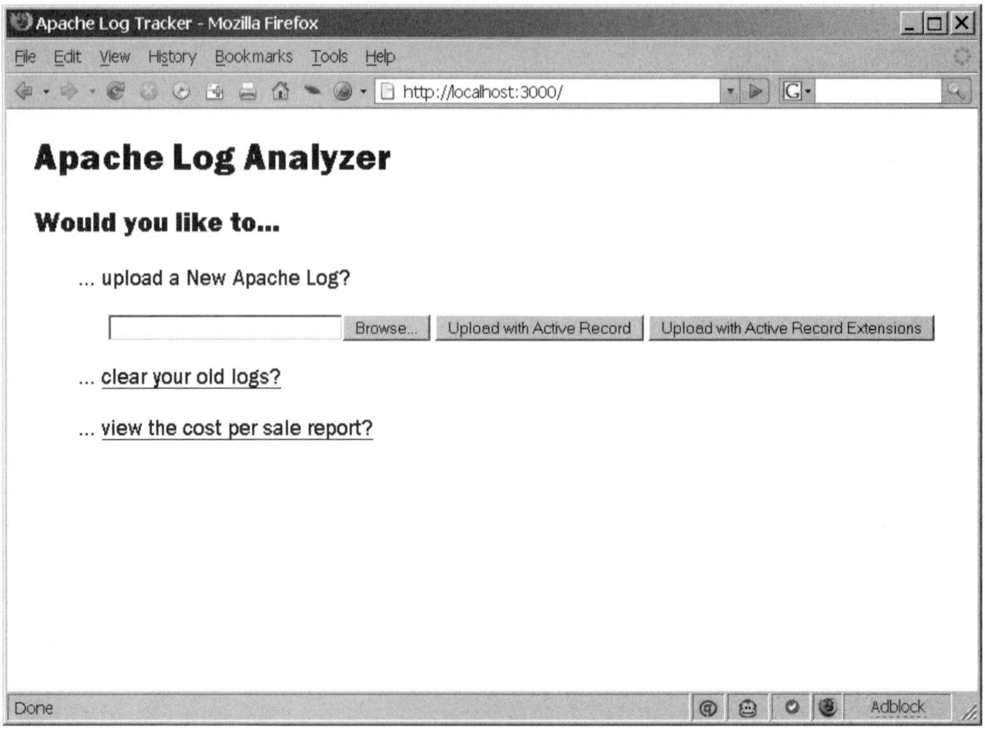

Figure 10-1. *Apache Analyzer Main Screen*

Now clear the database by choosing the link to clear your old logs, and then upload a new log, but this time, click the Upload with Active Record Extensions button.

In my tests, it took roughly 30 seconds to upload with Active Record, and roughly 10 seconds with ActiveRecord::Extensions. (My technical reviewer reported times of 15 seconds and 4 seconds, respectively.)

It becomes even more important to use ActiveRecord::Extensions if you have a number of indexes. For example, try adding the following indexes using the MySQL command-line client:

```
create index hits_path_info on hits(path_info);
create index hits_referrer on hits(http_referrer);
```

If you rerun the tests, you should find that the time to use Active Record should nearly double, but the time to use ActiveRecord::Extensions should barely increase at all. In my test, I got 50 seconds for Active Record and 13 seconds for ActiveRecord::Extensions, so Active Record took almost four times as long. With more indexes, it would take even longer. This is because after each query, all of the indexes are recalculated. It also takes longer and longer as the table gets larger.

After you've uploaded the log, click the link to view the report. This will display a PDF file in your browser (assuming you have a PDF viewer plug-in for your browser), as shown in Figure 10-2.

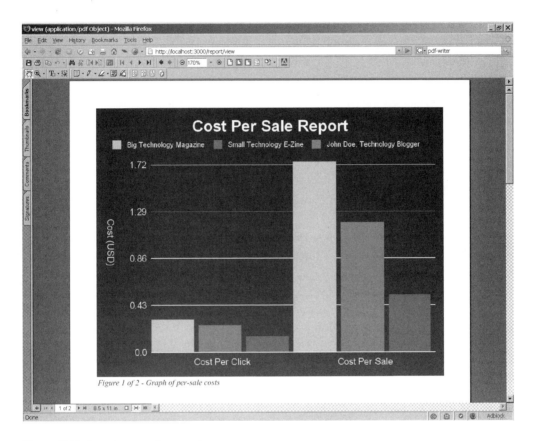

Figure 10-2. *A cost-per-sale report*

The chart graphically illustrates how each advertiser costs a different amount per sale. Of course, the more a sale costs, the less profit is made on each sale, so this is very valuable information. You can use this information to plan future spending, for example, since advertising dollars can be more fruitfully spent on advertisers who have a low cost per sale.

Now let's take a look at the important parts of the code.

Dissecting the Code

Users can take three actions in this application:

- Upload a log, which adds the data from that log to the application.

- Clear all of the data from the system, which can be useful if incorrect data was entered.

- View a report.

Let's examine the log uploader code (Listing 10-2), which is in app/controllers/ logs_controller.rb. The first thing that the script does is require a few libraries:

```
require 'benchmark'
require 'tempfile'
require 'ar-extensions'
```

Some developers would prefer to put these require statements in their config/ environment.rb file instead of at the top of the controller; I prefer this method, but it's not an extremely important distinction.

Next, this controller has just a single method, which controls the uploading. It has two different methods of uploading, and they are triggered by two different buttons. The first uploads with Active Record alone, which looks like this:

```
# If the user chose the "Upload with Active Record" button,
# then use regular Active Record to upload the records and
# measure the time it takes.
real_time_elapsed = Benchmark.realtime  do
  LogParser.new.parse_io_stream(params[:log][:file]) do |l|
    Hit.new do |h|
      h.user_agent    = l['HTTP_USER_AGENT']
      h.path_info     = l['PATH_INFO']
      h.remote_addr   = l['REMOTE_ADDR']
      h.http_referrer = l['HTTP_REFERER']
      h.status        = l['STATUS']
      h.visited_at    = l['DATETIME']
      h.save
    end
    count = count + 1
  end
end
```

The `Benchmark.realtime` call measures how long it takes to load the information, and the `LogParser` class parses the log for you. Specifically, the `parse_io_stream` method takes the uploaded file, parses it, and calls your block once for each record. The block is passed a hash, which looks like this:

```
---
HTTP_USER_AGENT: Mozilla/4.0 (compatible; a browser user agent here)
PATH_INFO: /some_url
HTTP_HOST: localhost
REMOTE_ADDR: 101.184.128.38
HTTP_REFERER: http://small-site.com.example/
STATUS: "200"
DATETIME: 1/Oct/2007:04:49:03 -0500
```

■**Note** HTTP_REFERER is intentionally spelled this way in the code, because that's the way it's spelled in the official HTTP standard. However, I've spelled *referrer* correctly in the schema, since the field in the `hits` table does not necessarily refer to the header but to the concept of the referrer in general. The `LogParser` class, on the other hand, uses the incorrect spelling so that it adheres to the standard.

The routine creates a new `Hit` object, sets the fields to the various values from the hash, and saves it. Then you add one to the `count` variable.

The ActiveRecord::Extensions code looks like this:

```
real_time_elapsed = Benchmark.realtime  do
  columns = [:user_agent, :path_info, :remote_addr,
             :http_referrer, :status, :visited_at]
  values = []
  LogParser.new.parse_io_stream(params[:log][:file]) do |l|
    values <<
            [ l['HTTP_USER_AGENT'],
              l['PATH_INFO'],
              l['REMOTE_ADDR'],
              l['HTTP_REFERER'],
              l['STATUS'],
              Date.parse(l['DATETIME']) ]
    count = count + 1
  end
  Hit.import columns, values, :validate=>false if values.length>0
  end
end
```

This code parses the log using `LogParser`, just as the plain Active Record code does, but it automatically uses the `import` method that ActiveRecord::Extensions adds to the `Hit` model. This `import` method imports all of the records in a single query.

Tip The `:validates=>false` option turns off validation. In this case, it doesn't make a difference, since the model doesn't include any validation. But, in general, if you're dealing with data that's guaranteed to be in a certain format, and you have expensive validations in your models, you can speed up ActiveRecord::Extensions inserts by including this optional parameter.

Finally, you create a flash notice with the number of uploaded records, the total number of records, the total time elapsed, and the rate of records being processed per minute.

```
flash[:notice] << " #{count} uploaded, #{Hit.count} total\n"
flash[:notice] << " #{'%0.2f' % real_time_elapsed} elapsed, " <<
                  "#{'%0.2f' % (count.to_f /
                           real_time_elapsed)*60
                  } records per minute ."

redirect_to :controller=>:home, :action=>:index

end
```

After creating the flash message, you redirect to the main page again. Note that you could have created a separate view that displayed the message and then offered a link back to the main page.

Next, let's take a look at the code that generates the reports. First, the report controller in app/controllers/report_controller.rb (Listing 10-3) uses rpdf to generate the PDF view.

```
class ReportController < ApplicationController

  def combined
    @rails_pdf_inline  = true

    @graph_files = {
            'Graph of per-sale costs'=>
                    get_sale_graph_tempfile,
          'Graph of total visitors from each advertiser'=>
                    get_visitor_graph_tempfile
                    }
```

```
# Note that the key is the label and the value is the
# graph filename. Note you could easily add more graphs in
# here if you'd like.

render :layout=>nil

# At this point, the images have already been embedded in the PDF,
# so we can safely delete them.

@graph_files.each do |label, filename|
  File.unlink filename
end
end
```

This code creates a hash with labels and graph file names. It uses the two graph-creation functions—get_sale_graph_tempfile and get_visitor_graph_tempfile—and passes them to the .rpdf view combined. rpdf uses the @rpf_pdf_inline variable to specify that the PDF should be displayed in the browser and not downloaded. If you set this variable to false, or don't set it at all, the PDF will be downloaded instead.

After that, the code loops through the graph temporary files and deletes them. (You cannot use Ruby's built-in Tempfile class here because you cannot specify a file extension, and both Gruff and rpdf use the file extension to determine the file format.)

The .rpdf view (Listing 10-7) is in app/views/report/combined.pdf.rpdf. As you can see, the code is reasonably straightforward:

```
pdf.select_font "Times-Roman"

figure_number = 1
@graph_files.each do |title, graph|
  pdf.image graph
  pdf.text "<i>Figure #{figure_number
                    } of #{@graph_files.length
                          }- #{title}</i>", :left=>6, :font_size=>12
  figure_number = figure_number  + 1
end
```

This code loops through the graphs passed by the controller and uses the image method from the PDF::Writer library to insert the image. Next, it labels each one with a figure number and a title.

Next, let's examine the three protected functions in the report controller, app/controllers/report_controller.rb (Listing 10-3). These functions are not publicly available as URLs. The first function creates temporary file names to save your Gruff graphs:

```
protected # Protected functions are for internal use only and
          # don't correspond to a URL.

# This function is used by the two graph functions to create a
# temporary filename.

def get_tempfile_name(prefix)
  File.join(RAILS_ROOT, "tmp/#{prefix}_#{request.env['REMOTE_ADDR']
                          }_#{Time.now.to_f
                          }_#{rand(10000)}.jpg")
end
```

Note that this solution does not absolutely guarantee unique file names, but it should work fine under most conditions. `Time.now.to_f` returns the unique timestamp in fractional seconds. It also appends a random number between one and 10,000. This should be more than sufficient to remove the possibility of collisions for your average intranet application. You would need to have the same IP accessing the same graph in the same millisecond or so to have a problem.

Note You could check if the file name has been used before using it, but this has race conditions. In situations where collisions are likely, you can look at a solution like the `ruby-stemp` library, which you can get from `http://ruby-stemp.rubyforge.org/`.

Next, let's take a look at the function in the report controller that shows the graph of visitors from each advertiser:

```
def get_visitor_graph_tempfile # Graph of visitor and purchasing visitors
  graph_tempfile_name = get_tempfile_name('visitor_graph')

  advertisers = Advertiser.find(:all)

  g = Gruff::Bar.new(1000)
  g.title = "Advertising Traffic Report"
  g.legend_font_size = 16
  advertisers.each do |a|
    visitor_addresses  = Hit.find(:all,
                     :group=>'remote_addr',
                     :conditions=>['http_referrer= ? ',
                     a.referrer_url]
                     ).map { |h| h.remote_addr }
```

```
    sale_count = Hit.count('remote_addr',
                  :conditions=>['remote_addr IN (?)
                                    AND
                                path_info LIKE "/cart/checkout%"',

                                visitor_addresses])

  g.data(a.company_name, [ visitor_addresses.length, sale_count ] )
  end

  g.labels = {0 => 'Visitors', 1 => 'Visitors With One or More Purchases' }

  g.write(graph_tempfile_name)
  graph_tempfile_name
end
```

This function uses Gruff (introduced in Chapter 3) to generate the graph. The function sets various parameters relating to the graph, and then loops through all of the advertisers. For each advertiser, it finds all of the visitors, as defined by visitors who arrive at the site by clicking a link on the referrer URL. It then finds all of the sale URLs for those visitors, which are defined as URLs that start with /cart/checkout. Note that if visitors check out multiple times, they will be counted as multiple sales, and if they click the referrer link more than once, that will be counted as multiple visits.

Then the company name of each advertiser, along with the total number of visitors and the number of visitors who have purchased something, is graphed, and the graph is written to the temporary file name created by the get_tempfile_name function. The temporary file name is returned, so that the calling function can use the graph.

Next, let's take a look at the get_sale_graph_tempfile function in the report controller:

```
def get_sale_graph_tempfile # Graph of per-click and per-sale costs

  graph_tempfile_name = get_tempfile_name('sale_graph_tempfile')

  advertisers = Advertiser.find(:all)

  g = Gruff::Bar.new(1000)

  g.title = "Cost Per Sale Report"
  g.legend_font_size = 16
  g.y_axis_label = 'Cost (USD)'

  advertisers.each do |a|
    visitor_addresses  = Hit.find(:all,
```

```
                       :group=>'remote_addr',
                       :conditions=>['http_referrer= ? ',
                       a.referrer_url]
                       ).map { |h| h.remote_addr }

    sale_count = Hit.count('remote_addr',
                     :conditions=>['remote_addr IN (?)
                        AND
                        path_info LIKE "/cart/checkout%"',
                          visitor_addresses])

    total_cost = visitor_addresses.length*a.cost_per_click
    cost_per_sale = total_cost / sale_count

    g.data(a.company_name, [a.cost_per_click, cost_per_sale ] )
  end

  g.labels = {0 => 'Cost Per Click', 1 => 'Cost Per Sale' }
  g.minimum_value = 0

  g.write(graph_tempfile_name)
  graph_tempfile_name
end
```

The graph options are slightly different from the get_visitor_graph_tempfile
function, but otherwise get_sale_graph_tempfile is similar to that function. The big difference is that instead of simply displaying the total number of visitors, it displays the cost
per click and cost per sale. It retrieves the cost per click from the advertiser, and it calculates the cost per sale by calculating the total cost of all of the clicks, then dividing it by
the total number of sales.

Summary

This chapter covered a great way to import data from Apache logs and then analyze that
data using Active Record. You can use analyses like these to intelligently choose how to
spend advertising dollars. By spending more money on advertisers with a low cost per
sale, you can be more efficient and increase your total sales.

Additionally, you saw how you can easily create PDF reports using just Ruby code,
and how you can speed up data import significantly using ActiveRecord::Extensions.
Both techniques are valuable. PDF reporting is a powerful and easy way to increase the

utility of your reports, and loading large amounts of data quickly is important to making your reports useful.

In the next chapter, you'll see how you can monitor public news about your company—or, for that matter, any RSS feed—using FeedTools, and then graph the data using CSS and HTML.

CHAPTER 11

■■■

Tracking the News with Google News

Due to the Internet, we live in a world with easy access to all types of information. Even local newspapers that were formerly inaccessible outside their locality are publishing stories online. As a result, you can catch up on localized news from all over the world. This is a significant step forward, of course, since it means you can get news about, say, Brazil, straight from the source, instead of from an Associated Press reporter who may have been in the country for only a few days. The downside is that there's an explosion of news sites—some good, some bad, and some mediocre. They are in such quantity that they can be hard to sift through, so it's difficult to extract the particular information you want from the mass of information you can access.

Fortunately, tools are available to help with the task of news organization. For example, just as Google web search makes searching for web sites easier, Google News makes searching news easier. Google News aggregates news from all over the world and lets you filter by useful constraints, such as keywords and dates. In fact, Google News can even eliminate duplicate stories (a result of news syndication companies such as the Associated Press and United Press International selling stories to dozens or hundreds of newspapers).

You can use Google News to track news topics easily and quickly. One way is to find news manually via the web interface at `http://news.google.com/`. Another approach is to use the Google News Really Simple Syndication (RSS) interface. Used in conjunction with a programming language such as Ruby, this interface allows you to manage news aggregation in ways limited only by the boundaries of your imagination.

In this chapter, you'll create a graphical report from Google News RSS data. To parse the data for this example, you'll use a handy utility called FeedTools, which we'll look at first. To create the graphs, you'll use a plug-in called CSS Graphs Helper. This is an easy-to-use tool for creating simple HTML charts, as you'll see when you create the Rails application later in the chapter.

Using FeedTools to Parse RSS

Google News provides its data in RSS form, which is an XML format, so you could parse it using a Ruby library like the standard REXML or the XmlSimple or Remarkably gems (both introduced in Chapter 9). However, FeedTools gives you the advantage of a powerful interface specific to news feeds, which makes your life much easier.

For example, here's how easy it is to print out the titles from the RubyForge news feed, which lists all the new software released on RubyForge:

```
require 'feed_tools'

newsfeed=FeedTools::Feed.open('http://rubyforge.org/export/rss_sfnews.php')

newsfeed.items.each do |item|
  puts item.title
end
```

This code results in the following output:

```
Net::NNTP Client Library:SCM is now Subversion
rb-appscript 0.5.0 released
Open Ruby on Rails Book:openrorbook Download Issues
Duration 0.1.0 released
votigoto 0.2.1 Released
Sequel 0.4.4.2 Released
```

The second line creates a new `FeedTools:Feed` object using the `open` method. The URL specified is `http://rubyforge.org/export/rss_sfnews.php`, which is the RSS feed for Ruby-Forge. The next line uses the `items` method of the feed and calls its `each` method to iterate through each feed item, and then the `title` method of each item is used to print the item titles. You can access other attributes of each item, such as the URL of the full view of the item, the date it was updated, and so forth. If it's included in the RSS feed, the full text of an item is available through the `description` method.

FeedTools can also parse Atom and Channel Definition Format (CDF) feeds, as well as generate news feeds in RSS, Atom, or CDF form. You can find out more about Feed-Tools at its home page: `http://sporkmonger.com/projects/feedtools/`.

■**Note** CDF is an obscure Microsoft format similar to RSS or Atom. You can find out more about CDF at `http://en.wikipedia.org/wiki/Channel_Definition_Format`.

Company News Coverage Reporting

Suppose your company is investing heavily in public relations in the hope that the media coverage will lead to sales. However, because so much money is being spent on a public relations firm, your managers don't want to spend additional money on a "press clipping" service. A press clipping service would monitor how well the public relations firm is doing by searching newspapers for stories, typically called *clippings*, about your firm.

Your boss hopes you can do something similar and create a report that details how many times in a day your company is mentioned in the press. Fortunately, it's easy to do this with Google News. You've decided to implement two programs to produce this report: a Ruby script that loads the Google News news reports into a database and a Rails application that performs the actual reporting.

Loading the Data

As noted, you'll use FeedTools to help load the data into a database. Install FeedTools using the following command:

```
gem install -y feedtools
```

```
Need to update xx gems from http://gems.rubyforge.org
...................
complete
Successfully installed feedtools-x.y.zz
Installing ri documentation for feedtools-x.y.zz...
Installing RDoc documentation for feedtools-x.y.zz...
```

You also need to create a database named `company_pr` and edit the `establish_connection` line at the top of the following loader script. (However, note that this code will automatically load a `config/database.yml` file if it exists, so if you run this application from the Rails application directory you'll create later, you don't need to edit the `establish_connection` line.)

Now create the loader script, as shown in Listing 11-1.

Listing 11-1. *RSS Loader (rss_loader.rb)*

```
require 'feed_tools'
require 'active_record'
require 'uri'
```

```ruby
(puts "usage: #{$0} query"; exit) unless ARGV.length==1

# If there's a config/database.yml file - like you'd find in a Rails app,
# read from that . . .

if File.exists?('./config/database.yml')
  require 'yaml'
  ActiveRecord::Base.establish_connection(
                  YAML.load(File.read('config/database.yml'))['development'])
else
  # . . . otherwise, connect to the default settings.

  ActiveRecord::Base.establish_connection(
    :adapter  => "mysql",
    :host     => "your_mysql_hostname_here",
    :username => "your_mysql_username_here",
    :password => "your_mysql_password_here",
    :database => "company_pr")
end

class Stories <  ActiveRecord::Base
end

unless Stories.table_exists?  # If this is the first time running this app,
                              # create the tables we need.

  ActiveRecord::Schema.define do
    create_table :stories do |t|
      t.column :guid, :string
      t.column :title, :string
      t.column :source, :string
      t.column :url, :string
      t.column :published_at, :datetime
      t.column :created_at, :datetime
    end
    create_table :cached_feeds do |t|
      t.column :url , :string
      t.column :title, :string
      t.column :href, :string
      t.column :link, :string
      t.column :feed_data, :text
```

```ruby
      t.column :feed_data_type, :string, :length=>25
      t.column :http_headers, :text
      t.column :last_retrieved, :datetime
    end

    # Without the following line,
    # you can't retrieve large results -
    # like those we use in this script.

    execute "ALTER TABLE cached_feeds
             CHANGE COLUMN feed_data feed_data MEDIUMTEXT;"
  end
end


output_format = 'rss'
per_page = 100
query = ARGV[0]
query_encoded = URI.encode(query) # URI.encode will escape values like "&"
                                  # that would mess up our URL.


feed_url = "http://news.google.com/news" <<
           "?hl=en&ned=us&ie=UTF-8" <<
           "&num=" << per_page <<
           "&output=" << output_format <<
           "&q=" << query_encoded

# Set up our cache:

FeedTools.configurations[:feed_cache] =  "FeedTools::DatabaseFeedCache"

# Create our feed object:

feed=FeedTools::Feed.open(feed_url)

if !feed.live?

  puts "feed is cached..."
  puts "last retrieved: #{ feed.last_retrieved }"
  puts "expires: #{ feed.last_retrieved + feed.time_to_live }"
```

```
else
  feed.items.each do |feed_story|
    if not (Stories.find_by_title(feed_story.title) or
            Stories.find_by_url(feed_story.link) or
            Stories.find_by_guid(feed_story.guid))
      puts "processing story '#{feed_story.title}' - new"
      Stories.new do |new_story|
        new_story.title=feed_story.title.gsub(/<[^>]*>/, '') # strip HTML
        new_story.guid=feed_story.guid
        new_story.sourcename=feed_story.publisher.name if feed_story.publisher.name
        new_story.url=feed_story.link
        new_story.published_at = feed_story.published
        new_story.save
      end
    else
      # do nothing
    end
  end
end
```

Save this script as `rss_loader.rb`.
You can run this script as follows:

```
ruby rss_loader.rb Microsoft
```

```
processing story 'Microsoft Exchange Troubleshooting Assistant v1.1 (MSI)
   - ZDNet' - new
processing story 'Being MVP and posting Microsoft copyrighted material without
.. - ZDNet UK' - new
. . .
```

Note You may get errors about `require_gem` being obsolete, but the script should still run fine.

Now, if you run the script again, it will detect that the feed was recently loaded and is in the cache, so it will exit:

```
ruby rss_loader.rb Microsoft
```

```
feed is cached...
last retrieved: Sun Sep 02 18:55:12 UTC 2007
expires: Sun Sep 02 19:55:12 UTC 2007
```

Not all reporting requires a script. SQL itself can be used for reporting from the MySQL client. This approach is very useful if you want to find a few pieces of information (or just one). Let's use a SQL query to verify that the data has been inserted into the MySQL database, as shown in Listing 11-2.

Listing 11-2. *SQL to Verify Data Loading*

```
mysql company_pr -u your_mysql_username -p
Password: your_password_here


mysql> SELECT id,
            CONCAT(LEFT(title,40),
                 CASE WHEN(LENGTH(title)>40)
                     THEN '...'
                     ELSE '' END) AS story_title
        FROM stories;
```

Running the query in Listing 11-2 produces results similar to the following:

```
+-----+---------------------------------------------+
| id  | story_title                                 |
+-----+---------------------------------------------+
|   1 | Judge approves final settlement in Iowa ... |
|   2 | Microsoft Webcast: Security Series (Part... |
|   3 | Security Showdown - Redmond Channel Part... |
|   4 | Linux: Hasta la Vista, Microsoft! - LXer... |
|   5 | Microsoft Vista desktops don&#39;t play... |
|   6 | Major Computer Viruses Over 25 Years - F... |
|   7 | Ford Syncs Up with Microsoft to Smooth t... |
|   8 | Sony connects with Microsoft&#39;s DRM ... |
|   9 | HP&#39;s MediaSmart Server Launch Delaye... |
|  10 | Customize Microsoft Management Console (... |
|  11 | Microsoft keeps businesses connected - B... |
|  12 | Yahoo! ups the ante in e-mail - Times On... |
|  13 | Microsoft Antitrust Settlement Is a Succ... |
|  14 | Microsoft settles eight year patent case... |
```

```
|  15 | Microsoft Delays Windows Server 2008 - C... |
 . . .
| 124 | Microsoft Exchange Troubleshooting Assis... |
| 125 | Being MVP and posting Microsoft copyrigh... |
+-----+--------------------------------------------+
95 rows in set (0.00 sec)
```

Of course, you'll get different results depending on the stories that are current when you run the script. Note that apostrophes are represented as ', which is an HTML entity equivalent to the ASCII character '. This means that the HTML entities will be correctly displayed on a web browser, although you'll need to decode them if you intend to display them in, say, a PDF or text file. (You might get more entities; they all begin with &#.)

Additionally, note the call to CONCAT, which has three parts. The first part is the call to CONCAT itself, which adds two strings together. The next two parts are the strings to add. The first string it concatenates is LEFT(title,40), which pulls out the leftmost 40 characters of the title of the story. The second string is CASE WHEN length(title)>40 THEN '...' ELSE '' END, which adds three periods after the title if the title is longer than 40 characters. In other words, if the title is longer than 40 characters, display the first 40 characters of the title followed by three periods.

■**Note** Strictly speaking, the notation after the 40-character maximum in this example should be an ellipsis, not three periods. An ellipsis is closer together, so the three periods are the width of a single character. However, text-only applications, like the MySQL console, don't have ellipses.

Now let's take a look at the code in the loading script.

Dissecting the Code

First, the script in Listing 11-1 needs to create a connection to the database:

```
# If there's a config/database.yml file,
# read from that . . .

if File.exists?('./config/database.yml')
  require 'yaml'
  ActiveRecord::Base.establish_connection(
            YAML.load(File.read('config/database.yml'))['development']
                )
```

```
else
  # . . . otherwise, connect to the default settings.
  # Note that if don't you have the default MySQL settings below,
  # you should change them.

  ActiveRecord::Base.establish_connection(
    :adapter  => "mysql",
    :host     => "your_mysql_hostname_here",
    :username => "your_mysql_username_here",
    :password => "your_mysql_password_here",
    :database => "company_pr")
end
```

If you run the script from the root of a Rails application, the information from the config/database.yml file and the parameters for the development environment are loaded. If not, it manually creates the connection with the default parameters. Note that you can change ['development'] to ['production'] on the first establish_connection line if you would prefer to use the connection parameters from the production environment.

Next, let's examine the code that contains the single model and the schema:

```
class Stories <  ActiveRecord::Base
end

unless Stories.table_exists?
  ActiveRecord::Schema.define do
    create_table :stories do |t|
      t.column :guid, :string
      t.column :title, :string
      t.column :source, :string
      t.column :url, :string
      t.column :published_at, :datetime
      t.column :created_at, :datetime
    end
    create_table :cached_feeds do |t|
      t.column :url , :string
      t.column :title, :string
      t.column :href, :string
      t.column :link, :string
      t.column :feed_data, :text
      t.column :feed_data_type, :string, :length=>25
      t.column :http_headers, :text
      t.column :last_retrieved, :datetime
    end
```

```
    # Without the following line,
    # you can't retrieve large results -
    # like those we use in this script.

    execute "ALTER TABLE cached_feeds
            CHANGE COLUMN feed_data feed_data MEDIUMTEXT;"
  end
end
```

This code creates a single model, Stories, and then creates a table for it. It also creates a second table named cached_feeds, which is used by FeedTools to store cached feeds. Note that the original schema was given in SQL on the FeedTools site, and it is a similar schema translated into a Rails migration. However, because the feed_data column contains too much data to be stored in a regular TEXT column, you use an ALTER TABLE ... CHANGE COLUMN statement to change the feed_data column to a MEDIUMTEXT type. (If Rails supported MEDIUMTEXT columns out of the box, you could have initially created it as a MEDIUMTEXT column.)

Tip You could create this database using Rails migrations as well, but in this case I've included it in this script. This is a simple way to create a database using Active Record, and it's independent of any Rails application, which means that you could use this loader and then make reports on the data from any reporting application. For example, if you did not have a Rails application and the developers in different departments of your company wrote the code to display the data as a Perl script, a Python program, an ASP.NET web application, a Crystal Reports report, or even a Microsoft Excel macro, they could still use this loader script.

Now that you have a database connection, a structure, and a model, you need to construct a Google News URL and download the data:

```
output_format = 'rss'
per_page = 100


query = ARGV[0]
query_encoded = URI.encode(query)

feed_url = "http://news.google.com/news" <<
           "?hl=en&ned=us&ie=UTF-8" <<
           "&num=" << per_page <<
           "&output=" << output_format <<
           "&q=" << query_encoded
```

```
FeedTools.configurations[:feed_cache] =  "FeedTools::DatabaseFeedCache"

feed=FeedTools::Feed.open(feed_url)
```

The URL was initially constructed by making a sample search on Google News, noting the RSS URL it generated, and creating code that generates the URL. You can follow a similar technique to create URL-generation code for other services, such as Google Blog Search, for example.

Two static variables, `output_format` and `per_page`, are used to create the URL. You can vary these as desired. Of course, you could have hard-coded them into the URL, but separating them makes it a bit easier to change. And note that you can simply change the `output_format` variable to `atom` to cause the output to be in Atom instead of RSS form. Since FeedTools can parse Atom instead of RSS seamlessly, the code will work with Atom without any other changes.

The third variable, `query_encoded`, is set by the application to be a URL-encoded version of the search string passed on the command line. The `URI.encode` function, provided by Ruby's built-in URI library, translates characters that have special meaning in URLs, such as the & character, into their encoded form.

■**Note** The difference between a Uniform Resource Identifier (URI) and a Uniform Resource Locator (URL) is generally unimportant. Strictly speaking, a URI can also be a Uniform Resource Name (URN), which can specify the identity of a thing, such as a book identified by its ISBN, without actually specifiying how to get it.

Next, you set the `FeedTools.configurations[:feed_cache]` variable to be equal to `"FeedTools::DatabaseFeedCache"`, which causes FeedTools to use its built-in `DatabaseFeedCache` class. If you're inclined to write a custom FeedTools cache class—one that stores information in, say, a `memcached` server—you can pass in a different class name. Note that it's passed in as a string, not as a class constant or a symbol.

Then you open the feed using the `FeedTools::Feed.open` method. This method is format-agnostic; it can be RSS, Atom, or CDF. Also, you don't need to use a separate method to download the URL and then pass it to FeedTools, because FeedTools downloads the feed and parses it in one step.

Finally, you add the stories to your MySQL database:

```
if !feed.live?
  puts "feed is cached..."
  puts "last retrieved: #{ feed.last_retrieved }"
  puts "expires: #{ feed.last_retrieved + feed.time_to_live }"
else
  feed.items.each do |feed_story|
```

```
    if not (Stories.find_by_title(feed_story.title) or
            Stories.find_by_url(feed_story.link) or
            Stories.find_by_guid(feed_story.guid))
      puts "processing story '#{feed_story.title}' - new"
      Stories.new do |new_story|
        new_story.title=feed_story.title.gsub(/<[^>]*>/, '') # strip HTML
        new_story.guid=feed_story.guid
        new_story.sourcename=feed_story.publisher.name if feed_story.publisher.name
        new_story.url=feed_story.link
        new_story.published_at = feed_story.published
        new_story.save
      end
    else
      # do nothing
    end
  end
end
```

If the feed isn't live—in other words, if it's cached—you print a brief message stating that, and then print the date of when it was last cached and when the cache will expire. (You could go through the data-insertion loop either way, but cached feed items are guaranteed to be in the database already, so that would just be a waste of time.) Note that some programmers believe that `unless feed.live?` is better written as `if not feed.live?`.

If the feed is live, you iterate through all of the items in the feed by using the `items` method. You check if any stories exist with the same `title`, `url`, or `guid`; if none exist, you add the story to the database. Otherwise, the story is a duplicate and you don't add the item. In most cases, it's sufficient to check by `guid` alone. However, for news items, checking by all three is a good idea, since you may eventually want to have more aggregators, which may assign the `guid` or `url` for items differently.

Creating the News Tracker Report Application

Next, let's take a look at creating a Rails application that shows the report. As noted at the beginning of the chapter, you'll use the CSS Graphs Helper plug-in to create the graphs. This provides a simple way to graph data, by creating HTML graphs using CSS. In Chapter 7, you generated custom HTML and CSS graphs using Markaby, which is the most flexible approach, but CSS Graphs Helper does this automatically.

In this example, you'll use the CSS Graphs Helper's `complex_bar_graph` method to create a thermometer-like chart. Also available are a `bar_graph` method, which creates vertical charts, and a `horizontal_bar_chart` method, which creates horizontal bar charts. You can get more information about CSS Graphs Helper and its various charts at `http://nubyonrails.com/pages/css_graphs`.

■Note Unfortunately, CSS Graphs Helper currently supports only one chart per page. And, while it's extremely easy to use, it has a limited range of chart types. If you're looking for more complicated charts or for many charts per page, consider using the Gruff graphing library (which was created by the same person who created CSS Graphs Helper). You can find examples of Gruff in Chapters 3, 4, and 10, and at the Gruff home page: `http://nubyonrails.com/pages/gruff`.

Before we start, if you haven't already installed the Rails gem, do so now:

```
gem install rails
```

Now create the framework of your Rails application as follows:

```
rails newstracker
```

```
    create  app/controllers
    create  app/helpers
    create  app/models
    create  app/views/layouts
    create  config/environments
    create  components
    create  db
    . . .
    create  log/server.log
    create  log/production.log
    create  log/development.log
    create  log/test.log
```

Next, create a report controller, as follows:

```
cd newstracker
ruby script/generate controller Reporter
```

```
    exists  app/controllers/
    exists  app/helpers/
    create  app/views/reporter
    exists  test/functional/
    create  app/controllers/reporter_controller.rb
    create  test/functional/reporter_controller_test.rb
    create  app/helpers/reporter_helper.rb
```

This controller covers a single action, which renders the report.

Your next step is to create the single model, which represents your `stories` table, as follows:

```
ruby script/generate model Story
```

```
  exists  app/models/
  exists  test/unit/
  exists  test/fixtures/
  create  app/models/story.rb
  create  test/unit/story_test.rb
  create  test/fixtures/stories.yml
  create  db/migrate
  create  db/migrate/001_create_stories.rb
```

Next, install CSS Graphs Helper by using the following command:

```
script/plugin install http://topfunky.net/svn/plugins/css_graphs
```

```
+ ./css_graphs/History.txt
+ ./css_graphs/MIT-LICENSE
+ ./css_graphs/Manifest.txt
+ ./css_graphs/README.txt
+ ./css_graphs/Rakefile
+ ./css_graphs/about.yml
+ ./css_graphs/generators/css_graphs/css_graphs_generator.rb
+ ./css_graphs/generators/css_graphs/templates/colorbar.jpg
+ ./css_graphs/generators/css_graphs/templates/g_colorbar.jpg
+ ./css_graphs/generators/css_graphs/templates/g_colorbar2.jpg
+ ./css_graphs/generators/css_graphs/templates/g_marker.gif
+ ./css_graphs/images/colorbar.jpg
+ ./css_graphs/init.rb
+ ./css_graphs/lib/css_graphs.rb
+ ./css_graphs/test/test_css_graphs.rb
```

After you install CSS Graphs Helper, you need to copy the files it uses into your `public/images` directory:

```
ruby ./script/generate css_graphs
```

```
create   public/images/css_graphs
create   public/images/css_graphs/colorbar.jpg
create   public/images/css_graphs/g_colorbar.jpg
create   public/images/css_graphs/g_colorbar2.jpg
create   public/images/css_graphs/g_marker.gif
```

Now, let's start filling in the code for the application. Add the code in Listing 11-3 to the Reporter controller.

Listing 11-3. *Reporter Controller (app/controller/reporter_controller.rb)*

```ruby
class ReporterController < ApplicationController
  def index
    custom_sql = "SELECT published_at_formatted,
                         count(*) as count

                  FROM (SELECT DATE_FORMAT(published_at,
                                           '%m-%d-%y')
                              AS published_at_formatted
                        FROM stories) AS grouped_table
                  GROUP
                     BY published_at_formatted
                  ;"

    @stories = Story.find_by_sql(custom_sql)
  end
end
```

Save this file as app/controller/reporter_controller.rb.
Next, create the single view, as shown in Listing 11-4.

Listing 11-4. *Reporter View (app/views/reporter/index.rhtml)*

```erb
<h1>Our Company In The Media</h1>

<p>
<%
  story_count_max = @stories.max { |a,b| a.count.to_i <=> b.count.to_i }.count.to_f

  story_data = @stories.map{|x| ["#{x.published_at_formatted} (#{x.count})",
                                 (x.count.to_f / story_count_max)*100]}
```

```
%>
    <%= complex_bar_graph story_data  %>
</p>
```

Save this view as `app/views/reporter/index.rhtml`.

You don't need to add any code into your model file. The defaults are fine, since the model doesn't need any relationships or other customizations. So, your application is all set.

At this point, you'll need to edit the `config/database.yml` file with your database connection parameters.

You can run this script using the following command:

```
ruby script/server
```

Now open a web browser and browse to `http://localhost:3000/reporter/`. You should see a screen similar to Figure 11-1.

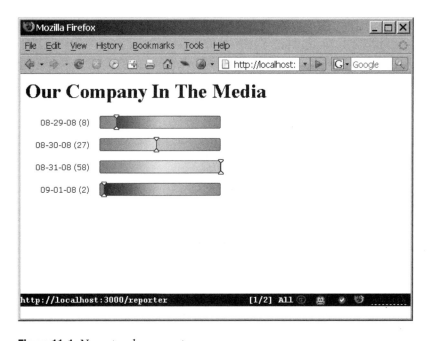

Figure 11-1. *News tracker report*

Next, let's take a look at this example line by line.

Dissecting the Code

First, let's take a look at the single method in the controller (Listing 11-3):

```
def index
  custom_sql = "SELECT published_at_formatted,
                      count(*) as count

                FROM (SELECT DATE_FORMAT(published_at,
                                         '%m-%d-%y')
                           AS published_at_formatted
                         FROM stories) AS grouped_table
              GROUP
                 BY published_at_formatted
              ;"

  @stories = Story.find_by_sql(custom_sql)
end
```

The SQL statement here pulls out each date on which a story was published and how
many stories where published that day. You use a nested query to group by a function
call. You could group by `published_at` directly, but then you would get each distinct time.
Since you cannot group by the result of a function call directly, you use a subquery to
return a set of rows with the date properly formatted, and then group by the new calculated field.

The list of stories is plugged into the `@stories` variable, which is used by the view
(Listing 11-4), as follows:

```
<h1>Our Company In The Media</h1>

<p>
<%
  story_count_max = @stories.max { |a,b| a.count.to_i <=> b.count.to_i }.count.to_f

  story_data = @stories.map{|x| ["#{x.published_at_formatted} (#{x.count})",
                                 (x.count.to_f / story_count_max)*100]}

%>
    <%= complex_bar_graph story_data  %>
</p>
```

The first two lines of code in the view prepare the data for the third line of code. The
`complex_bar_graph` method expects an array whose elements are each two-element arrays.
These two-element arrays consist of a label element followed by a value element. The
value element is expected to be in the range of 0 to 100, so you first calculate the maximum `count` value. Then you use Ruby's built-in `map` method to transform the array of

Story objects into an array of two-element arrays—what `complex_bar_graph` wants as an argument.

■**Note** Why isn't the data in Listing 11-4 in the controller instead of the view? The reason is that it's view-specific. If you were using, say, the Open Flash Chart component (introduced in Chapter 5), you would need the data in a different format. By separating the data from the presentation, as you've done here, you can change the way the data is graphed without changing the controller.

In this example, you use Ruby's built-in `max` method, which is part of `Enumerable`, to find the maximum count. You can use this method on hashes, arrays, or any other vaguely list-like structure. It might be faster to make an additional query in the database, but since you likely have only a few records, you use the Ruby built-in method instead. Generally, you should have database calls only in the controller, but you need to find the maximum input value because of a quirk in the `complex_bar_graph` method, which is a concern of the view only.

The call to `max` compares each of the element's `count` fields, but you convert them to an integer before comparing them. This is because Active Record doesn't automatically detect that the field is a string, so it compares them as strings unless you explicitly convert them.

Summary

Google News is a great news aggregator, which can be used to tap into a worldwide array of news sources. Fortunately, as you've seen in this chapter, FeedTools makes accessing it easy, and CSS Graphs Helper is a great way to present that and other data quickly and easily.

The next chapter shows how you can take data from a web application and make it easily accessible on a desktop machine with Windows and Microsoft Office. This way, Windows users can access data using familiar tools.

CHAPTER 12

■■■

Creating Reports with Ruby and Microsoft Office

For many businesspeople, knowing how to use a computer means knowing how to use Microsoft Office running under Microsoft Windows on a PC. While adoption of open source office software like OpenOffice.org and open source operating systems like Linux is on the rise—and many developers, including myself, strongly prefer them—Microsoft software in ubiquitous in corporate America. Of course, this is less of an issue for web-based applications, since HTML is well standardized, and with a relatively small amount of effort, you can produce applications that work across platforms. However, occasionally, you'll still need to interact directly with applications running on Microsoft Windows systems, which can be difficult, since Microsoft Office programs have proprietary, relatively closed formats.

In this chapter, we'll look at some ways to create reports with Ruby and Microsoft Office programs, and then work through an example of producing a web-based system that sends its data to an Access database.

Interacting with Microsoft Office

Microsoft Excel, Word, and Access are familiar to many users. Managers and other businesspeople are trained to manipulate data in Excel, and letting them use Excel as an input format gives them a great deal more power. In fact, you may not even get a choice whether to use Excel, since it may be already deeply ingrained in the business model or directly supplied to you by vendors. Microsoft Word is typically the word processor of choice for organizations of all types. Microsoft Access is also a convenient platform. End users can use data from Access to import data into Word and Excel; mail merges, for example, are often done using data from Access.

Let's look at some ways that you can create reports that interact with these familiar Microsoft Office programs.

Working with Microsoft Excel

Suppose you need to read data supplied in a Microsoft Excel file. Since this is a proprietary, closed format, there's no easy way to parse it. Fortunately, others in the open source community have already done the work in the form of the parseexcel gem. (Unfortunately, the parse-excel gem did not work with the Excel files I generated while writing this chapter, so I cannot recommend this technique at this time; however, by the time you read this, the situation may have changed.)

If you simply want to display an Excel spreadsheet in the browser, you can consider using unexcel, which is an open source Perl script that takes Excel files and converts them to HTML. You can find this tool at http://sourceforge.net/projects/unexcel.

When you need to directly export data to Excel, you can use the spreadsheet-excel gem, as discussed in detail in Chapter 4. Additionally, the example in Chapter 13 demonstrates how to use a trick to easily export an HTML file containing tabular data to Excel (and OpenOffice.org as well).

Working with Microsoft Word

You can convert Word documents into PDF or HTML with the Antiword or wvWare utilities, but support for formatting is spotty. I've deployed solutions based on both, and in my experience, clients become extremely displeased with tools that work great for some files but break down with other files.

In theory, at least, you could run an open source word processor like AbiWord or OpenOffice.org from the command line and generate Microsoft Word documents that way. Both are fairly large software packages, however, and you would likely encounter long startup times and need a lot of software you would otherwise not require on your deployment server. Also, both OpenOffice.org and AbiWord have imperfect Word filters, although support is improving. So, this is a conceivable solution, if that's the route you want to take.

When you want to write to Microsoft Word files, you'll typically need a small piece of software running on your clients' desktop machines under Windows. This software can use the Component Object Model (COM) to speak directly to your clients' Microsoft Office installation, and thus create the files using Word (or Access) itself. That's the approach we will take in this chapter's example.

Note COM is a platform used for, among other things, interprocess communication. It lets applications control other applications using an object-oriented interface. You can find out more about COM at http://en.wikipedia.org/wiki/Component_object_model.

To directly import data into Word, you can use the Win32OLE library. In fact, it can help you access any Windows COM library. Listing 12-1 shows a simple example of using Win32OLE to create a Word document (you'll need Microsoft Word installed to run this example).

Listing 12-1. *Creating a Word Document with Win32OLE (create_word_document.rb)*

```ruby
require 'win32ole'

word_app = WIN32OLE.new('Word.Application')
word_app.visible = true
word_document = word_app.Documents.add

current_selection = word_app.selection
current_selection.TypeText "Dear Mr Executive, \n"
current_selection.TypeText "I hereby resign my post as chief programmer. "
current_selection.TypeText "\n\n"
current_selection.TypeText "Sincerely,\n"
current_selection.TypeText "Mr. T. Tom\n"

word_document.SaveAs 'resignation_letter.doc'
```

If you run the code in Listing 12-1, you will see a screen similar to Figure 12-1.

The `TypeText` method in Listing 12-1 adds text to the resignation letter. You can find out more about this method at `http://msdn2.microsoft.com/en-us/library/6b9478cs(VS.80).aspx`.

A huge amount of other options are available through Win32OLE. For example, if you add the line `word_app.PrintOut` to the end of Listing 12-1, it will print the document before quitting. You can find out how to do virtually any kind of Object Linking and Embedding (OLE) Microsoft Office automation through the Microsoft Developer Network (MSDN) documentation.

You don't always need to use Win32OLE directly to control Microsoft Office programs. A number of other possibilities for working with Word are available. For example, you can use Word to do a mail merge from, say, a dynamically generated Excel document, as in the example in Chapter 4. Or, you can create a template .doc file, open it, and replace keywords with dynamically generated data. For details on the various ways you can use Microsoft Word, see the MSDN documentation at `http://msdn2.microsoft.com/en-us/library/kw65a0we(VS.80).aspx`. You'll need to translate the code from the languages these techniques provide into Ruby, but as demonstrated in Listing 12-1, that's reasonably straightforward.

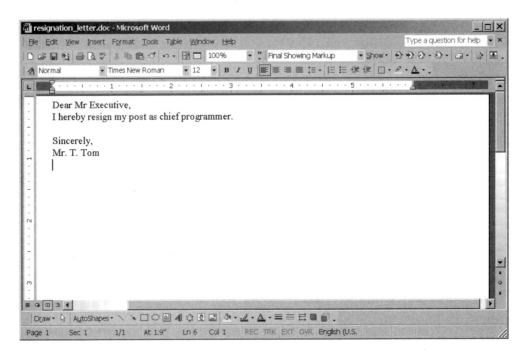

Figure 12-1. *Importing data into Word with Win32OLE*

Working with Microsoft Access

To export Microsoft Access files, you can use MDB Tools (`http://mdbtools.sourceforge.net/`), an open source project. You can use MDB to convert Access databases (which have the extension `.mdb`, hence the name MDB Tools) to a more open database architecture, such as PostgreSQL or MySQL. For that matter, you can also convert to proprietary databases that support standard SQL, such as Sybase and Oracle.

If you would like to manipulate an Access database without completely converting it, you can use DBI, which is a simple database library for Ruby. If you've used Perl's DBI, the version for Ruby is similar. It has support for a Perl DBI-style interface as well as a more familar Ruby interface. You'll take this approach in this chapter's example, in the "Importing the XML Data into Microsoft Access" section.

Importing Web-Form Data into an Access Database

Suppose that you work for a training company that has a large number of students from industry. Students are sent from client companies in the hope of getting them industrial certifications, and each student must pass two classes in order to be certified.

Currently, each trainer submits Excel spreadsheets with the grades of each student, and the training program administrator merges all of the spreadsheets into one master Access database. From that Access database, the administrator creates a report of all the students who have achieved a passing grade in both classes. Merging the data is time consuming, and often the Excel spreadsheets are created with different headings and notes in individual fields, which makes the import process harder.

The administrator would like you to create a reporting system to make the process smoother. She wants to replace Excel spreadsheets with a web form, but she is not willing to give up her Access database. Therefore, she wants you to create a web-based entry system with some way to automatically import the data into Access.

Fortunately, you can do this fairly easily with Ruby, Rails, and a few gems. The application will be split up into two parts: a web interface to enter data and then serve the data as XML, and a small, Windows-only, application that will go on the administrator's desktop. When the administrator wants to update her database, she simply drags her database onto the Update Program icon.

First, let's start creating the Rails application.

Creating the Web Interface

Begin the Rails application by creating the framework:

```
rails training_app
```

```
       create  app/controllers
       create  app/helpers
       create  app/models
       create  app/views/layouts
       create  config/environments
       create  components
       create  db
       create  doc
       create  lib
       . . .
       create  log/production.log
       create  log/development.log
       create  log/test.log
```

Next, create the first controller for this application, which will contain the main page of the application:

```
cd training_app
ruby script/generate controller homepage
```

```
       exists  app/controllers/
       exists  app/helpers/
       create  app/views/homepage
       exists  test/functional/
       create  app/controllers/homepage_controller.rb
       create  test/functional/homepage_controller_test.rb
       create  app/helpers/homepage_helper.rb
```

Now add the code for the home page controller, shown in Listing 12-2.

Listing 12-2. *Homepage Controller (app/controllers/homepage_controller.rb)*

```
class HomepageController < ApplicationController
  def index
  end
end
```

Save this file as app/controllers/homepage_controller.rb. This controller has just a single view, shown in Listing 12-3.

Listing 12-3. *Homepage Index View (app/views/homepage/index.html.erb)*

```
<h1>Training Log Application</h1>

<p>Actions:</p>

<ul><li><%=link_to 'Upload Log', :action=>:upload, :controller=>:log %>
    <li><%=link_to 'Download XML', :action=>:index, :controller=>:log %>
</ul>
```

Save this code as app/views/homepage/index.html.erb.
Next, create the log controller, which will keep a log of all of the students' grades:

```
ruby script/generate controller log
```

```
       exists  app/controllers/
       exists  app/helpers/
```

```
create  app/views/uploader
exists  test/functional/
create  app/controllers/log_controller.rb
create  test/functional/log_controller_test.rb
create  app/helpers/log_helper.rb
```

This controller will have an upload action to add new data and a view action to view the old data. Listing 12-4 shows the code.

Listing 12-4. *Log Controller (app/controllers/log_controller.rb)*

```ruby
class LogController < ApplicationController
  def upload
    if request.post?
      count = 0
      training_class = TrainingClass.find_by_id(params[:training_class_id])
      training_class_date = Date.parse(params[:training_class_date])
      params[:trainee].each do |index, t|
        next if t[:name]==''
        student = Student.find_or_create_by_name_and_employer( t[:name],
                                                               t[:employer])

        student.grades.create(:percentage_grade => t[:grade],
                    :training_class=>training_class,
                    :took_class_at=>training_class_date)
      count = count +1
      end
      flash[:notice]="#{count} Entries Uploaded!"
    end
  end
  def index
    @grades = Grade.find(:all)
    render(:layout=>false)
  end
end
```

Save this file as app/controllers/log_controller.rb.

Now create the views for the log controller's actions. The first view lets the students enter data, as shown in Listing 12-5.

Listing 12-5. *Log Uploader View (app/views/log/upload.html.erb)*

```erb
<%@title='Upload Training Log'
  number_of_elements_displayed = 10
%>
<% form_tag do %>
  <p>Class: <%=select ('training_class_id', nil,
                      TrainingClass.find(:all).map { |c|
                                          [c.name, c.id] } )%>
      Date: <%= calendar_date_select_tag "training_class_date",
                      Date.today.strftime('%B %d, %Y') %></p>

<table>
  <tr><th>Trainee Name</th> <th>Trainee Employer</th> <th>Grade</th></tr>
  <%1.upto(number_of_elements_displayed) do |i|%>
    <tr>
      <td><%=text_field "trainee", 'name',:index=>i %></td>
      <td><%=text_field "trainee", 'employer', :index=>i %></td>
      <td><%=text_field "trainee", 'grade', :index=>i, :size=>3, :value=>'0'%>%</td>
    </tr>

  <%end%>
  <tr><td><%=submit_tag 'Upload', :class=>'submit_button'%>

  </table>
<%end%>
```

Save this as app/views/log/upload.html.erb.

The other view lets you download the data as XML, as shown in Listing 12-6.

Listing 12-6. *XML Download View (app/views/log/index.xml.builder)*

```
xml.instruct! :xml, :version=>"1.0"
xml.instruct! 'xml-stylesheet', :href=>'/stylesheets/log.css'

xml.grades do
 xml.css :href=>'/stylesheets/log.css'
  @grades.each do |grade|
    xml.grade do
      xml.id          grade.id
      xml.student     grade.student.name
      xml.employer    grade.student.employer
```

```
      xml.class          grade.training_class.name
      xml.grade          grade.percentage_grade
      xml.took_class_at grade.took_class_at
    end
  end
end
```

Save this as `app/views/log/index.xml.builder`.

You'll notice a reference to a stylesheet for your XML. Let's create that now, as shown in Listing 12-7.

Listing 12-7. *XML Download Stylesheet (public/stylesheets/log.css)*

```
* {
  display:block;
  font-family: helvetica, verdana, sans-serif;
}
grades {
  padding:1em;
}
grade {
  margin-top:1em;
}
student {
  font-weight: bold;
}
```

Note that this stylesheet affects only your XML, not your HTML views.

You now have two views, but no layout. Let's create a layout for them, as shown in Listing 12-8.

Listing 12-8. *Application-Wide Layout (app/views/layout/application.html.erb)*

```
<html>
  <head>
    <title>Training Uploader Application <%=@title || ''%></title>
    <%= stylesheet_link_tag 'training.css'%>
    <%= javascript_include_tag :defaults %>
    <%= calendar_date_select_includes "silver"%>
  </head>
  <body>
    <h1><%=@title%></h1>
```

```
<%flash.each do |type,msg|%>
  <div class="flash_<%=type%>">
    <%=msg%>
  </div>
<%end%>
<%=yield%>
</body>
</html>
```

Save this as app/views/layout/application.html.erb.

Note that the layout includes a link to training.css, so you'll need to create that next, as shown in Listing 12-9.

Listing 12-9. *Application Stylesheet (public/stylesheet/training.css)*

```
* { font-family: helvetica, verdana, sans-serif; }

div.flash_notice { padding:1em; border: 2px dashed #cecece; margin: 1em 0;}

input.submit_button { width:120px; height:30px; }
```

Save this file as public/stylesheet/training.css.

Now generate a model, which represents students taking the course:

```
ruby script/generate model student
```

```
      exists  app/models/
      exists  test/unit/
      exists  test/fixtures/
      create  app/models/student.rb
      create  test/unit/student_test.rb
      create  test/fixtures/students.yml
      create  db/migrate
      create  db/migrate/001_create_students.rb
```

You'll notice it creates a migration for you automatically. Fill that in as shown in Listing 12-10.

Listing 12-10. *Create Students Table Migration (db/migrate/001_create_students.rb)*

```
class CreateStudents < ActiveRecord::Migration
  def self.up
    create_table :students do |t|
      t.string :name,    :limit=>45
      t.string :employer, :limit=>45
      t.timestamps
    end
  end

  def self.down
    drop_table :students
  end
end
```

Note that the `limit` clause sets a maximum amount of characters in each column. Listing 12-11 shows the code for your `student` model.

Listing 12-11. *Student Model (app/models/student.rb)*

```
class Student < ActiveRecord::Base
  has_many :grades
end
```

Save this as `app/models/student.rb`.

You also need to generate a `grade` model, which represents the grade each student received for each class:

```
ruby script/generate model grade
```

```
      exists   app/models/
      exists   test/unit/
      exists   test/fixtures/
      create   app/models/grade.rb
      create   test/unit/grade_test.rb
      create   test/fixtures/grades.yml
      exists   db/migrate
      create   db/migrate/002_create_grades.rb
```

Next, add the code shown in Listing 12-12 to your second migration.

Listing 12-12. *Create Grades Table Migration (db/migrate/002_create_grades.rb)*

```ruby
class CreateGrades < ActiveRecord::Migration
  def self.up
    create_table :grades do |t|
      t.integer :student_id
      t.integer :training_class_id
      t.integer :percentage_grade
      t.datetime :took_class_at
      t.timestamps
    end
  end

  def self.down
    drop_table :grades
  end
end
```

Listing 12-13 shows the code for the grade model.

Listing 12-13. *Grade Model (app/models/grade.rb)*

```ruby
class Grade < ActiveRecord::Base
  belongs_to :student
  belongs_to :training_class
end
```

Save this as app/models/grade.rb.
Finally, create the last model, training_class:

```
ruby script/generate model training_class
```

```
exists  app/models/
exists  test/unit/
exists  test/fixtures/
create  app/models/training_class.rb
create  test/unit/training_class_test.rb
create  test/fixtures/training_class.yml
```

```
exists  db/migrate
create  db/migrate/003_create_training_class.rb
```

The code for the third and last migration is shown in Listing 12-14.

Listing 12-14. *Create Training Classes Table Migration (db/migrate/003_create_training_class.rb)*

```ruby
class CreateTrainingClasses < ActiveRecord::Migration
  def self.up
    create_table :training_classes do |t|
      t.string :name, :limit=>45
    end
  end

  def self.down
    drop_table :training_classes
  end
end
```

Listing 12-15 shows the code for the `training_class` model.

Listing 12-15. *Training Class Model (app/models/training_class.rb)*

```ruby
class TrainingClass < ActiveRecord::Base
  has_many :grades
end
```

Save this as app/models/training_class.rb.

Now you need to create a database named `training_development`, and then edit your config/database.yml file with the MySQL connection settings for your machine.

Then you can run the three migrations:

```
rake db:migrate
```

```
(in /path/to/your/project)
== CreateStudents: migrating ===================================================
-- create_table(:students)
   -> 0.0310s
== CreateStudents: migrated (0.0310s) ==========================================
```

```
== CreateGrades: migrating ====================================================
-- create_table(:grades)
   -> 0.0000s
== CreateGrades: migrated (0.0000s) ===========================================

== CreateTrainingClasses: migrating ===========================================
-- create_table(:training_classes)
   -> 0.0150s
== CreateTrainingClasses: migrated (0.0150s) ==================================
```

Next, add some data to your `training_classes` table, as shown in Listing 12-16.

Listing 12-16. *Training Class Table Data (db/data/training_class_data.sql)*

```
INSERT INTO training_classes (name)
   VALUES ('Practical Exopaleontology'),
          ('Pro Quantum Biology');
```

Make a directory called `data` under the `db` directory, and save this as `db/data/training_class_data.sql`. Import it with the following command:

```
mysql training_development < db/data/training_class_data.sql
```

Next, set up your routes, as shown in Listing 12-17.

Listing 12-17. *Routes File (config/routes.rb)*

```
ActionController::Routing::Routes.draw do |map|
  map.root :controller => "homepage"

  map.connect '/log', :controller => 'log',
              :action => 'index', :format => 'xml'

  map.connect ':controller/:action/:id.:format'
  map.connect ':controller/:action/:id'
end
```

Note that to make the `index` action of your `homepage` controller the page for /, you also need to delete the file `public/index.html.erb`, so do that now.

To improve the interface, you'll use the Calendar Date Select plug-in, which gives you a nice calendar from which to pick dates. Users often prefer selecting dates from calendars, since they can verify the entry visually. Install the plug-in with this command:

```
ruby script/plugin install ➡
://calendardateselect.googlecode.com/svn/tags/calendar_date_select
```

Finally, run the script using the following command:

```
ruby script/server
```

You can see the application by pointing a web browser to `http://localhost:3000/`.

Click Upload Log. You should see a screen similar to Figure 12-2. Enter a few fictitious names, employers, and grades. A passing grade is 70, and the report groups by passing grades, so enter at least one grade of at least 70.

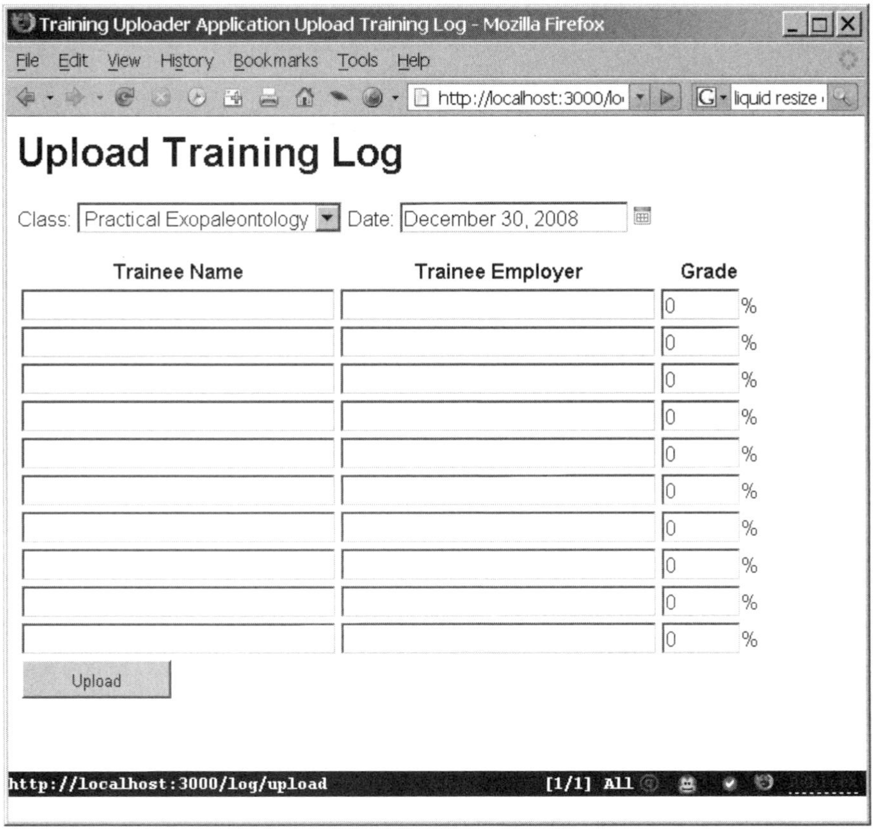

Figure 12-2. *Training Log Uploader*

Let's look at the important parts of the code.

Dissecting the Code

The log controller has two methods. The first controls uploading new logs. Let's examine its associated view (Listing 12-5):

```
<%@title='Upload Training Log'
  number_of_elements_displayed = 10
%>
<% form_tag do %>
  <p>Class: <%=select ('training_class_id', nil,
                    TrainingClass.find(:all).map { |c|
                                            [c.name, c.id] }) %>
    Date: <%= calendar_date_select_tag "training_class_date",
                    Date.today.strftime('%B %d, %Y') %></p>
```

These two input controls are used to set the TrainingClass (that is, either Practical Exopaleontology or Pro Quantum Ethnology) and the date for the rest of the form. The date control uses the calendar_date_select helper, which creates a regular text box with a button to select the date using a drop-down calendar.

The rest of the view is concerned with creating the individual rows to enter trainee grades:

```
<table>
  <tr><th>Trainee Name</th> <th>Trainee Employer</th> <th>Grade</th></tr>
  <%1.upto(number_of_elements_displayed) do |i|%>
    <tr>
      <td><%=text_field "trainee", 'name',:index=>i %> </td>
      <td><%=text_field "trainee", 'employer', :index=>i %></td>
      <td><%=text_field "trainee", 'grade', :index=>i, :size=>3, :value=>'0'%>%</td>
    </tr>

  <%end%>
  <tr><td><%=submit_tag 'Upload', :class=>'submit_button'%></td></tr>

  </table>
<%end%>
```

Note the :index option passed to each text_field element. This lets you submit multiple objects with the same name, and Rails turns them into an array before passing them to your controller.

Let's examine the controller part of this action next (in Listing 12-4):

```ruby
def upload
  if request.post?

    count = 0
    training_class = TrainingClass.find_by_id(params[:training_class_id])
    training_class_date = Date.parse(params[:training_class_date])
```

First, this code checks if the form has been submitted yet by checking the request.post? flag. If the request.post? flag is set, then the request is an HTTP POST request, which means that the user has submitted the form. After that, it sets a few variables. It finds the appropriate TrainingClass, which the user has selected using a drop-down list, and then parses the user-entered date. These variables will be used to assign a date and a TrainingClass to each grade entered on the form.

Next, you loop through the params[:trainee] array, which has one entry for each row of your form, and add a grade object for each of them:

```ruby
params[:trainee].each do |index, t|

  next if t[:name]==''



  student = Student.find_or_create_by_name_and_employer( t[:name],
                                                          t[:employer])

  student.grades.create(:percentage_grade => t[:grade],
                    :training_class=>training_class,
                  :took_class_at=>training_class_date)
    count = count +1
  end
  flash[:notice]="#{count} Entries Uploaded!"
  end
end
```

Note the use of find_or_create_by_name_and_employer. This dynamically generated finder returns an existing Student object with that name and employer if it already exists; if not, it creates a new one.

■Note Using the dynamically generated finder means that a typo in the name or employer field will create a new Student record, which may be a problem. If so, you might prefer to require that users maintain separate lists of trainees and employers and select them from a drop-down list. Although that would be more awkward, it would reduce the chances of incorrect data input.

In the log controller, the following code displays your data as XML:

```
def all
  @grades = Grade.find(:all)
  render :layout=>false # Only renders as XML...
end
```

This controller action is pretty simple. It finds all of the grades and renders all the action without a layout, since it's XML and the layout is a builder template. Here's the view itself (Listing 12-6):

```
xml.instruct! :xml, :version=>"1.0"
xml.instruct! 'xml-stylesheet', :href=>'/stylesheets/log.css'

xml.grades do
  @grades.each do |grade|
    xml.grade do
      xml.student        grade.student.name
      xml.id             grade.id
      xml.employer       grade.student.employer
      xml.class          grade.training_class.name
      xml.grade          grade.percentage_grade
      xml.took_class_at grade.took_class_at
    end
  end
end
```

This code is an XML builder template, which is the most common way to create XML output in Rails. The template gives you a builder object, and the builder object assumes undefined methods represent tag names, so the `xml.grades` call creates a `<grades>` element. The code then loops through all of the grades and creates a `<grade>` element for each grade with the various properties set: `student`, `id`, and so forth. The initial calls to `xml.instruct!` give various metadata about the document, including the XML version and the location of the stylesheet.

Note XML stylesheets affect the way the data looks when viewed in a browser. This approach is not as flexible as using XSLT, but it's much more straightforward.

Importing the XML Data into Microsoft Access

Now that you have a web application that serves up XML, you need a program to import the data into Access. For this example, you'll use the DBI database library for Ruby, mentioned earlier in the chapter. DBI comes with the Ruby one-click installer, but in order to get DBI to work with ActiveX Data Objects (ADO), you'll need to install the ADO driver. (ADO is one of many Microsoft technologies for accessing databases.)

Create a directory called C:\ruby\lib\ruby\site_ruby\X.Y\DBD\ADO. Replace X.Y with the appropriate Ruby version, and if your Ruby isn't installed in C:\ruby, modify the path appropriately). Grab the latest Ruby-DBI package from http://rubyforge.org/projects/ruby-dbi (you'll need at least version 0.1.1), and unzip the file src/lib/dbd_ado/ADO.rb into that directory. You'll need an appropriate decompression utility to unzip the tar.gz file, such as 7-Zip (http://www.7-zip.org/).

Of course, the ability to insert data into the database isn't enough, You also need to be able to retrieve the XML from the server and parse it. Let's use XmlSimple. As you saw in Chapter 9, XmlSimple is a very simple XML parser designed to turn complex XML data into a collection of hashes and arrays. (It's based on the Perl XML::Simple library, so if you've used that, it will be familiar.) You'll also need to install the rubyscript2exe gem. Install both gems as follows:

```
gem install -y xml-simple rubyscript2exe
```

Begin by creating the data loader, as shown in Listing 12-18.

Listing 12-18. *Access Data Loader (training_loader.rb)*

```
require 'dbi'
require 'xmlsimple'
require 'yaml'
require 'open-uri'
require 'swin'

database_path = ARGV[0]

unless database_path # If no path was specified on the command line,
                     # then ask for one.

  # You can find out more about Windows common dialogs here:
  # http://msdn2.microsoft.com/en-us/library/ms646949.aspx
  # You can find the header file with the full list of constants
  # here:
  # http://doc.ddart.net/msdn/header/include/commdlg.h.html
```

```ruby
    OFN_HIDEREADONLY   =   0x0004
    OFN_PATHMUSTEXIST  =   0x0800
    OFN_FILEMUSTEXIST  =   0x1000


    filetype_filter =[['Access Database (*.mdb)','*.mdb'],
             ['All files (*.*)', '*.*']]
    database_path = SWin::CommonDialog::openFilename(
                                      nil,
                                      filetype_filter,
                                      OFN_HIDEREADONLY |
                                      OFN_PATHMUSTEXIST |
                                      OFN_FILEMUSTEXIST,
                                      'Choose a database')

  exit if database_path.nil?
end

begin

  domain = '127.0.0.1'
  port = '3000'

  xml = open("http://#{domain}:#{port}/log/all").read
  grades = XmlSimple.xml_in(xml)['grade']
  puts YAML.dump(grades)
  imported_count = 0
  DBI.connect("DBI:ADO:" <<
              "Provider=Microsoft.Jet.OLEDB.4.0;" <<
              "Data Source=#{database_path}") do |dbh|

    grades.each do |grade_raw|
      g ={}
      grade_raw.each do |key,value|
        if value.length == 1
          g[key] = value.first
        else
          g[key] = value
        end
      end
      #g.map! { g.length==1 ? g.first  : g}
```

```
      sql = "SELECT COUNT(*)
            FROM grades
           WHERE id=?;"
      dbh.select_all(sql, g['id'].to_i) do |row|
        count = *row
        if count == 0
          sql = 'INSERT INTO  grades
                    (id, student,
                      employer, grade,
                      class_date, class_name)
                VALUES (?,?,?,?,?, ?);'
          dbh.do(sql, g['id'], g['student'],
               g['employer'], g['grade'],
               Date.parse(g['took_class_at']),
               g['class']
             );
          dbh.commit
          imported_count = imported_count + 1
        end
      end
    end
  end


  SWin::Application.messageBox  "Done! #{imported_count} records imported.",
                                "All done!"
rescue
  SWin::Application.messageBox  $!, "Error while importing"
end
```

Save this as training_loader.rb.

Before you run the example, make sure that the Rails application you created in the previous section is running. You can start it using the command ruby script/server. Then download the sample training.mdb file from the Source/Downloads area of the Apress web site (http://www.apress.com) or from http://rubyreporting.com/examples/training.mdb.

Run this loader as follows:

```
ruby training_loader.rb
```

It should present you with a file open dialog box similar to Figure 12-3. Select the training.mdb database, and you'll get a message box notifiying you how many records were imported.

■Tip You can also pass this script an argument on the command line. Users may like dialog boxes, but there is no reason not to make your scripts accessible via a more familar Unix-style command-line interface. For example, you could use the Windows scheduler to run this command once an hour, which means that the user would not need to update the database manually.

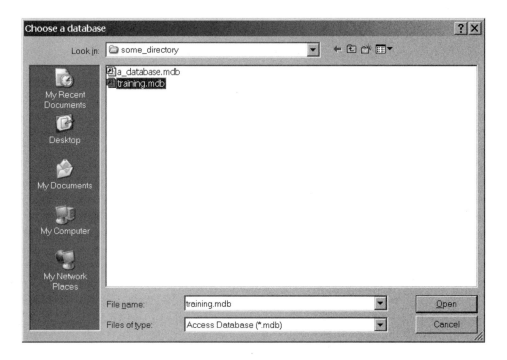

Figure 12-3. *Choosing a database*

Next, open the `training.mdb` database in Access, click the Reports tab, and then double-click the Passing Trainees report. You will see a report similar to Figure 12-4.

As you can see, your script successfully imported the data into Access. If you added more data to your application and reran the loader script, it would load only the new data, so it is safe to use repeatedly.

However, the solution is still not well suited for the administrator, since running the script requires a Ruby interpreter. It would be easier to install if it were just a single executable. Let's use `rubyscript2exe` to reduce this to an EXE file so that the end user can run it directly on her desktop.

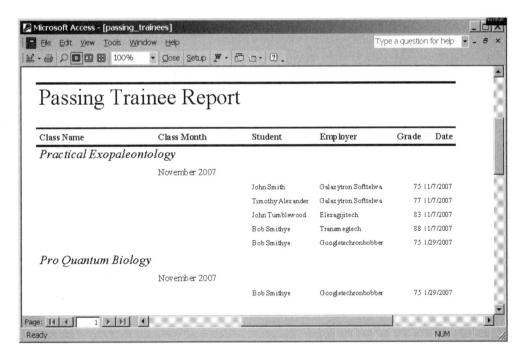

Figure 12-4. *Access passing trainees report*

First, install `rubyscript2exe`:

```
gem install rubyscript2exe
```

Next, compile it as follows:

```
rubyscript2exe training_loader.rb C:\full\path\to\training.mdb
```

```
Tracing training_loader...
Gathering files...
Copying files...
Creating training_loader.exe ...
```

This will create a `training_loader.exe` file, which can perform all of the functions that your original script performed. In fact, it will work even if you install it on a machine without Ruby installed, although you would need to change the hard-coded server address in the script, since it always looks for a Rails application running on `localhost`. You could store the information in a text file or in the Windows registry if you wanted.

■Note The reason the call includes the reference to the database is that when you use `rubyscript2exe`, it runs the program once to determine the required libraries. However, the database driver won't be loaded until the connection to the database is made, and if you don't run the script until that point, the driver won't be included.

Let's examine the code line by line.

Dissecting the Code

First, the loader script (Listing 12-18) checks to see whether a database was passed on the command line:

```
database_path = ARGV[0]

unless database_path # If no path was specified on the command line,
                     # then ask for one.

  # You can find out more about Windows common dialogs here:
  # http://msdn2.microsoft.com/en-us/library/ms646949.aspx
  # You can find the header file with the full list of constants
  # here:
  # http://doc.ddart.net/msdn/header/include/commdlg.h.html

  OFN_HIDEREADONLY  = 0x0004
  OFN_PATHMUSTEXIST = 0x0800
  OFN_FILEMUSTEXIST = 0x1000

  filetype_filter =[['Access Database (*.mdb)','*.mdb'],
                    ['All files (*.*)', '*.*']]

  database_path = SWin::CommonDialog::openFilename(
                                    nil,
                                    filetype_filter,
                                    OFN_HIDEREADONLY |
                                    OFN_PATHMUSTEXIST |
                                    OFN_FILEMUSTEXIST,
                                    'Choose a database')

  exit if database_path.nil?
end
```

If no database was passed, a Windows common dialog box is displayed, asking the user to choose a database file. This is achieved using the `SWin::CommonDialog::openFilename` method, which has the following parameters:

Parent window: Since you don't have any windows in this example, the parent window parameter is `nil`. In this case, having no owner window won't change anything. If you're interested in the cases where it does, you can read the gory details at `http://msdn2.microsoft.com/en-us/library/ms646839.aspx`.

Filter: The filter parameter is an array of two-element arrays. The first member of each two-element array is a string with a description, and the second is a string with a wildcard. This lets the user select the type of files displayed. The program has two filters: an Access database filter showing only files with an .mdb extension, and an "all files" filter showing all files. Although virtually all Access databases have an .mdb extension, it's convention to give the user the option of viewing all files. Note that this file-type filtration mechanism is intended for convenience and not for security. If the user types a new filter into the file name box and presses Enter, that filter will override the programmer-supplied filters.

Flags: This parameter is a bit field. You set individual options by bitwise ORing them together. (It would be more Ruby-like to instead use an options hash, but the designer of this interface has chosen to stick more closely to the Win32 API.) You set three options. The first is `OFN_HIDEREADONLY`, which hides the "read-only" check box. This check box exists by default and allows the users to indicate that they wish to open the file for reading only, but since this application has no function except to write to databases, there's no point in displaying that option. The other two options, `OFN_PATHMUSTEXIST` and `OFN_FILEMUSTEXIST`, guarantee that the user must select an existing path and file; otherwise, they could type in the name of a nonexistent file.

Once you have a database file to import into, you can start downloading the data:

```
begin

  domain = 'localhost'
  port = '3000'

  xml = open("http://#{domain}:#{port}/log/all").read
  grades = XmlSimple.xml_in(xml)['grade']
```

This code opens the address, reads the data, and then parses the XML using `XmlSimple.xml_in`. The reason you can use `open` to download a web page is that you `require`'d the `open-uri` at the top of the script. This allows the call to `open` to download data from remote URIs, which it normally cannot do.

■**Note** As noted in Chapter 11, a URL and a URI are the same in almost all situations you are likely to encounter. All URLs are URIs, and while some URIs are not URLs, most are, and the difference is rarely important even in academic contexts. You can find out more about URIs at http://en.wikipedia.org/wiki/Uniform_Resource_Identifier.

At this point, the grades variable looks something like this:

```
[{"grade"=>["88"],
  "student"=>["Bob Smithye"],
  "class"=>["Practical Exopaleontology"],
  "employer"=>["Transmegtech"],
  "id"=>["25"],
  "took_class_at"=>["Wed Nov 07 00:00:00 -0500 2011"]},
 {"grade"=>["83"],
  "student"=>["John Tumblewood"],
  "class"=>["Practical Exopaleontology"],
  "employer"=>["Elexagijitech"],
  "id"=>["26"],
  "took_class_at"=>["Wed Nov 07 00:00:00 -0500 2011"]},
  . . .
```

The grades variable is an array of hashes. Each value of the resultant hash is an array, even though they are all single values. This is because although each row will have only one id, one grade, and so forth, that isn't evident from the XML. The structure of the XML is such that you could have more than one student or class for each row, so it puts them all in single-element arrays. It's easy to work around, though, since you can simply take the first element of each array to access its single value.

Next, the code connects to the database and loops through each grade from the XML:

```
imported_count = 0

DBI.connect("DBI:ADO:" <<
            "Provider=Microsoft.Jet.OLEDB.4.0;" <<
            "Data Source=#{database_path}") do |dbh|

  grades.each do |grade_raw|
    g ={}
    grade_raw.each do |key,value|
      if value.length == 1
        g[key] = value.first
      else
```

```
        g[key] = value
    end
  end
```

The loop goes through each grade and pulls out the single value from each member, which makes it a bit easier to access.

Then you need to check if this particular grade has already been processed:

```
sql = "SELECT COUNT(*)
          FROM grades
        WHERE id=?;"

dbh.select_all(sql, g['id'].to_i) do |row|
  count = *row
  if count == 0
```

The select_all method calls your block once for each row of the result. The query returns only one result, so your block is executed only once. The row is an array, so you use the * operator to pull that single value into the count variable, and check if the result is zero. If the result is zero, this data is missing from your local database, and you can insert it as follows:

```
sql = '       INSERT INTO grades
                    (id, student,
                     employer, grade,
                     class_date, class_name)
              VALUES (?,?,?,?,?,?);'

dbh.do(sql,  g['id'], g['student'],
             g['employer'], g['grade'],
             Date.parse(g['took_class_at']),
             g['class']
      );
dbh.commit
imported_count = imported_count + 1
```

Note Adding missing records isn't the only way to synchronize databases. You could also delete all of the records every time you import the data from the XML, and simply insert all of the records again. However, this will cause problems if the end user wants to add new fields to the table. With the current technique, adding fields isn't a problem—the importer will leave them alone.

If the import was successful, you pop up a message box telling the user you're finished and how many records were imported. If the import failed, you need to display an error message.

```
    SWin::Application.messageBox "Done! #{imported_count} records imported.",
                                 "All done!"
rescue
  SWin::Application.messageBox $!, "Error while importing"
end
```

The `SWin::Application.messageBox` displays a pop-up dialog box with a simple message. You pass it two parameters: the first is the message itself, and the second is the title. Note that the second call to `messageBox` uses the $! special variable, which contains a description of the error. You might prefer to output a generic message and log the error to a file, which you can do using the following code:

```
rescue
  SWin::Application.messageBox "There was an error during the import process.",
                              "Error while importing"
  File.open("training_loader.log", "a").puts $!

end
```

At this point, you have a web application for entering data, which gives you flexibility and easy deployment, and it exports XML. You also have a desktop application, which imports this XML into your Access database. This lets the administrator easily create customized reports and present other information in a familiar, easy-to-use environment. Even better, the importer is very easy to use and familiar. It is activated with a double-click and communicates information with simple dialog boxes that most Windows users will find comfortable to use.

Summary

Microsoft Office is used every day by businesspeople everywhere, and those businesspeople often have extensive experience using Microsoft Office programs to analyze data. You can often enhance the utility of your software by using Microsoft Office output formats. Access or Excel can be a "catchall" analysis tool for a host of miscellaneous questions not directly answered by your reporting, and therefore you can empower your users, which is what reporting—and, for that matter, open source software—is all about.

The next chapter covers how you can plan Google AdWords advertising campaigns using Hpricot, Active Record, and HTML reports.

## CHAPTER 13

Tracking Your Ads with Google AdWords

According to a 2005 report by PricewaterhouseCoopers, $385 billion dollars are spent on advertising annually. This report estimated that by 2010, worldwide advertising spending will exceed $500 billion. As you can imagine, such a gigantic flow of money requires a similarly gigantic infrastructure. Of course, the most common advertising formats—print, radio, and television—have a relatively long history, with a very entrenched methodology for analyzing how money is spent. On the other hand, web advertising is a relatively new phenomenon, and many organizations do not have a coherent system for tracking Internet advertising.

Perhaps the most popular online advertising system is Google AdWords, which allows people to buy text advertising space in small blocks to the right of Google's main search results. Additionally, Google allows Google AdWords ads to be placed on other web sites using the Google AdSense program, which further increases the potential market of Google AdWords advertisers.

Ads in Google AdWords are priced on a per-click basis, so the more your ad is clicked, the more you pay, and you pay only when people click your ad. Each advertisement has a list of keywords for which it will appear, and a maximum per-click bid on each keyword. (You can find out more about AdWords at `http://adwords.google.com`.)

Because Google AdWords is a type of Vickrey auction, you pay only what the second-highest bidder paid, so you can bid your maximum without fear of overpaying. However, a number of ads can appear on a single page, with progressively lower bidders receiving progressively lower locations. Some Google AdWords advertisers attempt to bid as low as possible while still having their ad appear on the search results page.

Additionally, advertisers often attempt to purchase obscure keywords or misspelled keywords. In reality, such attempts are often stymied by the fact that keywords without competition usually do not receive many search results, so the total amount of clicks available for purchase is likely low. As a result, advertisers attempt to construct the most attractive ad possible, so they can get more clicks for obscure, and therefore cheaper, keywords.

Obviously, conducting an effective Google AdWords campaign requires some strategy. This chapter's example is a reporting system that will help you optimize a selection of ads, so that each click is as cheap as possible.

Obtaining Google AdWords Reports

For the example in this chapter, you need to start with a report on the past performance of your ads. Fortunately, you can do this fairly easily. Google AdWords offers a number of different report types, each of which can be viewed in several ways, ranging from HTML to XML or CSV format.

If you don't have access to a Google AdWords account, you can feel free to download a sample XML file in the Source/Downloads area of the Apress web site (`http://www.apress.com`) or from `http://rubyreporting.com/examples/google_adwords_sample.xml`.

However, if you already have a Google AdWords account with some data in it, you can retrieve your own report as follows:

1. From the Google AdWords site, click the Report tab.

2. Click Create a New Report. You should see a screen similar to Figure 13-1.

3. Select Ad Performance.

4. At this point, you can filter the data using the available options. For example, you can limit the data to just a few days. For this example, just click Create Report to generate the report.

Figure 13-1. *Google report creation page*

5. You should see some notification that your report is being prepared. This screen will automatically refresh, and when your report is ready, you should see a screen similar to Figure 13-2. Under the Export Results label, click the XML download link.

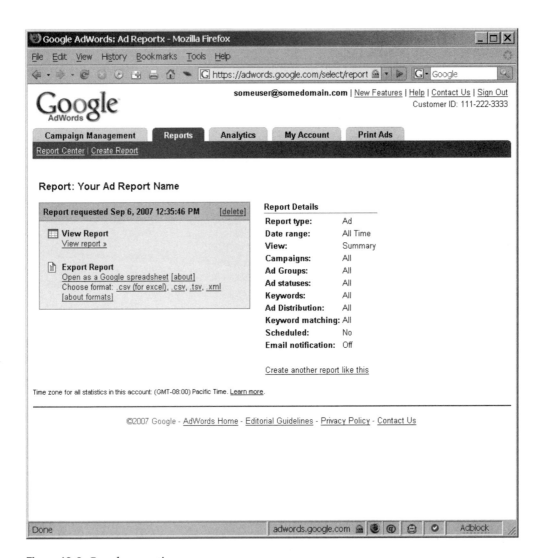

Figure 13-2. *Google reporting page*

6. Save this file and use it for this chapter's example.

The XML source in the sample file you can download looks like Listing 13-1.

Listing 13-1. *Google AdWords Sample XML (google_adwords_sample.xml)*

```
<?xml version="1.0" standalone="yes"?>
<report>
  <table>
    <columns>
      <column name="month"/>
      <column name="campaign"/>
      <column name="adgroup"/>
      <column name="preview"/>
      <column name="headline"/>
      <column name="desc1"/>
      <column name="desc2"/>
      <column name="creativeVisUrl"/>
      <column name="creativeid"/>
      <column name="creativeType"/>
      <column name="creativeStatus"/>
      <column name="agStatus"/>
      <column name="creativeDestUrl"/>
      <column name="campStatus"/>
      <column name="imps"/>
      <column name="clicks"/>
      <column name="ctr"/>
      <column name="cpc"/>
      <column name="cost"/>
      . . .(may vary depending on fields selected). . .
    </columns>
    <rows>
  <row month="December 2009" campaign="Campaign #1"
      adgroup="Python" preview="Not available"
      headline="We Write Apps in Python"
      desc1="We're not a sweatshop,"
      desc2="so we only need to write it once."
      creativeVisUrl="berubeconsulting.com"
      creativeid="554433221"
      creativeType="text"
      creativeStatus="Disabled"
      agStatus="Enabled"
      creativeDestUrl="http://berubeconsulting.com"
      campStatus="Paused" imps="6230"
      clicks="41" ctr="0.00658105939004815"
      cpc="160000" cost="6560000" />
```

```
<row month="December 2009" campaign="Campaign #1"
    adgroup="Ruby" preview="Not available"
    headline="We Write Apps in Ruby"
    desc1="We're not a sweatshop,"
    desc2="so we only need to write it once."
    creativeVisUrl="berubeconsulting.com"
    creativeid="112233445"
    creativeType="text"
    creativeStatus="Disabled"
    agStatus="Enabled"
    creativeDestUrl="http://berubeconsulting.com"
    campStatus="Paused" imps="4099"
    clicks="48" ctr="0.0117101732129788"
    cpc="130000" cost="6240000" />

    . . .

<row month="March 2010" campaign="Campaign #1"
    adgroup="Haskell" preview="Not available"
    headline="We Write Apps in Haskell"
    desc1="We're not a sweatshop,"
    desc2="so we only need to write it once."
    creativeVisUrl="berubeconsulting.com"
    creativeid="000112233"
    creativeType="text"
    creativeStatus="Disabled"
    agStatus="Enabled"
    creativeDestUrl="http://berubeconsulting.com"
    campStatus="Paused" imps="1614"
    clicks="55" ctr="0.0340768277571252"
    cpc="140000" cost="7700000" />
    </rows>
</table>
<totals>
  <subtotal imps="43999"
    clicks="321" ctr="0.00729562035500807"
    cpc="159158" cost="51090000" name="January 2010" />
  <grandtotal imps="136770"
    clicks="1133" ctr="0.00828398040505959"
    cpc="163459" cost="185200000"  />
  <subtotal imps="30753"
    clicks="235" ctr="0.00764153090755374"
```

```
    cpc="110553" cost="25980000" name="December 2009" />
   <subtotal imps="28779"
    clicks="212" ctr="0.00736648250460405"
    cpc="195377" cost="41420000" name="March 2010" />
   <subtotal imps="33239"
    clicks="365" ctr="0.0109810764463432"
    cpc="182767" cost="66710000" name="February 2010" />
  </totals>
</report>
```

Note that XML is whitespace-agnostic, and the original format that the XML comes in has much less whitespace, so files downloaded from PayPal will be less readable than the file shown here. (Functionally, though, there isn't any difference; the XML structure is the same.)

Planning an AdWords Campaign

Suppose you work for a technology company that specializes in developing software for a variety of open source languages. Since the company is small and does not have a full-time sales staff, it uses Google AdWords to get leads on new clients.

The problem is that the company's developers prefer different languages, and the company wants to determine which language should receive the most ad revenue. In order to answer this question, your company is temporarily spending an equal amount of money for one ad for each of the languages. The plan is to use the data gathered to decide how to spend a smaller budget efficiently. The company wants you to create a Rails application that lets the user specify a target number of clicks for the ad campaign, regardless of the language advertised, and returns a list of the cheapest ads to achieve that many clicks.

You've retrieved the Google report on the past performance of the ads (Listing 13-1). The catch with the reports generated by Google is that results greater than 100MB can be retrieved only in XML format. A sizable campaign could conceivably exceed that limit. To be prepared, you'll parse the XML version, so you won't need to change input formats if the size of your results changes. After you've retrieved that result, you can analyze it and then determine the cheapest ad mixture to meet your target number of clicks.

Loading the XML into a Database

Listing 13-2 shows the script that loads the report XML into a MySQL database. You'll need Active Record and Hpricot (introduced in Chapter 6) installed to use this script. You can install Hpricot with the following command:

```
gem install hpricot
```

You'll also need MySQL installed and a blank database named text_ad_report set up. You can create this database with the following command:

```
mysqladmin create text_ad_data
```

Listing 13-2. *Google AdWords Database Loader (google_adwords_loader.rb)*

```ruby
require 'hpricot'
require 'active_record'

class AdResult < ActiveRecord::Base
end

ActiveRecord::Base.establish_connection(
            :adapter=>'mysql',
            :database=>'text_ad_performance',
            :host=>'your_mysql_host_here',
            :username=>'your_mysql_username_here',
            :password=>'your_mysql_password_here')


unless AdResult.table_exists?
  first_row = rows.first # We'll use this row as a model
                         # to create the database schema

  field_override_types = {
            'imps'=>:integer,
            'clicks'=>:integer,
            'ctr'=>:float,
            'cpc'=>:integer,
            'cost'=>:integer
                    }

  ActiveRecord::Schema.define do
    create_table :ad_results do |t|
        first_row.attributes.each do |attribute_name, value|
            if field_override_types.include?(attribute_name)
              t.column attribute_name, field_override_types[attribute_name]
            else
              t.column attribute_name, :text, :length=>25
            end
        end
      end
```

```
      end
    end
end

hpricot_doc = Hpricot.XML(ARGF)
rows = (hpricot_doc/"rows/row")

rows.each do |row|
    AdResult.new do |n|
      row.attributes.each do |attribute_name, attribute_value|
        n.send("#{attribute_name}=", attribute_value)
      end
      n.save
    end
end
```

Save this script as google_adwords_loader.rb.

You can run the script as follows:

```
ruby google_adwords_loader.rb google_sample_report.xml
```

Of course, if you've downloaded the file to a different name than google_sample_
report.xml, you should change the file name in this command.

Now, let's take a look at this example line by line.

Dissecting the Code

First, the code in Listing 13-2 connects to a MySQL database and defines a single model,
similar to examples in preceding chapters. Next, you create a table for your single model,
AdResult, if it doesn't already exist:

```
unless AdResult.table_exists?
  first_row = rows.first # We'll use this row as a model
                         # to create the database schema

  field_override_types = {
                'imps'=>:integer,
                'clicks'=>:integer,
                'ctr'=>:float,
                'cpc'=>:integer,
                'cost'=>:integer
                        }
```

```
ActiveRecord::Schema.define do
  create_table AdResults.table_name do |t|
      first_row.attributes.each do |attribute_name, value|
          if field_override_types.include?(attribute_name)
            t.column attribute_name, field_override_types[attribute_name]
          else
            t.column attribute_name, :text, :length=>25
          end
      end
    end
  end
end
```

This code pulls out the first extracted row of your data and uses it as a template to create a schema for your table. For each attribute of the row, you add a column to your table with that attribute's name. The default type for each column is a text field with a length of 25, but you also have a field_override_types hash. If an attribute name is present in that hash, the new type is used instead. As a result, if Google AdWords adds a new column to the XML schema, this script will adjust.

In fact, the only parts of the entire script that are specific to this schema are the name of the model, AdResult, the field_override_types hash, and the "table/rows/rows" selector. If you change those elements, you can load many different types of XML using a script like this. (You would need to modify the code slightly if the fields are stored as children instead of attributes, and Chapter 6 has an example of doing just that.)

Note that the schema has a columns element, which has one child column element for every field in each row. You could have parsed that columns element instead and ended up with the same information, but the approach used here is more flexible, since many XML files do not contain headers describing their children's attributes.

■**Note** This automatic creation of the schema is very convenient, since it avoids hard-coding values, and it guarantees you'll get all of the data from the XML input for future processing. However, in many cases, you may want to create your schema by hand. For example, you may wish to load only a few fields, or you may wish to have a more controlled table schema, such as one with carefully selected text field lengths. Additionally, you may need to normalize one row in an XML schema into multiple tables. In any case, the techniques are similar to what you've done here. This approach can also be used for quick scripts outside Rails applications. Of course, there's nothing preventing you from using standard Rails migrations.

Next, the code parses your input XML:

```
hpricot_doc = Hpricot.XML(ARGF)
rows=(hpricot_doc/"table/rows/row")
```

The first line creates an HTML document from the special `ARGF` variable. This variable acts like a `File` object, but automatically refers to either one or more files passed on the command line or to standard input if a file is not specified. In other words, the following commands are equivalent:

```
ruby google_adwords_loader.rb google_sample_report.xml
ruby google_adwords_loader.rb < google_sample_report.xml
cat google_sample_report.xml | ruby google_adwords_loader.rb
```

If you aren't familar with shell redirection, you can treat `ARGF` as if it simply lets you read from the file or files specified on the command line.

The second line divides the `hpricot_doc` object by `"table/rows/rows"`. This looks for any `table` elements containing `rows` elements and returns any `row` element that they contain. As you can see from the XML in Listing 13-1, you have just one `table` and `rows` element, so it will return every `row` element in the XML document.

Finally, now that you are guaranteed to have a connection, a model, and a correctly structured database, you can begin inserting data into the database, as follows:

```
rows.each do |row|
   AdResult.new do |n|
    row.attributes.each do |attribute_name, attribute_value|
      n.send("#{attribute_name}=", attribute_value)
    end
    n.save
   end
end
```

This code loops through all of the rows, creating a new `AdResult` object for each. You then loop through all the various attributes of each `row`, and use the `send` method to call the setter method for that attribute. The `send` method takes a string naming the method to call as well as a list of parameters. In other words, the following two lines are identical:

```
some_object.send('some_method', an_argument)
some_object.some_method(an_argument)
```

The advantage of using the `send` method is that you can call it with a method name that you build dynamically, as you do here.

Now that your data is stored in the database, let's create a simple Rails reporting application that helps your boss spend his advertising revenue.

Creating the AdWords Campaign Reporter Application

The Rails reporting application will let you specify a number of clicks, and using past data, create an ad campaign that gives you that many clicks for the least money.

First, create the framework for the application:

```
rails adwords_reporter
```

```
create  app/controllers
create  app/helpers
create  app/models
create  app/views/layouts
create  config/environments
create  components
create  db
create  doc
create  lib
. . .
create  log/production.log
create  log/development.log
create  log/test.log
```

Next, create your single controller for this application:

```
cd adwords_reporter
ruby script/generate controller budget_optimizer
```

```
exists  app/controllers/
exists  app/helpers/
create  app/views/budget_optimizer
exists  test/functional/
create  app/controllers/budget_optimizer_controller.rb
create  test/functional/budget_optimizer_controller_test.rb
create  app/helpers/budget_optimizer_helper.rb
```

Finally, create the single model:

```
ruby script/generate model ad_results
```

```
exists   app/models/
exists   test/unit/
exists   test/fixtures/
create   app/models/ad_results.rb
create   test/unit/ad_results_test.rb
create   test/fixtures/ad_results.yml
create   db/migrate
create   db/migrate/001_create_ad_results.rb
```

Note that at this point, you'll need to edit your `config/database.yml` file to reflect your database connection parameters.

Put the code in Listing 13-3 in your single controller.

Listing 13-3. *Budget Optimizer Controller (app/controllers/budget_optimizer_controller.rb)*

```ruby
class BudgetOptimizerController < ApplicationController
  def index
  end

  def report
    @excel_view = params[:view_as_excel]
    @target_clicks=params[:target_clicks].to_f

    results_raw=AdResult.find(:all,
                        :select=>'headline,
                                  AVG(cost) as cost,
                                  AVG(clicks) as clicks',
                        :group=>'headline')

    results_raw.sort! { |x,y| (x.cost/x.clicks <=> y.cost/y.clicks) }
    @results = []
    click_sum = 0.0
    results_raw.each do |r|
     @results << r
     click_sum += r.clicks
     break if click_sum > @target_clicks
    end
    @estimated_clicks = click_sum
    @avg_cost_per_click = (
                  @results.inject(0.0) { |sum,r|  sum+=r.cost } )  / (
                  @results.inject(0.0) { |sum,r|  sum+= r.clicks } )
```

```
    if @excel_view
      headers['Content-Type'] = "application/vnd.ms-excel"
      headers['Content-Disposition'] = 'attachment; filename="adwords_report.xls"'
    end
  end
end
```

Save this file as app/controllers/budget_optimizer_controller.rb.

Next, create a single helper file, as shown in Listing 13-4.

Listing 13-4. *Budget Optimizer Helper (app/helpers/budget_optimizer_helper.rb)*

```
module BudgetOptimizerHelper
  def format_google_currency(currency_value)
      "#{'%0.2f' % (currency_value/10000.0) } cents"
  end
end
```

Save this file as app/helpers/budget_optimizer_helper.rb.

Listing 13-5 shows the file for a layout, which will wrap around your views.

Listing 13-5. *Budget Optimizer Application-Wide Layout (app/views/layouts/application.rhtml)*

```
<head>
  <html>
    <style type="text/css">
    body {
      font-family: sans-serif;
    }
    #create_report {

      padding: 0.3em;
    }
    table tr th {
      text-align:left;
    }
    td, th {
      padding:0.3em;
      border: 2px solid #cecece;
      margin:0;
    }
```

```
    th {
      background-color: #f0f0f0;
    }
    table {
      padding:0;
      border-spacing:0;
      border-collapse:collapse;
    }
  </style>
  </head>
  <body>
    <%=@content_for_layout%>
  </body>
</html>
```

Save this as `app/views/layouts/application.rhtml`.

The application will have two views. Listing 13-5 shows the first view, which repre-sents your report creation form.

Listing 13-5. *Report Creation Form (app/views/budget_optimizer/index.rhtml)*

```
<h1>Create AdWords Report</h1>

<div>
  <% form_tag(:action => 'report') do %>
  Target number of clicks: <%=text_field_tag 'target_clicks', '10',
                                              :size=>4%>
  <%=submit_tag 'Create Report', :id=>'create_report'%>
  <% end %>
</div>
```

Save this view as `app/views/budget_optimizer/index.rhtml`.
Listing 13-6 shows the second view, which contains the actual report.

Listing 13-6. *Report Display Page (app/views/budget_optimizer/report.rhtml)*

```
<h1>Google AdWords Campaign Plan </h1>
<%unless @excel_view %>
<p><%=link_to '[download as excel]',
              :params=>{
                        'view_as_excel'=>true,
                        'target_clicks'=>@target_clicks
```

```
                              }
      %></p>
<%end%>
<table>
  <tr>
    <th>Ad Headline</th>
    <th>Avg Clicks</th>
    <th>Cost Per Click</th>
  </tr>
<%@results.each do |r| %>

  <tr>
    <td><%=r.headline%> </td>
    <td><%=r.clicks%> clicks </td>
    <td><%=format_google_currency(r.cost/r.clicks) %></td>
  </tr>
<%end%>
</table>


<h2>Summary</h2>
<table>
  <tr>
    <th>Goal Clicks</th>
    <td><%=@target_clicks%></td>
  </tr>
  <tr>
    <th>Estimated Available Clicks</th>
    <td><%=@estimated_clicks%></td>
  </tr>
  <tr>
    <th>Estimated Cost Per Click (CPC)</th>
    <td><%=format_google_currency(@avg_cost_per_click )%></td>
  </tr>
</table>
```

Save this view as app/views/budget_optimizer/report.rhtml.

You can run this example by using the following command:

```
ruby script/server
```

```
=> Booting Mongrel (use 'script/server webrick' to force WEBrick)
=> Rails application starting on http://0.0.0.0:3000
```

```
=> Call with -d to detach
=> Ctrl-C to shutdown server
** Starting Mongrel listening at 0.0.0.0:3000
** Starting Rails with development environment . . .
** Rails loaded.
** Loading any Rails specific GemPlugins
** Signals ready.  INT => stop (no restart).
** Mongrel available at 0.0.0.0:3000
** Use CTRL-C to stop.
```

Open your web browser and enter the address http://127.0.0.1:3000/budget_
optimizer. You should see a screen similar to Figure 13-3. Type **100** into the text box and
click Create Report. Then you should see a screen similar to Figure 13-4.

Figure 13-3. *AdWords reporter application form for creating a report*

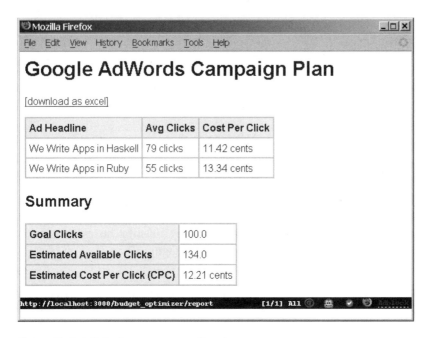

Figure 13-4. *AdWords reporter application report*

Let's look at a few lines from the application.

Dissecting the Code

First, let's take a look at the controller, apps/controllers/budget_optimizer_controller.rb
(Listing 13-3):

```
class BudgetOptimizerController < ApplicationController
  def index
  end

  def report
      @excel_view = params[:view_as_excel]
      @target_clicks=params[:report][:target_clicks].to_f

      results_raw=AdResult.find(:all,
                                :select=>'headline,
                                          AVG(cost) as cost,
                                          AVG(clicks) as clicks',
                                :group=>'headline')

      results_raw.sort! { |x,y| ((x.cost/x.clicks) <=> (y.cost/y.clicks)) }
```

The first method, `index`, just displays a form allowing the user to select a goal with a number of clicks. The second method, `report`, actually creates the report. You first grab the parameters passed to the action, and then grab the average cost and number of clicks for each distinct headline. This means that for each time period in the report, the cost and number of clicks will be averaged and returned for that headline.

■**Note** This code analyzes ads by headline, so multiple ads with the same headline and different body copy will be grouped together. In most cases, an ad with an identical headline and different body copy is simply going to be a variation on a theme, such as an attempt to see which ad has a higher click-through rate, not an ad with a completely different subject matter. However, if you wish to look at each headline as a different group, you could easily group by `creativeid`, which is guaranteed to be distinct for each ad, and then display the `creativeid` instead of the headline. In that case, it would be difficult to tell ads with the same headline apart, so you would need to devise a way to distinguish them, such as by including the body copy on each line of the report.

The code then sorts the `results_raw` array by the ratio of cost per click of each item. This will be used by the next chunk of code to determine which ads should be used first. The source XML has a `cpc` field, which is, in theory, equal to the cost divided by the clicks; however, this field is heavily rounded, despite being in units of one-millionth of a cent. Instead of using this field, the code calculates the cost per click by dividing the cost by the number of clicks, which is more accurate. In fact, in this example, replacing instances of calculating the cost per click on the fly with the precalculated `cpc` field leads to several rounding errors, including one that is 50 cents or so. Such errors would only get worse as the scale of the calculation increased.

Next, you iterate through the results, adding each one to an array until the required number of clicks is reached:

```
@results = []
click_sum = 0
results_raw.each do |r|
 @results << r
 click_sum += r.clicks
 break if click_sum > @target_clicks
end

@estimated_clicks = click_sum
@avg_cost_per_click = (
                @results.inject(0.0) { |sum,r|  sum+=r.cost } )  / (
                @results.inject(0.0) { |sum,r|  sum+= r.clicks } )
```

As you can see, the loop through `results_raw` is used to fill the `@results` array. It loops through all of the results and adds them into the array. It also adds to the `click_sum` counter, and when that's equal to the number of clicks you are looking for, you stop adding values to the array. Since you sorted by the cost per click, you end up with an array of the ads with the lowest cost per click that totals the amount of clicks you are seeking.

The two `@results.inject` structures look complicated, but they simply sum the `cost` and the `clicks` fields, respectively. The division of the sum of the `cost` values and the `clicks` value is the average. (Technically, what most people call the average is actually the mean, and strictly speaking, this calculates the mean value.) The `@avg_cost_per_click` is used to show the average cost per click of the entire campaign.

Finally, you get ready to display your report:

```
    if @excel_view
      headers['Content-Type'] = "application/vnd.ms-excel"
      headers['Content-Disposition'] = 'attachment; filename="adwords_report.xls"'
    end
  end
end
```

The `if` statement checks if you are trying to generate the report in Excel format; if so, it sends the appropriate headers that mark the file as being an Excel document. But notice that no special action is taken to generate the report as an Excel document.

Chapter 4 showed how you can use the `spreadsheet-excel` gem to generate Excel spreadsheets, and you could have used that technique here. However, this application uses a very odd trick: you mark the application as having an Excel `content-type` header (specifically, `application/vnd.ms-excel`). Since it's an HTML file containing tabular data, both Excel and OpenOffice.org will import the document seamlessly. You can see the results of opening the Excel document in Microsoft Excel in Figure 13-5 and in OpenOffice.org in Figure 13-6. But note that although this application's tables are imported neatly in both applications, there's no guarantee that more complex HTML layouts will work well. (Of course, if you have HTML that's not in tabular form, you probably shouldn't be trying to import it into a spreadsheet.)

If you're thinking that this trick is counterintuitive and does not sound like it would work, you're correct: it is counterintuitive and does not sound like it would work. But it does work, apparently because while your web browser uses the MIME type (represented by the `content-type` header) to determine the format of the page, the spreadsheet applications examine the data to determine the format. Because both programs can open HTML pages as spreadsheets, the trick works.

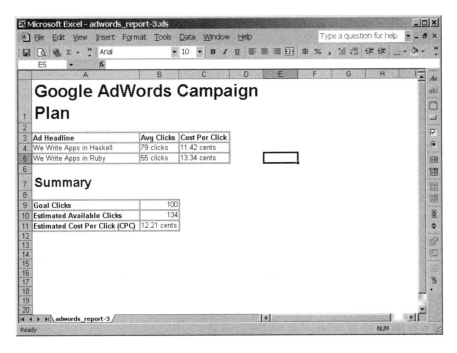

Figure 13-5. *AdWords reporter Excel report in Microsoft Excel*

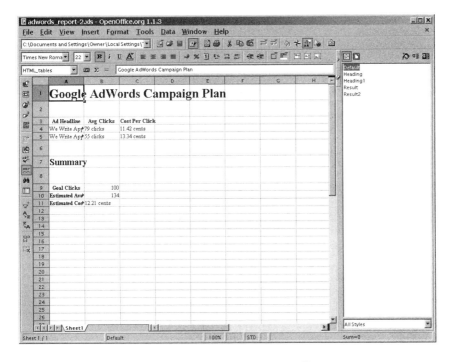

Figure 13-6. *AdWords reporter Excel report in OpenOffice.org*

This trick is perhaps the easiest way to add Excel views to your application. However, note that you cannot use spreadsheet-specific features like formulas with this technique. Another odd consequence is that if the user modifies the spreadsheet and then saves it, the spreadsheet will still be saved in HTML format, even though it has an Excel extension. This could conceivably be a problem if the user wants to import the file into an application and expects a genuine Excel-format file. (If you are writing the application into which they will import such a file, you could simply write the importer to expect HTML as input.)

The application has two views: index.rhtml, which simply displays a form and is self-explanatory, and report.rhtml (Listing 13-6), which begins like this:

```
<h1>Google AdWords Campaign Plan </h1>
<%unless @excel_view %>
<p><%=link_to '[download as excel]',
             :params=>{
                     'view_as_excel'=>true,
                     'report[target_clicks]'=>@target_clicks
                     }
    %></p>
<%end%>
```

The link to download the page as an Excel file is visible unless the current page is already in Excel format. (You could, if you so desired, include a link to the regular HTML version of the page on the Excel version, since Excel spreadsheets can contain HTML links.)

Next, let's take a look at the actual display of the ads:

```
<table>
  <tr>
    <th>Ad Headline</th>
    <th>Avg Clicks</th>
    <th>Cost Per Click</th>
  </tr>
<%@results.each do |r| %>

  <tr>
    <td><%=r.headline%> </td>
    <td><%=r.clicks%> clicks </td>
    <td><%=format_google_currency(r.cost/r.clicks) %></td>
  </tr>
<%end%>
</table>
```

This code loops through each of the ads from your report, displaying the headline, the number of estimated clicks, and the cost per click formatted as a number of cents. The formatting is controlled by the format_google_currency helper, which is defined in app/helpers/budget_optimizer_helper.rb. The clicks are only estimated, of course, because there's no guarantee that next month will have an identical number of clicks (or cost) for a given keyword. However, it's likely that things will remain similar, even if they aren't completely identical. If this were not true—if the market were completely random—we couldn't make any intelligent reporting in any event.

Note that the helper methods are automatically available to your controller and to your view, so they can automatically be used in your view. The format_currency_helper (Listing 13-4) looks like this:

```
def format_google_currency(currency_value)
    "#{'%0.2f' % (currency_value/10000.0) } cents"
end
```

As you can see, the helper divides by 10,000 and then formats the value with two decimal points, followed by the word "cents." If you wanted to display a dollar format instead, you could use a helper like this:

```
def format_google_currency(currency_value)
    "#{'$%0.2f' % (currency_value/1000000.0) } "
end
```

This alternate helper displays values like $0.23 instead of 23 cents. It divides by 1,000,000 instead of 10,000, since the units of currency in the XML files are millionths of a dollar, which is equivalent to ten thousandths of a cent.

The remainder of the code in report.rhtml (Listing 13-6) just prints out a few variables from your controller that relate to the entire campaign:

```
<h2>Summary</h2>
<table>
  <tr>
    <th>Goal Clicks</th>
    <td><%=@target_clicks%></td>
  </tr>
  <tr>
    <th>Estimated Available Clicks</th>
    <td><%=@estimated_clicks%></td>
  </tr>
  <tr>
    <th>Estimated Cost Per Click (CPC)</th>
    <td><%=format_google_currency(@avg_cost_per_click )%></td>
```

```
    </tr>
</table>
```

Note that if you so desired, you could use just one table by replacing this following chunk:

```
</table>
<h2>Summary</h2>
<table>
```

with this:

```
<tr><td colspan=2><h2>Summary</h2></td></tr>
```

Using a single table would affect the appearance of your report.

Summary

Google AdWords is a powerful platform for delivering your ad content. It has a variety of powerful reporting tools available online, but, like virtually any reporting tools, they have their limits. Here, you saw how to use the Google AdWords XML export and Hpricot to create a more complicated report. In fact, in just a few lines of code, you created a tool that will read in Google AdWords data and generate an estimated campaign plan that optimizes spending to get the most clicks in the least amount of money—potentially saving a huge amount of advertising money.

This completes the examples of specific Ruby reports. Over the course of the book, you've seen a lot of different techniques for using Ruby and related tools to find answers to reporting questions. You've also seen a number of different ways to present those answers in convenient forms. I've shown you how you can use Ruby, SQL, and a few gems to quickly create flexible reports that perform well and can be used in almost any context—from the Web, to a command-line batch process, to a desktop application, to a cell phone. Many other techniques are available—ranging from using commercial charting products such as amCharts to libraries that aim to replace SQL with pure Ruby, like Ambition or Ruport—and you'll find that you now have a firm foundation for exploring other solutions.

If you would like to comment on anything in this book, or if you would like to share with me how you've been able to use Ruby and related tools to do reporting, please visit the book's web site at http://rubyreporting.com/—I'd love to hear from you.

Index

Special Characters

$! variable, 260
& character, 124, 129, 130

A

AbiWord, 234
Access
    creating reports, 236
    importing web-form data into database,
        236–260
        creating web interface, 237–250
        importing XML data into, 251–260
        overview, 236–237
Accident model, 21
accident_count column, 21
Active Record database access library, 5–17,
        19–32
    calculating player salaries, 6–11
    calculating player wins, 11–17
    grouping and aggregation
        analyzing data with, 22–31
        overview, 19–22
    overview, 5–6, 19
ActiveRecord::Base class, 9, 141, 163
ActiveRecord::Base.establish_connection
        method, 9
ActiveRecord::Extensions, 190–191
ActiveRecord::Migration relationship, 79
ActiveRecord::Schema.define method, 143
ActiveX Data Objects (ADO), 251
actor model, 84
actor object, 90
actor_schedule application, 76
adapter parameter, 9, 141
add command, 37
addTimeout method, 184
ADO (ActiveX Data Objects), 251
AdResult model, 269
ads, Google AdWords, 261–284
    obtaining reports, 262–267
    overview, 261–262
    planning campaigns, 267–284
Advertiser model, 203

Adwords campaign reporter application,
        272–284
aggregation, 19
    analyzing data with, 22–31
        calculating drink/win distribution, 26–31
        calculating salary distribution, 25–26
        overview, 22–24
    overview, 19–22
Ajax.Updater function, 102
all_players.rb script, 47
ALTER TABLE . . . CHANGE COLUMN
        statement, 224
analyzing data, with grouping and aggregation,
        22–31
    calculating drink/win distribution, 26–31
    calculating salary distribution, 25–26
    overview, 22–24
Apache Web logs, 189–213
    ActiveRecord::Extensions, 190–191
    cost-per-sale reporting, 192–212
        controllers, 193–198
        database, 201–202
        layout, 198–200
        log analyzer, 203–212
        models, 203
        parser libraries, 201
        routing files, 201
        schema, 201–202
        views, 198–200
    overview, 189
    PDF::Writer, 191–192
apache_sales_tracker directory, 193
APIs, eBay, 111–113
app/controller/reporter_controller.rb file, 229
app/controllers/budget_optimizer_controller.rb
        file, 274
app/controllers/home_controller.rb file, 85, 94
app/controllers/homepage_controller.rb file,
        238
app/controllers/log_controller.rb file, 239
app/controllers/logs_controller.rb file, 206
app/controllers/report_controller.rb file,
        208–209
appendItem method, 71

appendItem parameter, 71

app/helpers/budget_optimizer_helper.rb file, 274, 283

AppleScript library, 52

app/models directory, 84

app/models/actor.rb file, 84

app/models/grade.rb file, 244

app/models/student.rb file, 243

app/models/training_class.rb file, 245

apps/controllers/budget_optimizer_controller. rb controller, 278

app/view/layout/application.html.erb file, 242

app/views/budget_optimizer/index.rhtml file, 275

app/views/budget_optimizer/report.rhtml file, 276

app/views/home/index.html.erb file, 96

app/views/home/index.rhtml file, 86

app/views/homepage/index.html.erb file, 238

app/views/layouts/application.html.erb file, 98

app/views/layouts/application.rhtml file, 87, 275

app/views/layouts/show.text.erb file, 97

app/views/log/index.xml.builder file, 241

app/views/log/upload.html.erb file, 240

app/views/performance/show.html.erb file, 97

app/views/performance/show.text.erb view, 106

app/views/reporter/index.rhtml file, 230

ar-extensions gem, 193

ARGF variable, 271

*ARGV construct, 149

assigned_user_id foreign key, 163

average_price_report.rb file, 121

average_time element, 106

average_time value, 104

AVG function, 20

B

bar charts, 37–45

Benchmark.realtime call, 207

booking model, 84

C

cached_feeds table, 224

calculate function, 20–26

calculate_rewards.rb file, 160

calculating

    drink/win distribution, 26–31

    player salaries, 6–11

    player wins, 11–17

    salary distribution, 25–26

calendar_date_select helper, 248

CallName parameter, 124

Cascading Style Sheets (CSS), 33

CDF (Channel Definition Format), 216

Channel Definition Format (CDF), 216

clicks field, 280

clippings, 217

COALESCE function, 150

columnize method, 142

columns element, 270

COM (Component Object Model), 171, 234

COMBOBOX_STATIC | FRAME_SUNKEN parameter, 71

COMBOBOX_STATIC constant, 71

comma-separated values (CSV) data, converting, 138–144

company news coverage reporting, 217–232

    loading data, 217–226

    news tracker report application, 226–232

company_pr database, 217

complex_bar_graph method, 226, 231–232

Component Object Model (COM), 171, 234

CONCAT command, 222

:conditions parameter, 11

config/database.yml file, 78, 93, 201, 217, 223, 230, 245, 273

config/environment.rb file, 206

config/routes.rb file, 100, 201

connect method, 71

Content-Type header, 179

content-type header, 280

controllers, cost-per-sale reporting, 192–198

correlated subquery, 150

cost field, 280

cost-per-sale reporting

    controllers, 193–198

    database, 201–202

    layout, 198–200

    log analyzer, 203–212

    models, 203

    parser libraries, 201

    routing files, 201

    schema, 201–202

    views, 198–200

count aggregate function, 44

count fields, 232

COUNT function, 20, 25

count method, 60

count variable, 207, 259

count_by_sql method, 144

:counter_cache=>true option, 165

cpc field, 279

create method, 63
create_table statement, 90
CRM systems, SugarCRM. *See* customer
        relationship management systems,
        SugarCRM
CSS (Cascading Style Sheets), 33
CSV (comma-separated values) data,
        converting, 138–144
current_row method, 58
<CurrentPrice> elements, 125, 126
Customer model, 11
customer relationship management (CRM)
        systems, SugarCRM
    installing, 155–156
    overview, 155
    sales force reporting with, 156–169

D
data
    analyzing, PayPal accounts, 144–153
    analyzing, with grouping and aggregation,
            22–31
        calculating drink/win distribution, 26–31
        calculating salary distribution, 25–26
        overview, 22–24
    exporting to spreadsheets, 52–60
        creating spreadsheet report, 53–60
        generating Excel spreadsheet, 52–53
    gathering from PayPal, 133–136
    report, writing small servers to get, 171–172
    XML, importing into Microsoft Access,
            251–260
data center (DC) component, 37
data directory, 246
data method, 37, 45
data_format format, 57
DatabaseFeedCache class, 225
databases, 3–17
    Active Record, 5–17
        calculating player salaries, 6–11
        calculating player wins, 11–17
        overview, 5–6
    choosing, 3–4
    cost-per-sale reporting, 201–202
    overview, 3
Date class, 151
DATE_ADD function, 82
db directory, 246
db/data/training_class_data.sql file, 246
DC (data center) component, 37
DELETE FROM statement, 82
description column, 190

description method, 216
desktop, creating reports on, 51–73
    choosing format, 51–52
    creating GUIs with Ruby, 60–73
    exporting data to spreadsheets, 52–60
    overview, 51
desktop_team_performance_graph.rb
        script, 67
development environment, 78, 93, 223
div tag, 101
.doc file, 235
document element, 131
domain column, 190
down method, 79, 90
drink field, 30
drink_win_distribution.rb script, 29

E
each method, 216
eBay, 111–131
    overview, 111
    using APIs, 111–113
    web services, 113–131
        coding report, 115–131
        Hpricot, 114–115
        LaTeX, 114–115
eBaySearch class, 116
EMBED tags, 106
Erubis::Eruby object, 164
eruby_object variable, 164
escape_latex method, 128
establish_connection class, 9
establish_connection line, 217
evalScripts parameter, 102
evaluate method, 164
event element, 106
Event.observe function, 102
events table, 39
<events> element, 105
Excel
    creating reports, 234
    spreadsheets, 52–53
:except parameter, 105
expenses, reporting, 136–153
    analyzing data, 144–153
    converting CSV data, 138–144
    overview, 136–137
    using FasterCSV, 137–138
exporting data to spreadsheets, 52–60
    creating spreadsheet report, 53–60
    generating Excel spreadsheet, 52–53

F

FasterCSV, 136, 137–138
fastercsv gem, 173
feed_data column, 224
FeedTools, 216
FeedTools.configurations[:feed_cache]
    variable, 225
"FeedTools::DatabaseFeedCache" variable, 225
FeedTools:Feed object, 216
FeedTools::Feed.open method, 225
Fidelity CSV file, 173
Fidelity investments, 171–187
    overview, 171
    tracking stock portfolio, 173–187
        creating graphical XML ticker, 180–187
        creating XML server with Mongrel,
            173–180
        overview, 173
    writing small server to get report data,
        171–172
field_override_types hash, 270
File object, 271
find method, 11
find_by_sql column, 21, 26
find_or_create_by_name_and_employer class,
    249
format_column method, 57
format_currency_helper, 283
format_google_currency helper, 283
format_row method, 58
FOX GUI library, 180
FRAME_SUNKEN constant, 71
FXApp object, 62, 70, 184
FXApp.instance() method, 72
FXButton control, 63
FXCheckButton control, 63
FXComboBox object, 70–71
FXImageView object, 72
FXLabel object, 70
FXMainWindow class, 70
FXMainWindow object, 62
FXMatrix object, 70
FXRadioButton object, 63
FXRuby, 52, 60, 61–63
fxruby gem, 180
FXRuby object, 63
FXTextField object, 63
FXTickerApp class, 183–187

G

Game class, 15, 16
game method, 15
games table, 39
gem install rmagick command, 33
gem install -y gruff command, 33
generate model command, 84
GET request, 112
get_average_price class, 130
get_label_text function, 186
get_sale_graph_tempfile function, 209, 211–212
get_tempfile_name function, 211
get_visitor_graph_tempfile function, 209, 212
getItemData method, 69
GetSearchResults parameter, 124
Ghostscript source utility, 157
go method, 187
Google AdWords, 261–284
    obtaining reports, 262–267
    overview, 261–262
    planning campaigns, 267–284
        creating Adwords campaign reporter
            application, 272–284
        loading XML into database, 267–271
        overview, 267
Google News, 215–232
    company news coverage reporting, 217–232
        loading data, 217–226
        news tracker report application, 226–232
    overview, 215
    using FeedTools to parse RSS, 216
google_adwords_loader.rb script, 269
grade model, 243
grade object, 249
grades variable, 258
<grades> element, 250
graphical reporting, 91–107
    creating controller for, 92–95
    creating models for, 95
    creating view for, 96–98
    examining application, 99–107
graphical user interfaces (GUIs), creating,
    60–73
    graphing team performance on desktop,
        63–73
    using FXRuby, 61–63
graphical XML ticker, 180–187
graphs, 33–49
    bar charts, 37–45
    choosing graphing utilities, 33–37
    choosing utilities for creating, 33–37

line charts, 45–49
overview, 33
team performance, 63–73
group parameter, 21
grouping, 19
analyzing data with, 22–31
calculating drink/win distribution, 26–31
calculating salary distribution, 25–26
overview, 22–24
overview, 19–22
gruff gem, 193
Gruff::Bar class, 43, 48
Gruff::Line class, 48
gsub method, 128
guid method, 226
GUIs, creating. *See* graphical user interfaces, creating

H

has_many :bookings relationship, 84
has_many relationship, 11, 84, 163
has_one relationship, 11
Hello world! text, 192
Hit model, 203
Hit object, 207
home controller, 85, 92, 201
homepage controller, 246
horizontal_bar_chart method, 226
Hpricot, 113, 114–115, 125, 267
hpricot_doc object, 271
hpricot_doc/:SearchResultItem expression, 126
HTML (Hypertext Markup Language), 33, 157–169
html2ps source utility, 157
HTTP_REFERER statement, 207
Hypertext Markup Language (HTML), 33, 157–169

I

id property, 250
;id=>false option, 90
if statement, 127, 280
image method, 209
import method, 208
importing XML data into Microsoft Access, 251–260
:include parameter, 105
IncludeSellers parameter, 124
index action, 201, 246
index method, 279
:index option, 248
index.rhtml view, 282

initialize method, 68, 176, 178, 183, 186
inner_html method, 115
innerHTML method, 126
INSERT DELAYED statement, 191
INSERT statement, 191
is_weekend? method, 151
Item model, 5
itemData array, 71
ItemData method, 69
items method, 216, 226
ItemTypeFilter parameter, 127

J

JRuby, 60

K

kernel::spintf function, 11
Korundum, 60

L

labels attribute, 34
LaTeX, 114–115
layout, cost-per-sale reporting, 198–200
LAYOUT_FILL_X flag, 72
LAYOUT_FILL_Y flag, 72
legend_font_size attribute, 43
LIMIT clause, 11, 243
:limit parameter, 11
line charts, 45–49
Linux, 114
live intranet reporting, 76–91
creating controller for, 85
creating models for, 82–84
creating view for, 85–87
examining application, 87–91
setting up database, 78–82
LOAD DATA INFILE statement, 191
load_csv method, 177, 179
log analyzers, cost-per-sale reporting, 203–212
log_parser.rb library, 201
LogParser class, 207
logs controller, 201

M

Mac OS X, 114
map method, 101, 231
Markaby, 136
Markaby::Builder object, 152–153
MATRIX_BY_COLUMNS flag, 70
MATRIX_BY_ROWS flag, 70
max function, 20
max method, 232

maximum_value attribute, 44
.mdb extension, 257
.mdb file, 236
MEDIUMTEXT type, 224
Meetings model, 165
meetings table, 163
meetings_count column, 165
memcached server, 225
messageBox method, 260
method function, 184
Method object, 184
method parameter, 102
method_missing technique, 178
Microsoft Access. *See* Access
Microsoft Developer Network (MSDN), 235
Microsoft Excel. *See* Excel
Microsoft Office. *See* Office, Microsoft
Microsoft Word, 234–235
migrations, 78
MIN function, 20
minimum_value attribute, 44
Model-View-Controller (MVC) framework, 75
Mongrel, 172, 173–180
mongrel gem, 173
Mongrel::HttpHandler instance, 178
Mongrel::HttpServer instance, 180
MSDN (Microsoft Developer Network), 235
MVC (Model-View-Controller) framework, 75
MySQL, 3, 268
mysql -u my_mysql_user -p < player_4.sql
    command, 64

N

n flags, 168
name method, 10
Net::HTTP library, 185
Net::HTTP.get method, 125
net/http.rb download library, 136
new method, 10
new parameter, 48
news tracker report application, 226–232
not is_admin condition, 164
numVisible attribute, 71

O

Object Linking and Embedding (OLE), 235
object-relational mapping (ORM) library, 5
Office, Microsoft, 233–236
    Microsoft Access, 236
    Microsoft Excel, 234
    Microsoft Word, 234–235
    overview, 233

OFN_FILEMUSTEXIST command, 257
OFN_HIDEREADONLY command, 257
OLE (Object Linking and Embedding), 235
onComplete callback, 103
open method, 216
open-flash-chart.swf file, 92
OpenOffice.org, 234
Order model, 11
ORM (object-relational mapping) library, 5
output_format static variable, 225

P

p tags, 115
padding property, 62
page_header_format format, 58
params hash, 124, 127
params[:trainee] array, 249
parse method, 137
parse_io_stream method, 207
parseexcel gem, 234
parse-excel gem, 234
parser libraries, 201
PayPal, 133–153
    gathering data from, 133–136
    overview, 133
    reporting expenses, 136–153
        analyzing data, 144–153
        converting CSV data, 138–144
        overview, 136–137
        using FasterCSV, 137–138
paypal gem, 133
paypal_expense_report.rb code, 148
paypal_load_data.rb script, 140
paypal_source_file variable, 141
paypal_transactions table, 141
PayPalTransaction model, 141
PaypalTransaction object, 144
PaypalTransaction.new method, 144
PDF creation, 128–131
pdf object, 192
pdf_source variable, 169
PDFs, creating from HTML documents,
    157–169
PDF::Writer, 191–192
pdf-writer gem, 193
per_page static variable, 225
Performance controller, 102–103
performance/game_id/player_id form, 100
performance/game_id/player_id.html type,
    100
performance/game_id/player_id.xml type, 100
Perl DBI-style interface, 236

Person model, 20
PLACEMENT_SCREEN constant, 63, 187
PLACEMENT_SCREEN flag, 72
Player class, 9–15
player method, 15
Player model, 15
Player object, 10
player_bar_charts.rb script, 42
player_graph_pics directory, 42
player_name_format method, 58
player_salary_ratio.rb script, 8
player_schema_2.sql file, 13
player_schema.sql file, 7
player_wins.rb script, 14
Player.find class method, 11
plays table, 39
POST request, 112, 249
PostgreSQL, 4
process method, 179
production environment, 78, 223
ps2pdf tool, 157
public/images directory, 228
public/index.html file, 94, 201
public/index.html.erb file, 246
public/stylesheet/training.css file, 242
published_at method, 230
puts method, 153

Q

QtRuby, 60
quantity attribute, 15
Query parameter, 124
query_encoded variable, 225

R

Rails
    graphical reporting with, 91–107
        creating controller for, 92–95
        creating models for, 95
        creating view for, 96–98
        examining application, 99–107
    live intranet reporting with, 76–91
        creating controller for, 85
        creating models for, 82–84
        creating view for, 85–87
        examining application, 87–91
        setting up database, 78–82
Rails PDF plug-in (rpdf), 192
rake command, 81
Really Simple Syndication (RSS), 215, 216
remarkably gem, 173
render method, 90

report data, writing small servers to get,
        171–172
report method, 279
Reporter controller, 229
report.html script, 148
report.pdf file, 161
report.rhtml view, 282
reports, 233–260
    creating on desktop, 51–73
        choosing format, 51–52
        creating GUIs with Ruby, 60–73
        exporting data to spreadsheets, 52–60
        overview, 51
    creating with Microsoft Office, 233–236
        Access, 236
        Excel, 234
        overview, 233
        Word, 234–235
    importing web-form data into Access
            database, 236–260
        creating web interface, 237–250
        importing XML data into, 251–260
        overview, 236–237
    overview, 233
request.post? flag, 249
require statements, 206
respond_to block, 104
response method, 179
results_raw array, 279
reward method, 163
rewards table, 157, 167
rewards_data.sql file, 157
rewards_report_template.rhtml file, 164
r\n flags, 168
routing files, cost-per-sale reporting, 201
row element, 271
rpdf (Rails PDF plug-in), 192
.rpdf view, 42, 192, 200, 209
RSS (Really Simple Syndication), 215, 216
rss_loader.rb script, 220
Ruby
    creating GUIs with, 60–73
        graphing team performance, 63–73
        using FXRuby, 61–63
    graphing data with, 33–49
        bar charts, 37–45
        choosing graphing utilities, 33–37
        line charts, 45–49
        overview, 33
ruby script/server command, 253
RubyCocoa, 60
Ruby-DBI package, 251

Ruby-GNOME, 60
RubyOSA, 52
rubyscript2exe command, 254
RubyScript2Exe gem, 72, 251
ruby-stemp library, 210

S

salary field, 26
salary method, 10
salary_distribution.rb script, 26
sales force reporting, with SugarCRM, 156–169
   creating PDFs from HTML documents,
     157–169
   updating database, 156–157
save method, 144
schema, cost-per-sale reporting, 201–202
scroll_label class, 184
scroll_label function, 186
scroll_label method, 186
scroll_timer method, 184
SearchResultItem elements, 125
<SearchResultItem> elements, 126
SEL_COMMAND constant, 71
select tag, 101
select_all method, 259
sellers array, 130
send method, 144, 271
show method, 63
show_report function, 102
simple subquery, 150
:skip_types=>true parameter, 105
small servers, writing to get report data,
     171–172
spreadsheet_report.xls file, 55
spreadsheet_team_performance.rb code, 55
spreadsheet-excel gem, 52, 234, 280
spreadsheet/excel library, 56
spreadsheets, exporting data to, 52–60
   creating spreadsheet report, 53–60
   generating Excel spreadsheet, 52–53
src/lib/dbd_ado/ADO.rb file, 251
startx command, 61, 183
stftime function, 91
stock portfolios, tracking, 173–187
   creating graphical XML ticker, 180–187
   creating XML server with Mongrel, 173–180
   overview, 173
StocksList class, 176, 179
StocksListHandler class, 176, 178
Stories model, 224
stories table, 228
Story objects, 231

String class, 128, 141
student model, 243
Student object, 249
student property, 250
style element, 152
subqueries, 150
SugarCRM
   installing, 155–156
   overview, 155
   sales force reporting with, 156–169
     creating PDFs from HTML documents,
       157–169
     updating database, 156–157
SUM function, 20
super method, 178
SWin::Application.messageBox method, 260
SWin::CommonDialog::openFilename method,
     257
Symbol column, 177
symbol nodes, 185
symbols node, 178

T

table element, 271
tabular element, 131
tar.gz file, 251
team performance, graphing, 63–73
Tempfile class, 209
Tempfile object, 69
testing environment, 78
text property, 63
text_ad_report database, 268
text_field element, 248
Time.now.to_f variable, 210
title method, 216, 226
to_csv method, 138
to_xml method, 105, 177
total_wins method, 16–17
tracking news coverage, 215–232
   company news coverage reporting, 217–232
     loading data, 217–226
     news tracker report application, 226–232
   overview, 215
   using FeedTools to parse RSS, 216
tracking stock portfolio, 173–187
   creating graphical XML ticker, 180–187
   creating XML server with Mongrel, 173–180
   overview, 173
training_class model, 244
training_classes table, 246
training_development model, 245
training_loader.exe file, 255

training_loader.rb file, 253
TrainingClass class, 246–249
training.css file, 242
training.mdb file, 253
transaction_id method, 143
Transmegtech Studios, 6
TransmegtechGraphWindow class, 68
TypeText method, 235

U

Uniform Resource Identifier (URI), 225
Uniform Resource Locator (URL), 225
Uniform Resource Name (URN), 225
up method, 79, 90
update_display method, 68–71
upload action, 239
URI (Uniform Resource Identifier), 225
URI.encode function, 225
URL (Uniform Resource Locator), 225
url method, 226
URN (Uniform Resource Name), 225
User model, 163
users table, 167
users variable, 164

V

valid_symbol_labels array, 177
vehicle_model column, 21
VERSION=x option, 80
views, 76, 198–200
vSpacing property, 62

W

wb+ flags, 168
Web reporting, 75–108
    overview, 75
    Rails
        graphical reporting with, 91–107
        live intranet reporting with, 76–91
    selecting web frameworks, 75–76
web services, eBay, 113–131
    coding report, 115–131
    Hpricot, 114–115
    LaTeX, 114–115
webhosts table, 190
WEEKDAY function, 150
weekday_bar class, 152
weekend_bar class, 152
weeks array, 151
WHERE clause, 11
widget_chart_scruffy.rb file, 36
widgets_and_sprockets.png file, 36

Win model, 15
Win32OLE directly, 235
Windows, 114
Windows COM library, 235
wins property, 16
Word, Microsoft, creating reports, 234–235
word_app.PrintOut, 235
worksheet object, 58
worksheet.write method, 58
write method, 58

X

x axis line, 107
x_axis_colour control, 107
XHR (XmlHttpRequest) request, 104
XML
    importing into Access, 251–260
    loading into database, 267–271
xml method, 178
XML servers, creating with Mongrel, 173–180
xml_server.rb file, 175
xml_ticker.rb script, 183
xml.grades call tag, 250
XmlHttpRequest (XHR) request, 104
xml-simple gem, 180
XML::Simple library, 251
XML::Simple module, 180

Y

y_ticks parameter, 107
yahoofinance gem, 180
YahooFinance module, 180
YahooFinance::get_standard_quotes function,
    187

You Need the Companion eBook

Your purchase of this book entitles you to buy the companion PDF-version eBook for only $10. Take the weightless companion with you anywhere.

We believe this Apress title will prove so indispensable that you'll want to carry it with you everywhere, which is why we are offering the companion eBook (in PDF format) for $10 to customers who purchase this book now. Convenient and fully searchable, the PDF version of any content-rich, page-heavy Apress book makes a valuable addition to your programming library. You can easily find and copy code—or perform examples by quickly toggling between instructions and the application. Even simultaneously tackling a donut, diet soda, and complex code becomes simplified with hands-free eBooks!

Once you purchase your book, getting the $10 companion eBook is simple:

❶ Visit **www.apress.com/promo/tendollars/**.

❷ Complete a basic registration form to receive a randomly generated question about this title.

❸ Answer the question correctly in 60 seconds, and you will receive a promotional code to redeem for the $10.00 eBook.

2855 TELEGRAPH AVENUE | SUITE 600 | BERKELEY, CA 94705

Offer valid through 7/08.